THE WORLD OF
UCL
1828-2004

First edition 1978
Second edition 1991
Third edition 2004

Published for UCL by UCL Press
The Glass House
Wharton Street
London WC1X 9PX

ISBN 1-84472-025-X (pbk)
ISBN 1-84472-068-3 (hbk)

A CIP catalogue record for this
book is available from the British
Library.

Designed and produced by
Richard Bryant
Past Historic, Kings Stanley,
Gloucestershire

Printed in Great Britain

THE WORLD OF
UCL
1828-2004

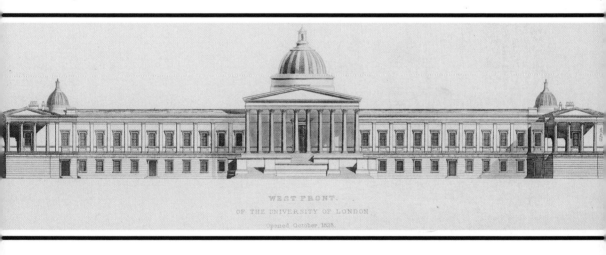

WEST FRONT.
OF THE UNIVERSITY OF LONDON
Opened October 1828.

NEGLEY HARTE AND JOHN NORTH

Foreword by
MALCOLM GRANT
President and Provost

Contents

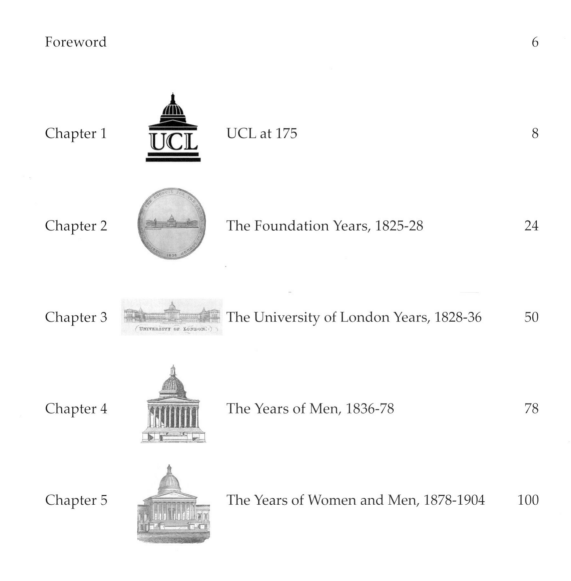

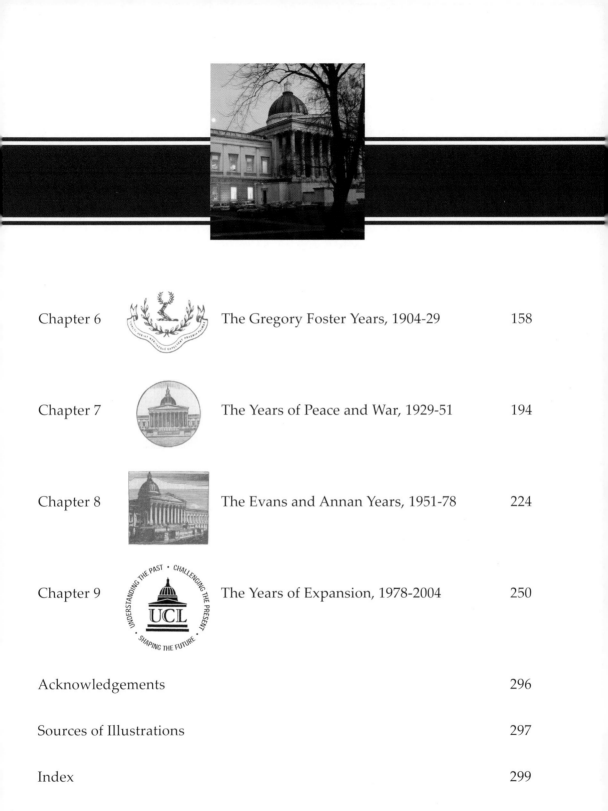

Foreword

Institutional histories are rarely riveting.

But UCL is, in this as in so many other areas, a clear exception. It has throughout its time been a university of innovations and firsts, with no fewer than 19 Nobel Prize winners to show for it. And from the beginning its focus has been international: indeed that very word was coined by Jeremy Bentham, who is still today a dominating presence at UCL (not only intellectually but physically).

Even UCL's early foundation in 1826 — as a secular institution as distinct from Oxford and Cambridge — set a precedent that was quickly followed in New York with the foundation of New York University (NYU), and it provoked a small flurry of other university foundations in England, amongst them King's College London and Durham University.

In 1863, UCL was the destination for some of the earliest Japanese students to study in the west. Upon their return, they were to have a remarkable role in founding the modern state of Japan. One was Ito Hirobume, who was eventually elected four times to be Prime Minister. Others participated in the foundation of the University of Tokyo, the Mint, and the railway system. The ties remain close: the current Prime Minister of Japan, Junichiro Koizumi, is a former UCL student.

Today, UCL is a truly international community. More than a quarter of our staff (including the Provost) come from 84 countries outside the UK; and more than a quarter of our 12,000 undergraduate and 7,000 postgraduate students come from 130 different countries outside the UK.

This internationalism, and the cosmopolitan character that it gives rise to, is a very special feature of UCL, both historically and even more so today. It reflects London's status as a major world city, and UCL's place as London's founding university. But it is also an intellectual quality, of an institution that has a global vision, that sets out to address, through its teaching and research, problems which have universal significance.

We at UCL are proud of the history and the ethos of this university, and I am delighted to introduce this new edition of *The World of UCL* and to share with a wider audience this remarkable history of a leading university.

Malcolm Grant
President and Provost

Professor Malcolm Grant, since 2003 the ninth Provost – and the third President – of UCL.

Chapter 1
UCL at 175

You are celebrating the termination and crown of a very great century, a very great hundred years, which began, not as a mere arbitrary or accidental date, but with the opening, one might say, almost, of the modern world, certainly with the opening of those great hopes which existed a hundred years ago, which it is difficult to define in few words. Perhaps there are none better than those hackneyed words which are said to have been uttered by the great German poet when he was dying. The desire for light and for liberty and for the expansion of the mind which possessed the beginning of the nineteenth century and the end of the eighteenth century created a vast number of institutions that are still with of tremendous significance and historic importance, this great College among them.

G. K. Chesterton in his address on the occasion
of the celebration of the
Centenary of the College, 28 June 1927

Unlike the modern civic universities which grew from some local patriotism, University College London grew from an idea. Originally that idea was based upon a belief in freedom of investigation without any distinction of creed or race or sex. That quest, which made University College the pioneer in modern university development in England, also led the founders to find a place in the College for studies which had previously been outside the university curriculum. The freedom to investigate was not an idle phrase: it meant breaking into new fields. This is still the central tradition of the College.

Sir Ifor Evans in UCL: A Survey, 1950-55 *(1955)*

Alma Mater, loved and splendid. This chapter deals only with University College and with my experiences as a student and a member of its academic staff. It is of interest only to those who have known (and loved) that great and splendid establishment. Those unfortunates, who do not possess that knowledge and affection, need therefore have no qualms in skipping this chapter and going on to the next!

Margaret Murray, My First Hundred Years *(1963)*

1. *Aerial photograph of the central UCL site, taken in May 2004.*

The aerial photograph taken in 2004 reveals that the world of
UCL, in its hundred and seventy-fifth year, was undergoing
a high degree of rapid change. The dome of the original
building, as designed by Wilkins, can be seen in the centre, facing
the Cruciform Building, the former Hospital, already refurbished as
the Wolfson Institute for Biomedical Research. The new University
College Hospital building (top right) and the new Wellcome
Foundation building on Euston Road are shown almost completed.

No fewer than five building sites can be seen in and around
the original 'rectangle'. Almost finished is the new Andrew
Huxley Building, mainly for neuroscience, built to the south
of the original Wilkins building and sandwiched between the
Bernard Katz Building for the Eisai Laboratories for Studies in
Neurodegeneration and the MRC Laboratory for Molecular Cell

2

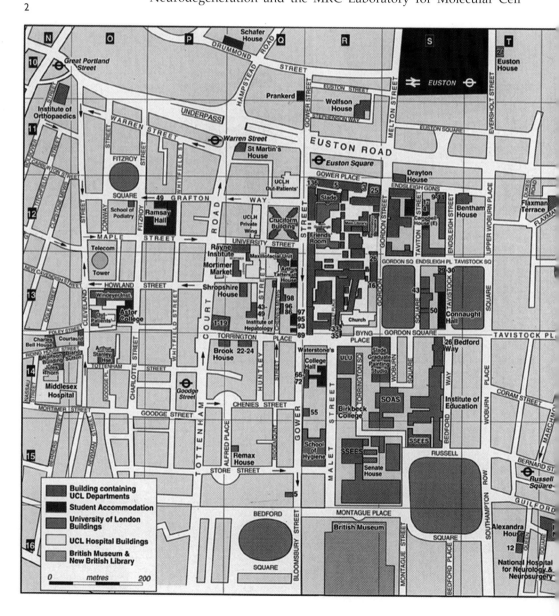

Biology, both of which were opened in 1993. Marked by the yellow crane and screened, is the new building for the London Centre for Nanotechnology, a joint initiative between UCL and Imperial College, due to be opened in 2005. The new building for Computer Science and for Medical Physics and Bioengineering is seen nearing completion in the former Engineering Yard. The building site in the foreground, marked by a white pole, is for the School of Slavonic and East European Studies, squeezed in at the back of Chemistry; its foundation stone was laid by the President of Poland in May 2004. Marked by the red crane, on the other side of Gower Street, is the cleared space for the Institute for Cancer Sciences. One more site remains for a possible future building: the gap between the UCL Bloomsbury Theatre and 26 Gordon Square has been earmarked for a new building to house some of the UCL's 'treasures'.

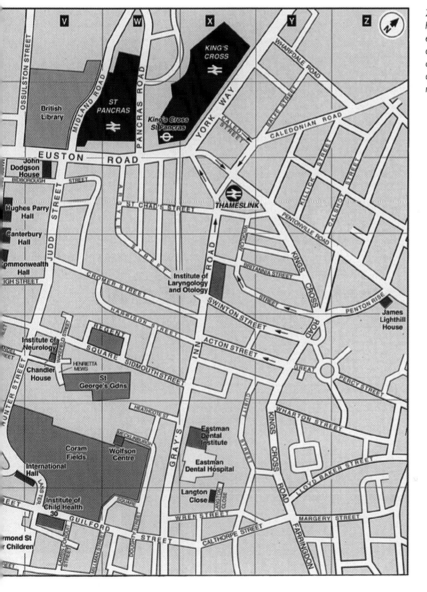

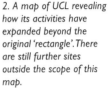

2. A map of UCL revealing how its activities have expanded beyond the original 'rectangle'. There are still further sites outside the scope of this map.

Gower Street Site

INDEX OF MUSEUMS, LIBRARIES, LECTURE THEATRES

Facility	Building	Map	Grid
Lecture Theatres			
Anatomy Theatre	Anatomy	2	E5
Archaeology	Inst of Archaeology	2	I4
Basement Theatres	Cruciform Building	2	D3
Basement Theatre	1-19 Torrington Place	2	A8
Bentham House	Bentham House	2	M1-2
Biochemistry	Darwin	2	E7
Bland Sutton	Bland Sutton	3	O14
Bloomsbury Theatre	Bloomsbury Theatre	2	H3
Chemistry Auditorium	Christopher Ingold	2	I3
Chemistry Theatre	Christopher Ingold	2	I3
Courtauld	Middlesex Hospital	3	N1
Darwin	Darwin	2	E7
Edward Lewis	Windeyer	3	O13
Embryology	Anatomy	2	E5
Fleming	Engineering	2	F8
Garwood	South Wing	2	F4
Gustave Tuck	South Wing	2	F4
Haldane	Wolfson House	3	R11
Harrie Massey	25 Gordon Street	2	H1
Lankester	Medawar	2	G7
Pearson	Pearson	2	E2
Physiology	Medical Sciences	2	F5
Torrington	1-19 Torrington Place	2	A8
Watson	Medawar	2	G7
Library Services (EISD)			
Boldero	Bland Sutton	3	O14
Child Health	Inst of Child Health	3	V16
Clinical Sciences	Cruciform Building	2	D3
Environmental Studies	Wates House	2	I1
Human Communication	Chandler House	3	V14
Institute of Archaeology	Inst of Archaeology	2	I4
Laryngology & Otology	Inst of Laryngology	3	X13
Library Store	140 Hampstead Rd	1	
Main Library	Wilkins	2	G3
Neurology	Inst of Neurology	3	U16
Ophthalmology	Inst of Ophthalmology	1	
Orthopaedics	Inst of Orthopaedics	3	N14
R.N.I.D	Inst of Laryngology	3	U16
Science	DMS Watson	2	F6
Museums			
Bentham Auto-Icon	Wilkins (South)	2	F3
College History	Wilkins (North)	2	G1
Grant Museum (Zoology)	Darwin	2	E7
Petrie (Egyptology)	DMS Watson	2	F6
Strang Print Room	Wilkins (South)	2	F3

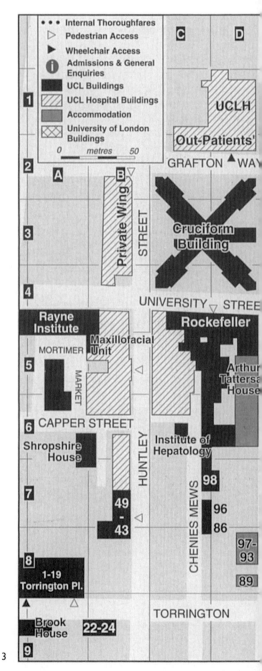

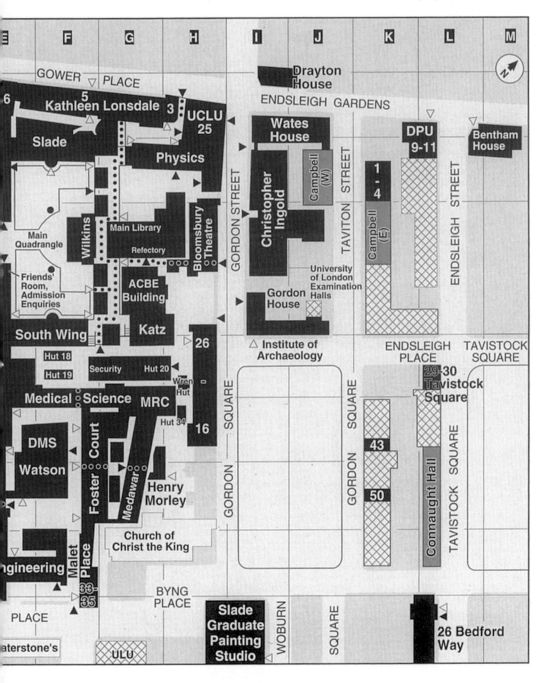

3. A map of UCL showing how activity continues more and more intensively on the original 'rectangle', spilling over into many adjacent streets.

Between 1986 and 1999, no fewer than twelve previously separate institutions joined the expanding UCL. The first was the Institute of Archaeology in August 1986, formerly an 'institute' of the University of London, now flourishing as a department in the Faculty of Social and Historical Sciences, having absorbed the former UCL departments of Classical Archaeology and Egyptology and the sub-department of Medieval Archaeology. In 1987 there was an outbreak of medical amalgamations, with the Middlesex Hospital Medical School and three of the constituent parts of the former British Postgraduate Medical Federation – the Institute of Urology, the Institute of Orthopaedics and the Institute of Laryngology and Otology.

Mergers started up again after Sir Derek Roberts had succeeded Sir James Lighthill as Provost in 1989. It was observed that there was a sharp difference in style between the first round of mergers under Lighthill and the second round under Roberts: Lighthill held elaborate negotiations first, and then agreed the mergers; Roberts decided to merge first and negotiated afterwards. The result was a dramatic transforming sequence of events. Medicine became an increasingly dominant part of UCL and its finances.

4

5

4. The first of the current round of new buildings to be brought into use is that for the Molecular and Cellular Neuroscience Laboratories, named after Sir Andrew Huxley, Nobel prize-winner and former Professor of Physiology.

5. The architect's projection of the new building for the School of Slavonic and East European Studies currently under construction in Taviton Street.

In 1995, there were two mergers. The Institute of Ophthalmology, founded nearly fifty years previously in conjunction with the Moorfields Eye Hospital in the City Road, brought into UCL what became the largest single site for eye research as well as eye care in the world. The National Hospital's College of Speech Sciences, which had evolved from the speech therapy clinic established in 1918 at the West End Hospital for Nervous Diseases, became the Department of Human Communication Science in the Faculty of Life Sciences. In 1996, the Institute of Child Health joined UCL, as did the Institute of Neurology in 1997, each of them the leading centre of research in its field. In 1998 the whole of the Royal Free Hospital Medical School followed, as, in 1999, did the Eastman Dental Institute, originally from 1931 part of the Royal Free Hospital, but a separate institute from 1948. These medical expansions were to some extent balanced by the amalgamation with the School of Slavonic and East European Studies, founded in 1915 as the country's leading centre for research and teaching in those fields. For a time the School of Podiatric Medicine in connection with the London Foot Hospital was also part of UCL, but all the other twelve institutions have become permanent parts of the world of UCL.

6. The Royal Free Hospital and its Medical School – since 1999 amalgamated with the UCL Medical School – seen across the ponds on Hampstead Heath.

6

T he expansion, evident enough in terms of new buildings and merged institutions, is even more striking in terms of student numbers. There were barely 6,000 students in total when the first edition of this book appeared in 1978, nearly 10,000 when the second edition appeared in 1991; today, the total is approaching as many as 20,000. The chart (7) shows how the postgraduates made up an increasing proportion of the increasing total, so that postgraduate students now constitute 37% of the total student body. 4,242 of them are taking Masters' degrees (1,592 of them part-time) and 2,736 research degrees (734 of them part-time). There has also been a steady increase in the percentage of women in the total of UCL students; by 1997, the number of women had reached the point of parity; in 2004, women were 52% of the student body.

This expansion was not achieved without a good deal of misgiving. More students meant more income, but also more pressure on limited resources and space. The unit of resource per student fell. In many areas the overcrowding became too serious to overlook readily. Nevertheless, as quality assessments and research assessments both consistently proved, the highest academic standards were maintained.

7. *Total student numbers, 1990-2004, showing the percentage of postgraduates.*

7

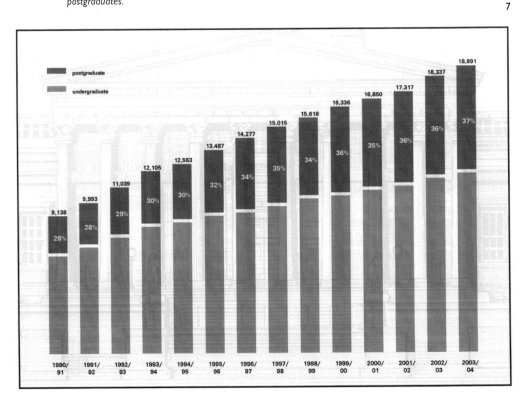

8. *Three of the six Sabbatical Officers – the Sabbs – of the UCL Union, plotting strategy in 2004; they are, from the left, Alex Coles, Education and Welfare Officer, Andreas von Maltzahn, Media and Communications Officer, and Sinan Rabee, Finance and Administration Officer.*

9. *The new emphasis on 'widening access' promoted by the Blair government led to great efforts in UCL to encourage well-qualified applicants from state schools; here, sixth-formers from Haringey in 2001 anticipate university life in the company of Professor Michael Worton, Vice-Provost for Teaching and Learning.*

8

9

Besides the nearly 20,000 students, UCL has nearly 9,000 people on its payroll, making it the biggest employer in the London Borough of Camden. This includes over 4,000 academic and research staff, 627 of whom are professors — almost as many professors as there were students in 1828. The financial turnover now approaches £500m per annum, of which rather less than a third is provided by the Higher Education Funding Council for England, the government body that since 1993 has performed the functions of the former UGC and UFC, albeit in a more directive manner. Rather more than a third comes from research grants and contracts, some from the research councils, but far more from industry and charitable funds.

Since 1986, there have been official periodic assessments of the quality of the research undertaken in British universities. First called the Research Selectivity Exercise in 1986 and 1989, renamed in 1992 as the Research Assessment Exercise and conducted again in 1996 and 2001, the RAE became a haunting presence in academic life. In all five exercises the large majority of UCL's submissions have received one of the top two ratings. In the most recent RAE, for instance, forty of forty-eight submissions were graded either 5 or 5*, the top rating. Only Cambridge and Oxford won more 5* ratings than UCL's sixteen. The place of UCL among the top multi-faculty universities in Britain has repeatedly been confirmed.

UCL's international distinction cannot be quantified so readily. Besides the many examples of international research collaboration, the efforts of the Development Office and the new emphasis on fund-raising and on alumni relations have been global in scope. It has been a difficult task to remain competitive internationally at a time when successive British governments in the 1990s have lamentably failed to increase spending in line with the expansion in student numbers. In real terms, academic salaries continue to fall, while academic work-loads increase. The present government's legislative proposals involving changes in the structure and level of tuition fees go only a little way towards dealing with the financial problem. UCL has grown dramatically over 175 years; its ever-present funding shortage has grown with it.

10. A chart showing how substantial has been the shift in the structure of the College's finances during the last quarter-century. The proportion provided by the government grant, from successively the UGC, the UFC and now HEFCE, has halved. In this period too, UCL's turnover has increased from about £20 million per annum to nearly £500 million.

10

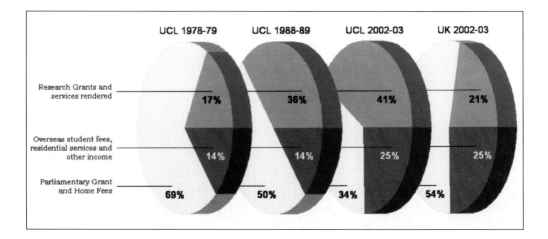

	UCL 1978-79	UCL 1988-89	UCL 2002-03	UK 2002-03
Research Grants and services rendered	17%	36%	41%	21%
Overseas student fees, residential services and other income	14%	14%	25%	25%
Parliamentary Grant and Home Fees	69%	50%	34%	54%

11. A poster advertising the range of 'UCL merchandise', available at the re-vamped College Shop, revealing the new attitude towards the corporate image that emerged in the 1990s.

12. Professor John Midwinter, FRS, Pender Professor of Electrical Engineering since 1988 and Vice-Provost of UCL, 1994-99, refusing to be swamped by the quantity of information required by the 1997 Teaching Quality Assessment (TQA) of his Department, the other new national inquisition, imposed on universities in the 1990s.

13. The Provost's Weekly Meeting with Vice-Provosts and Deans: at the far end of the table is the Provost, presiding, with Professor Michael Worton, Vice-Provost (International), on his right, and Professor Leon Fine, Dean of the Faculty of Clinical Sciences, on his left; next along is Marilyn Gallyer, Vice-Provost (Administration). Nearest the camera on the left is Professor Michael Spyer, Vice-Provost and Dean of the Royal Free and University College Medical School.

It is paradoxical that two seemingly quite inconsistent developments are happening at UCL in 2004. As these words are being written, UCL is the scene of extensive building activity with five new buildings under construction, a sixth in the planning stage and many other departments being re-housed or enhanced; at the same time, the financial deficits that have plagued recent years continue to demand ever more stringent efforts to contain expenditure on day-to-day running. Outstanding success in research and intellectual achievement has attracted the funding for so many capital projects, but the income from fees and grants needed to underpin such a programme of expansion never reaches the proper level. So those who have to suffer the inconvenience of the noise and disruption caused by the building works, are denied even the comfort of feeling that this is the price to be paid for financial security. It has become possible to expand and run a deficit simultaneously. Over 175 years, UCL has seen earlier moments of intellectual triumph in the teeth of financial adversity, but the speed and scale of the current expansion is far greater than ever before and so too is the financial shortfall.

The new Provost has made a vigorous start towards tackling these intractable problems. In February 2004, he launched a much applauded consultation throughout UCL on the basis of a 'Green Paper'; in June, after extensive debate in Departments and Faculties, in Committees and Union Meetings, the corresponding 'White Paper' has been approved by the Academic Board and the College

13

Council. One key recommendation is to re-inforce UCL's standing as a university of global consequence; another is to place UCL's finances on a permanently sounder footing by focusing investment in areas of world-leading excellence and increasing annual and endowment income through a major capital campaign.

14. The front quad at the beginning of the academic year in 2003, adorned in purple to greet the year's freshers at the Union's 'Freshers' Fayre'.

14

Chapter 2
The Foundation Years, 1825-28

There is one matter which I beg you to bring to the King's notice yet again before your departure; this is the proposed foundation of a university of London. You have my authority to tell His Majesty of my absolute conviction that the implementation of this plan would bring about England's ruin.

Metternich's instructions to the Austrian Ambassador
in London, 8 September 1825

Come bustle, my neighbours, give over your labours,
Leave digging and delving, and churning:
New lights are preparing to set you a staring,
And fill all your noddles with learning.
Each dustman shall speak, both in Latin and Greek,
And tinkers beat bishops in knowledge –
If the opulent tribe will consent to subscribe
To build up a new Cockney College.

'The Cockney College' in John Bull, *July 1825*

… we will venture to cast the horoscope of the infant Institution. We predict, that the clamour by which it has been assailed will die away, - that it is destined to a long, a glorious, and a beneficent existence, - that, while the spirit of its system remains unchanged, the details will vary with the varying necessities and facilities of every age, - that it will be the model of many future establishments, - that even those haughty establishments which now treat it with contempt, will in some degree feel its salutary influence, - and that the approbation of a great people, to whose wisdom, energy and virtue, its exertions will have largely contributed, will confer on it a dignity more imposing than any which derive from the most lucrative patronage, or the most splendid ceremonial.

T. B. Macaulay in the Edinburgh Review, *1826*

I t is generally but wrongly believed that Jeremy Bentham was the founder of University College London. This myth is sustained in a bizarre manner by the display of the body of the great

15

15. Henry Tonks's remarkable but completely unhistorical painting of the building of the College, showing William Wilkins offering his plans up to Jeremy Bentham for approval.

philosopher of ethics, jurisprudence and government, 'in the attitude', as he himself instructed before his death in 1832, 'in which I am sitting when engaged in thought'. The 'Auto-Icon' has been in the possession of the College since 1850.

Besides the box with Bentham in it, the College possesses over 200 more boxes full of his writings, a collection that has been called 'one of the most remarkable monuments to the mind of a single man in all its aspects to be found anywhere'. Prominently displayed in the Flaxman Gallery, moreover, is the huge painting undertaken in 1922 by Henry Tonks, the then Slade Professor of Fine Art, portraying William Wilkins, the architect, offering the original College plans up to Bentham for his approval, while Henry Brougham, Thomas Campbell and Crabb Robinson look on.

In fact Bentham played no such close personal role in the establishment of the College. When the College first opened its doors to students as the self-styled 'University of London' in October 1828, Bentham was an old withdrawn man of 80. He gave his blessing and financial support to the moves to found a university in the largest city in Europe and almost the only capital without one, and the founders certainly owed a very considerable intellectual debt to him.

Since 1959 the Bentham Project, based in the College, has been engaged in the massive enterprise of preparing for publication Bentham's collected works and correspondence; twenty-five volumes have appeared so far, and about thirty-five more are planned. The 'Auto-Icon' attended the sesquicentennial meeting of the College Committee in 1976, the minutes recording 'Jeremy Bentham present but not voting'.

16. An extraordinary possession of the College is the clothed skeleton of Jeremy Bentham, as displayed with a wax head, in its box in the South Cloisters. As presented today, Jeremy seems a less rotund figure than he does in this photograph, owing to the professional anxieties of modern textile conservators.

17. An even more extraordinary possession is Bentham's actual mummified head, now kept in the College safe.

16

17

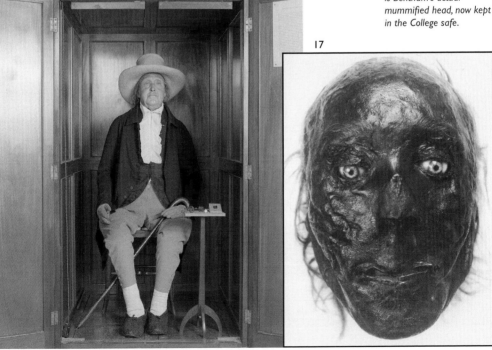

The College was founded by what Bentham called 'an association of liberals', a description he used in a letter written in August 1825 to Bolivar, the South American liberator. The leading roles were played by an improbable duo formed by a poet and a lawyer.

Credit for the original proposal must go to Thomas Campbell, the now forgotten Scottish poet whose *Pleasures of Hope* (1799) brought him popular fame and a rapid entrée into London literary society. In 1820, on a visit to Bonn, he was impressed by the religious toleration of the re-founded university there and formed the idea of establishing 'a great London University' for 'effectively and multifariously teaching, examining, exercising and rewarding with honours, in the liberal arts and sciences, the youth of our middling rich people...' In February 1825 *The Times* printed a powerful open letter on this subject from Campbell to Henry Brougham, another Scot, a brilliant man, one of the founders of the *Edinburgh Review*, who had moved to London to seek commanding outlets in the law and in politics for his versatility and energy. An MP first in 1810, he became particularly involved with the cause of popular education, associating himself with George Birkbeck and the mechanics' institutes and founding in 1826 the Society for the Diffusion of Useful Knowledge, the papers of which are now in the College Library, as are Brougham's own papers.

Brougham regarded himself as a Benthamite, as a believer in the utilitarian principle of 'the greatest happiness of the greatest

18. The first of the effective founders of the College, the poet Thomas Campbell (1777-1844), an engraving based on his portrait by Sir Thomas Lawrence.

19. The second and even more effective of the founders of the College, the lawyer and politician Henry Brougham, FRS, MP (1778-1868), after 1830 Lord Brougham and Vaux, as painted by James Lonsdale.

18

19

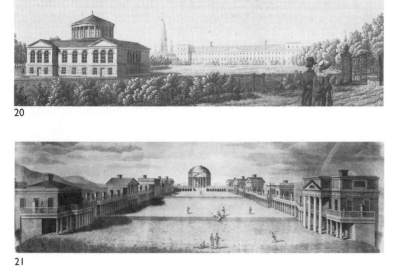

20

21

20. *The University of Bonn as it appeared when visited by Campbell in 1820.*

21. *A second university which provided a model for the new university in London was Jefferson's carefully planned University of Virginia, seen here soon after its opening in 1825.*

number' – though it has been claimed that in his view the greatest number was number one. His extravagant style smacked of humbug to many, but he was a man who got things done. Under his direction Campbell's dreams for a London University were turned into reality.

22. *The University of Edinburgh was the most powerful model of all, familiar as it was to Brougham and many of the founding professoriate in London.*

22

THE UNIVERSITY, SOUTH BRIDGE STREET.

24

23

W hen Campbell and Brougham began to organise a university for London, the only existing universities in England
were those long established at Oxford and Cambridge –
'the two great public nuisances', Bentham called them, 'storehouses
and nurseries of political corruption...' Membership of the Church
of England was necessary for admission to the one and for
graduation from the other. All nonconformists, Catholics and Jews
were thus excluded, while many Anglicans were kept out by the
social restrictiveness, by the cost or by the characteristic intellectual
backwardness. The old universities were seen to be increasingly out
of touch with a rapidly changing society. The population doubled
in the first half of the nineteenth century and the combined effects
of industrialisation and of urbanisation were making for new social
patterns with new pressures and new demands. The industrial
revolution necessitated an extended system of higher education.

The main appeal of the new university was therefore to the interests excluded from the established system, such as it was, and to
the various new social groups. Isaac Lyon Goldsmid, a millionaire
financier and later to be the first Jew to become a baronet, played
an especially significant role. He it was who brought Campbell and
Brougham together on the project and he ensured the considerable
support of the Jewish community. The nonconformists were actively

among your friends with a view to an early 'ainment of the important objects of the Institution. We have the honor to be

London, 20th March 1826

Your most obedient Servants

J. Abercrombie.
Auckland
Alex. Baring
George Birkbeck
H. Brougham
Thos. Campbell
Dudley & Ward
Isaac Goldsmid
Olynthus Gregory.
Geo. Grote
Joseph Hume
Lansdowne
Z. Macaulay
J. Mackintosh
J. Mill
Norfolk
Russell
B. Shaw
John Smith.
Wm. Tooke
Henry Warburton
H. Waymouth
J. Whishaw
Thomas Wilson

All communications on the subject of subscriptions or otherwise to be addressed to "Mr. Coates" (Clerk to the Council) "No.7, Furnivals Inn."

25

25. The signatures of all the twenty-four members of the original Council.

26. James Mill, disciple of Bentham and father of John Stuart Mill.

27. Zachary Macaulay, campaigner against slavery and the slave-trade.

28. George Grote, banker, MP and historian of ancient Greece.

led by Francis Augustus Cox, the Baptist minister of Hackney, while a different dissenting strand was represented by the support of Zachary Macaulay, whose main work had been devoted to the abolition of the slave trade. The Catholics were represented by the Duke of Norfolk, and the Whig establishment provided a number of other titled luminaries. James Mill, the utilitarian philosopher, actively represented Benthamism, and the various progressive influences rubbed shoulders readily with supporters from the City.

29. George Birkbeck, founder in 1823 of the Mechanics' Institute, later Birkbeck College.

As the result of a year-long series of meetings both public and private chaired by Brougham, the College came into formal existence on 11 February 1826 with the signing of an elaborate Deed of Settlement. It was agreed to raise a substantial sum of between £150,000 and £300,000 by the selling of shares of £100 each. From among the 'proprietors', as the shareholders were called, twenty-four persons were to be elected as the Council, the all-powerful body which was to control the University's property, appoint the professors and regulate the education of the students. It was a fundamental principle of the new institution that religion in any form should be neither a requirement for entry, nor a subject for teaching. As a corollary it was decided that no minister of religion should sit on the Council. The Revd Dr Cox served therefore as Honorary Secretary of that body until becoming Librarian in 1827.

30

30. The bust of the Revd Dr Francis Augustus Cox, long displayed in the room of his successors as Librarian, now in the Special Collections room.

31

31. One of the share certificates as issued to the original proprietors.

32. Cruikshank's cartoon of Brougham hawking shares
in the projected University around Lincoln's Inn.

From the outset the promoters sought incorporation. Brougham's soundings towards a royal charter in 1825 were rebuffed by the Tory government of the day, and his subsequent efforts to achieve an Act of Parliament were defeated by the influence of Oxford and Cambridge. Parliamentary assistance was provided by Joseph Hume, one of the members of the original Council, a leading radical who was indefatigable in support of the College as well as of those other great progressive causes of the age, catholic emancipation and parliamentary reform. After 1832 he was joined in the House of Commons by another member of the original Council, William Tooke, a prominent solicitor who became the first Treasurer of the College and of the Hospital. The strength of the combined opposition of Oxbridge and of the London medical profession to legal recognition of the College as a 'University' could not easily be overcome in Parliament, despite the efforts also of Brougham in the House of Lords, where he had astonishingly gone in 1830 as Lord Chancellor. When the College did eventually get its first charter in 1836, it took an unexpected form.

33

34

33. William Tooke, FRS, an engraving published in the Illustrated London News after his death in 1863: one of the members of the original Council who as a radical MP fought for full recognition and incorporation for the College.

34. Joseph Hume, FRS, as painted by John Lucas in the largest portrait on display in the College: another member of the original Council who was a radical MP.

UNIVERSITY OF LONDON.

PROSPECTUS.

THE PLAN of the UNIVERSITY of LONDON is now so much matured, that the Council, chosen to superintend its affairs, deem themselves bound to lay an outline of it before the public, in order that the friends of public instruction may have the fullest opportunity of determining how far the Institution deserves their support, and of considering in what particulars it may seem to them capable of improvement.

The number and names of the Subscribers sufficiently evince the strong conviction of its utility which prevails in the class of men for whom the Institution is peculiarly destined, and who consult their own interest, as well as that of the public, in contributing towards its establishment.

The City of London is nearly equal in population, and far superior in wealth, to each of the Kingdoms of Denmark, Saxony, Hanover, and Wirtemburgh, every one of which has at least one flourishing University. Supposing the annual rate of increase, in the last five years, to have been the same as in the preceding ten, the present population cannot be less than fourteen hundred thousand souls,* of whom there are about forty thousand males, between the ages of sixteen and twenty-one; the usual period of academical education. It may safely be affirmed, that there is no equal number of youths in any other place, of whom so large a portion feel the want of liberal education, are so well qualified for it, could so easily obtain all its advantages at home, and are so little able to go in quest of them elsewhere. No where else is knowledge more an object of desire, either as a source of gratification, a means of improvement, or an instrument of honest and useful ambition. The exclusion of so great a body of intelligent youth, designed for the most important occupations in society, from the highest means of liberal education, is a defect in our institutions, which, if it were not become familiar by its long prevalence, would offend every reasonable mind. In a word, London, which, for intelligence and wealth, as well as numbers, may fairly be deemed the first City in the civilized world, is at once the place which most needs an University, and the only great Capital which has none.

Public Lectures, combined with examinations by the Professors, and with mutual instruction by the pupils, will form the general system of this Institution. It is intended, that the Professors shall derive their income at first principally, and, as soon as may be, entirely, from the fees paid by their pupils; and they will hold their offices during good behaviour. We are assured, that Professors will be found of eminent ability, and of such established reputation, as to give authority and lustre to their instructions, so that the University will not be wanting in the means of exciting and guiding superior faculties in their ascent to excellence, as well as of speedily and easily imparting the needful share of knowledge to all diligent students. The number of the Professors, the allotment of particular branches to individuals, and the order in which the Lectures ought to be attended, are matters not yet finally settled, and some of them must partly depend, in the first instance, on the qualifications of candidates; all of them will permanently be regulated by the demand for different sorts of instruction. Some Professorships may hereafter be consolidated; more are likely, in process of time to be subdivided; many entirely new will doubtless be rendered necessary by the progress of discovery, and by the enlarged desire of the community for knowledge. The Course of Instruction will at present consist of Languages, Mathematics, Physics, the Mental and the Moral Sciences, together with the Law of England, History, and Political Economy;—and the various branches of knowledge which are the objects of Medical Education. In the classification of these studies there is no intention to adhere strictly to a logical order, whether founded upon the subjects to which each relates, or on the faculties principally employed on it. Without entirely losing sight of these considerations, our main guide is the convenience of teaching, which for the present purpose is more important than a scientific arrangement; even if such an arrangement could be well made without a new nomenclature of the sciences, and a new distribution of their objects.

Some LANGUAGES will probably be studied only by those whose peculiar destination requires such attainments, and in this department generally, it will be fit to seek for every method of abridging the labour by which the majority are to attain that proficiency to which they ought to confine themselves. But the structure of human speech is itself one of the worthiest objects of meditation: the comparison of various languages, makes each of them better understood, and illustrates the affinity of nations, while it enlarges and strengthens every vigorous understanding; even the minute and seemingly unfruitful study of words is a school of discrimination and precision; and in the arts which employ language as their instrument, the contemplation of the original models, not only serves to form the taste of the youth of genius, but generally conduces to expand and elevate the human faculties.

The MATHEMATICAL SCIENCES are so justly valued as a discipline of the reasoning faculties, and as an unerring measure of human advancement, that the commendation of them might seem disrespectful to the judgment of the reader, if they did not afford by far the most striking instance of the dependance of the most common and useful arts upon abstruse reasoning. The elementary propositions of Geometry were once merely speculative; but those to whom their subserviency to the speed and safety of voyages, is now familiar, will be slow to disparage any truth for the want of present and palpable usefulness.

It is a matter of considerable difficulty to ascertain the distribution of PHYSICS, a vast science, or rather class of sciences, which consists in the knowledge of the most general facts observed by the senses in the things without us. Some of these appearances are the subject of calculation, and must, in teaching, be blended with the Mathematics; others are chiefly discovered and proved by experiment; one portion of physical observation relates to the movements of conspicuous masses, while another relates to the reciprocal action of the imperceptible particles or agents which we know only by their results; and a great part are founded on that uniformity of structure, and those important peculiarities of action, which distinguish vegetable and animal life. The subjoined division of professorships in this province, though chiefly adapted to the practical purpose of instruction, is influenced by some regard to the above considerations.

* By the returns of 1821, the numbers were 1,274,030.

35. The following three pages: the Prospectus produced by the original Council of February 1826 laying out in some detail the scheme of education to be offered.

2

As the Physical Sciences aim at ascertaining the most general facts observed by sense in the things which are the objects of thought, so the MENTAL SCIENCES seek to determine the most general facts as relating to thought or feelings, made known to the being who thinks, by his own consciousness.

The sub-division of this part of knowledge, would be very desirable on account of its importance and intricacy; but the close connexion of all the facts with each other renders it peculiarly difficult.

A separate Professorship of LOGIC is proposed, not only because it supplies the rules of argument, and the tests of sophistry, but still more for that mental regimen by which it slowly dispels prejudice and strengthens habits of right judgment.

Perhaps, also, RHETORIC, or the Art of Persuasion, may in time merit a separate Professorship, of which one main object would be to undeceive those rigid censurers, and misguided admirers, who consider it as a gaudy pageant; and to imbue the minds of youth with the wholesome assurance that when guided by morality, and subjected to logic, it is the art of rendering truth popular, and virtue delightful; of transforming conviction into persuasion; and of engaging the whole man, the feelings as well as the understanding, on the side of true wisdom.

The object common to the MORAL SCIENCES, is the determination of the rules which ought to direct the voluntary actions of men; and they have generally been subdivided into Ethics and Jurisprudence; though the important distinction between these sciences has seldom been accurately traced, still less steadily observed. The direct object of Ethics is the knowledge of those habitual dispositions of mind which we approve as moral, or disapprove as immoral, and from which beneficial or mischievous actions ordinarily flow. Particular actions themselves are estimated by the motives from which they arise. Ethics is co-extensive with the whole character and conduct of man; it is the science of virtues and duties; of those dispositions which are praiseworthy, and of that course of action which is incumbent on a reasonable being, apart from the consideration of the injunctions of law, and the authority of civil government.

The first object of JURISPRUDENCE, (taking that term in an enlarged sense,) is the ascertainment of rights, or of those portions of power over persons or things which should be allotted to each individual for the general welfare. The second is to determine what violations of these rights are so injurious in their effects and consequences to society, as to require prevention by the fear of adequate punishment. It is the science of rights and of crimes; it pre-supposes the authority of government, and is limited in its direct operation to the outward actions of men as they affect each other. Ethics, though it has a wider scope, contemplates its objects more simply and generally. Jurisprudence, within its more limited sphere, considers its objects in more points of view; prescribes more exact rules, and is therefore compelled to make minute and even subtle distinctions. The confusion of these two branches of Moral Science has contributed to disturb the Theory of Ethics, and to corrupt the practice of legislation.

The study of the LAWS OF ENGLAND has for centuries been confined to the Capital, where alone there is a constant opportunity of observing its administration in Courts of Justice, and of acquiring skill in peculiar branches under private instructors. These exclusive advantages of London for the Study of the Law would surely be enhanced by combination with Lectures and Examinations, while systematic instruction in Law, and in general knowledge, would be rendered accessible to those branches of the legal profession which are now shut out from them by the impediments common to them with the Youth of the Metropolis in general.

The maxims which ought to be observed by independent communities towards each other, and of which the fitness is generally acknowledged by civilized states, constitute what is metaphorically called the LAW OF NATIONS.

POLITICAL PHILOSOPHY, which considers what are the rights and duties of Rulers and Subjects in relation to each other, may be conveniently taught by the Professor of Ethics.

In an arrangement which does not affect a rigid method, History and Political Economy may be classed either as parts or appendages of Moral Science. A minute knowledge of HISTORY cannot be communicated by Lectures. But the outline of General History, directions to the Student for historical reading, the subsidiary sciences of Geography and Chronology, together with some information respecting Numismatics and Diplomatics, and the rules of Historical Criticism will furnish ample scope for one Professor.

The science of POLITICAL ECONOMY seeks to ascertain the laws which regulate the production, distribution, and consumption of wealth, or the outward things obtained by labour, or needed or desired by men. It is now too justly valued to require any other remark, than that the occasional difficulty of applying its principles, and the differences of opinion to which that difficulty has given rise, form new reasons for the diligent cultivation of a science which is so indispensable to the well being of communities, and of which, as it depends wholly on facts, all the perplexities must be finally removed by accurate observation and precise language.

For the studies which are necessary in all the branches of the PROFESSION of MEDICINE, the greatest city of Europe possesses peculiar and inestimable advantages. It is in large towns only that a Medical School can exist. The means of acquiring anatomical knowledge, medical experience, and surgical dexterity, must increase in exact proportion to the size of the town. At this moment the great majority of those who are called general practitioners, who take no degree, confine themselves to no single branch of the profession; but in whose hands the whole ordinary practice of England is placed, receive their systematic instruction from Lectures in London, for one or two years, while many of them attend hospitals. Their annual average is about seven hundred. Many of the Lecturers have been, and are men of very eminent ability; and the body of practitioners thus educated are, doubtless, very respectable for information and skill. It is no reflexion on either, to affirm, that Medical Education would be improved if the teachers of most distinguished ability who are now scattered over London, were gradually attracted to one Institution, where they would be stimulated to the utmost exertion of their faculties, by closer rivalship, larger emolument, and wider reputation. To what cause but to the present dispersion of eminent teachers can it be ascribed, that the greatest city of the civilized world is not its first School of Medicine?

The young men who are intended for the scientific profession of a CIVIL ENGINEER, which has of late been raised so high by men of genius, and exercised with such signal advantage to the public, have almost as strong reasons as those who are destined for the practice of Medicine, for desiring that a System of Academical Education should be accessible to them in the City, where alone they can be trained to skill and expertness under Artists of the first class.

The Council are rather encouraged than disheartened by the consideration that their undertaking rests on the voluntary contributions of individuals, on which, after the experience of a season of public difficulty, they now rely with firmer assurance. They are satisfied, that experience of its advantages will, in due time, procure for it such legal privileges as

3

may be found convenient for its administration. For the good effects expected in other Seminaries from discipline, the Council put their trust in the power of Home and the care of Parents: to whom, in this Institution, which is equally open to the youth of every religious persuasion, the important duty of religious education is necessarily, as well as naturally left. That care, always the best wherever it can be obtained, will assuredly be adequate to every purpose in the case of the Residents in London, who must at first be the main foundation of the Establishment. When its reputation attracts many Pupils from the Country and the Colonies, the houses of Professors may afford those means of private instruction, and domestic superintendence, which have been found in other places to be excellent substitutes for parental care, and in the conduct of which the most justly celebrated men of this age have not disdained to take a part. They are not unwilling that the value of testimonials of proficiency and conduct, granted by the University, should, at least for the present, depend on the opinion entertained by the Public, of the judgment, knowledge, vigilance, and integrity, of the Professors.

Finally. The Council trust, that they are now about to lay the Foundation of an Institution well adapted to communi-cate liberal instruction to successive generations of those who are now excluded from it, and likely neither to retain the machinery of studies superseded by time, nor to neglect any new science brought into view by the progress of reason; of such magnitude as to combine the illustration and ornament which every part of knowledge derives from the neighbourhood of every other, with the advantage which accrues to all from the outward aids and instruments of Libraries, Museums, and Apparatus; where there will be a sufficient prospect of fame and emolument to satisfy the ambiton, and employ the whole active lives of the ablest Professors; which may thus contribute to restore the most eminent places in Education to their natural rank among the ultimate and highest objects of pursuit; where the least remission of diligence must give instant warning of danger, and an attempt to pervert its resources to personal purposes cannot fail to cut off the supply sought to be perverted; where the inseparable connexion of ample income, and splendid reputation with the general belief of meritorious service, may prove at once a permanent security for the ability of the Teachers, an incentive to their constant activity, and a preservative of the Establishment from decay.

I. -LANGUAGE.

1. Greek Language, Literature, and Antiquities.
2. Roman Language, Literature, and Antiquities.
3. English Literature and Composition.
4. Oriental Literature, subdivided into,--
   A. Languages from the Mediterranean to the Indus.
   B. Languages from the Indus to the Burrampooter.
5. French Language and Literature.
6. Italian and Spanish Literature.
7. German and Northern Literature.

II. MATHEMATICS.

8. Elementary Mathematics.
9. Higher Mathematics.

III. HISTORY.

10. History.

IV. PHYSICS.

11. Mathematical Physics.
12. Experimental Physics
13. Chemistry.
14. Geology and Mineralogy.
15. Botany and Vegetable Physiology.
16. Zoology and Comparative Anatomy.
17. Application of Physical Sciences to the Arts.

V. MENTAL SCIENCE.

18. Philosophy of the Human Mind.
19. Logic.

VI. MORAL SCIENCES.

20. Moral and Political Philosophy.
21. Jurisprudence, including International Law.
22. English Law, with (perhaps) separate Lectures on the Constitution.
23. Roman Law.

VII. POLITICAL ECONOMY.

24. Political Economy.

VIII. MEDICAL SCIENCES.

25. Anatomy.
26. Physiology.
27. Surgery.
28. Midwifery and Diseases of Women and Children.
29. Materia Medica and Pharmacy.
30. Nature and Treatment of Diseases, together with
31. Clinical Lectures as soon as an Hospital can be con-nected with this Establishment.

(Signed, by Order of the Council,)

THOMAS COATES.

It is due to the Promoters of this Institution, to state the privileges and advantages to which they will be entitled in respect of their contributions, whether by subscription or donation to its funds.

The Deed of Settlement, fully provides for the protection of the Proprietors from all liability beyond the amount of the sums respectively subscribed by them. While it confers large powers on the Council, it also interposes every proper check on any irregularity in the exercise of those powers by the appointment of Auditors, and by General and Special Meetings of Proprietors for the revision of the proceedings of the Council and the adoption of such new By-Laws and Regulations as in the progress of the Establishment may from time to time be required.

The rights and privileges of the Proprietors under such Deed may thus shortly be recapitulated ;—

   1. Absolute right of presentation of one Student, in respect of each Share, at such reduced rate of annual payment, and subject to such rules and restrictions as may be prescribed by the Council.

   2. Interest on Shares not exceeding £4 per cent out of surplus income, (if any.)

   3. Privilege of Transfer and Bequest of Shares.

   4. In cases of Ballot, a Proprietor of one Share is entitled to one vote; of five Shares, to two votes; and of ten Shares, or upwards, to three votes, with privilege of voting by proxy at Elections.

   Donors of £50 and upwards are entitled to all the privileges and advantages of Proprietors except as regards the transfer and devolution of their interest, and have no more than one vote on any occasion.

   In addition, Proprietors and Donors will have the right of personal admission to the Library, and the various Collections of the University.

36. The College and its environs
as mapped to show the new
parliamentary borough of St
Marylebone after the 1832
Reform Act. The site was on the
fringe of the built-up area of
the expanding metropolis, with
fields virtually in sight before the
building of Euston station.

36

One of the first acquisitions for the College, even before it was officially constituted, was a building site. Nearly eight acres in Bloomsbury were bought in August 1825 for £30,000 by three of the richest promoters, Goldsmid, John Smith and Benjamin Shaw, and held by them until it could be transferred to the new University. Previously the site had served variously as a drilling ground, a place for duelling and as a rubbish dump. It had been intended to develop it as Carmarthen Square, a projected addition to the yet unfinished Bloomsbury.

37. The 'Catch Me Who Can' in a cartoon ascribed to Rowlandson of the first experimental passenger railway designed by Trevithick in 1808 which had been erected more or less on the future site of the College. The present Faculty of Engineering like to think it was on the site of their original building.

37

38. A plan of the projected
Carmarthen Square
development dated
December 1824, before
the site was acquired for
the College.

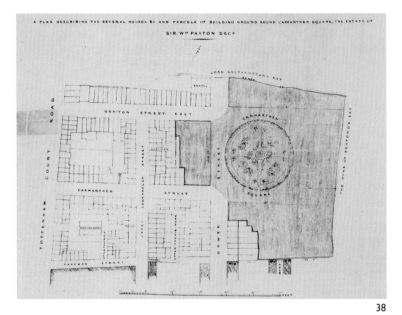

38

By the time of the holding of the first meeting of the proprietors at the end of October 1826, 1,300 shares in the University had been sold, 200 fewer than the minimum believed necessary. Plans for the building were nevertheless being pressed ahead, and the foundations were already being dug. Despite the bad weather of the winter of 1826-27 work was sufficiently advanced by 30 April 1827 for the ceremony of laying the foundation stone. This was undertaken with full masonic rights by the brother of George IV, the Duke of Sussex, the only member of the royal family with any intellectual pretensions, well known for his liberal sympathies. A copper plate with an inscription duly read out by Cox was placed in

39. An invitation to the
foundation ceremony for
the College on 30 April
1827.

40. The Duke of Sussex,
who laid the foundation
stone, as painted by Guy
Head.

40

39

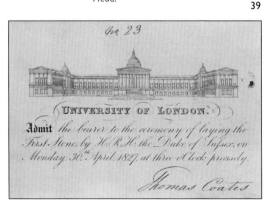

a cavity in the stone together with the traditional coins. Afterwards some 500 people gathered for a dinner at the Freemasons' Tavern at which many speeches were made, many healths drunk and £8,000 raised. Brougham made a memorably sarcastic oration attacking the opponents of the University, but annoyed Campbell's friends by appearing to accept credit for founding the University single-handed. Campbell was absent from the foundation ceremony being occupied as Lord Rector of the University of Glasgow and he did not serve on the Council beyond the first year. Squeezed out by Brougham, Campbell's connection with the University he had proposed ended as it was coming into being.

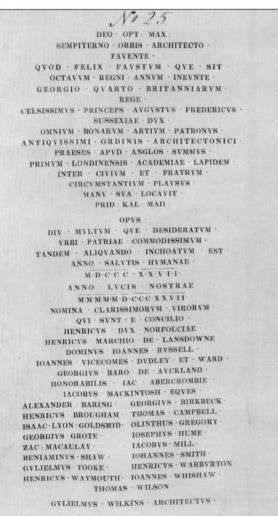

41. An invitation to the grand dinner in the Freemasons' Tavern following the foundation ceremony.

42. The inscription placed inside the foundation stone, the precise whereabouts of which are now unknown.

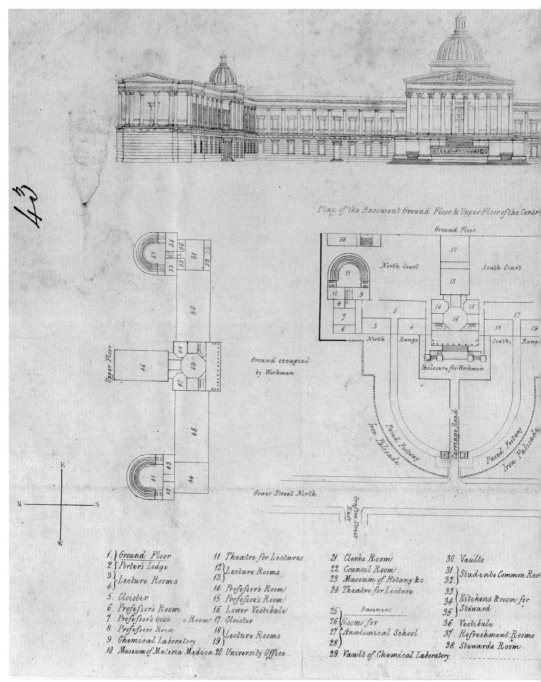

43. The original plan for the College designed by William Wilkins.

The architect chosen for the College was William Wilkins whose fashionable neo-Grecian design submitted in response to public advertisement in August 1825 was found exceedingly fine. Wilkins had previously designed new college buildings for Downing and King's at Cambridge, as well as Haileybury College. University College is Wilkins's greatest work, much more distinguished than the National Gallery he built in Trafalgar Square a few years later. The main entrance was to be at the top of a wide

Plan of the Basement Ground Floor & Upper Floor of the Centr

Ground Floor

North Court

South Court

North Range

South Range

Ground occupied by Workmen

Inclosure for Workmen

Upper Floor

Ground Floor

Iron Palisade

Paved Footway

Carriage Road

Paved Footway

Iron Palisade

Gower Street North

Grafton Street East

1 } Ground Floor
2 } Porter's Lodge
3 } Lecture Rooms
4 }
5. Cloister
6. Professor's Room
7. Professor's Room
8. Professor's Room
9. Chemical Laboratory
10. Museum of Materia Medica

11. Theatre for Lectures
12 } Lecture Rooms
13 }
14. Professor's Room
15. Professor's Room
16. Lower Vestibule
17. Cloister
18 } Lecture Rooms
19 }
20. University Office

21. Clerks Room
22. Council Room
23. Museum of Botany &c.
24. Theatre for Lecture

25 } Basement
26 } Rooms for
27 } Anatomical School
28 }
29. Vault of Chemical Laboratory

30. Vaults
31 } Students Common Roo
32 }
33 }
34 } Kitchens & room for
35 } Steward
36. Vestibule
37. Refreshment Rooms
38. Stewards Room

staircase under a ten-column Corinthian portico topped by an elegant dome. A chapel was conspicuous by its absence, the main entrance being intended to give on to the three principal rooms, the Museum of Natural History to the left, the Library to the right, and the Great Hall directly ahead. Lecture theatres of various sizes led off generous cloisters running to the impressive wings containing further suites of rooms. In the event, shortage of money meant that Wilkins' splendid design was only partially carried out.

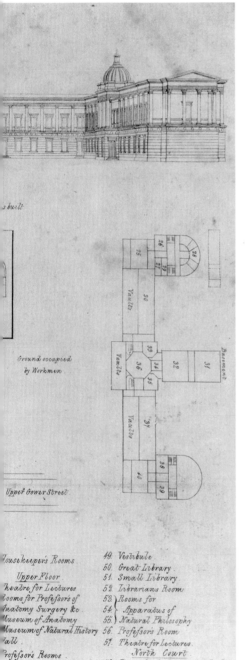

s built

Ground occupied
by Workmin

Upper Gower Street

ousekeepers Rooms   49. Vestibule
                           50. Great Library
   Upper Floor   51. Small Library
heatre for Lectures   52. Librarians Room
ooms for Professors of   53. Rooms for
natomy Surgery &c   54. Apparatus of
useum of Anatomy   55. Natural Philosophy
useum of Natural History   56. Professors Room
all   57. Theatre for Lectures
rofessors Rooms   North Court
                           58. Rooms for Anatomical School

44

44. The bust of William Wilkins by E. H. Bailey now in the Fitzwilliam Museum in Cambridge.

45. The foundation medal showing Wilkins's design for the College including the original wings.

46. Lord Auckland, later a Whig cabinet minister and Governor-General of India, 1835-42, who chaired the committee which supervised the building of the College in 1826-28.

47. A rejected design for the College on a grandiose scale submitted by C. R. Cockerell, later a distinguished Victorian architect who succeeded Wilkins as the Royal Academy's professor of architecture in 1840.

The lowest tender received from a builder for the construction of Wilkins's building was £110,000, almost as much as the College had raised in toto by autumn 1826. 'The wish of the Council will appear to have been', it was confidently declared, 'rather to select a great design suited to the wants, the wealth, and the magnitude of the population for whom the Institution is intended, than one commensurate with its present means...'. To this heroic decision the College owes the distinctive centre to its present rambling and otherwise unimpressive premises. It was decided to build the central range of the building with the portico and dome as envisaged by Wilkins, but to put off the addition of the two wings until the financial position improved. Together with the stone ornamentation, various fittings and the two front lodges, the cost was not to exceed £86,000. Financial stringency also involved postponement of the Great Hall, and strict curtailment

45

46

47

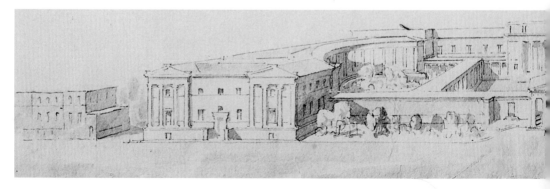

of expenditure on the Museum and Library, and thus the steps
under the Portico became something of a lavish white elephant;
'the grandest entrance in London', it has been called, 'with nothing
behind it'.

Despite the financial setbacks, the great hopes for the new institution continued. Before the building had begun, the College was
treated to the publication of what Thomas Babington Macaulay,
the historian, called its 'horoscope' in the pages of the *Edinburgh
Review*. 'We predict', he wrote, 'that the clamour by which it has
been assailed will die away, that it is destined to a long, a glorious,
and a beneficent existence, that, while the spirit of its system remains
unchanged, the details will vary with the varying necessities and
facilities of every age, that it will be the model of many future
establishments, that even those haughty foundations which now
treat it with contempt, will in some degree feel its salutary influence,
and that the approbation of a great people to whose wisdom, energy
and virtue, its exertions will have largely contributed, will confer
upon it a dignity more imposing than any which it would derive
from the most lucrative patronage or the most splendid ceremonial.'
A very rash prediction at the time, it turned out to be remarkably
percipient.

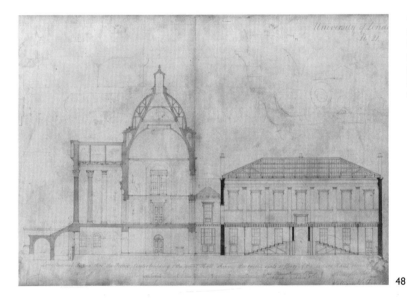

48

48. An architectural cross-section through the Great Hall and the Portico, one of a fine series of such plans drawn by Wilkins himself and used during construction.

THE COCKNEY UNIVERSITY.
Tune—"OVER THE WATER TO CHARLEY."

COME bustle, my neighbours, give over your labours,
  Leave digging and delving, and churning :
New lights are preparing to set you a staring,
  And fill all your noddles with learning.
Each Dustman shall speak, both in Latin and Greek,
  And Tinkers beat Bishops in knowledge—
If the opulent tribe will consent to subscribe
  To build up a new Cockney College.

We've had bubbles in milk—we've had bubbles in silk,
  And bubbles in baths of sea-water;
With other mad schemes, of rail-roads and steams,
  Of tombstones, and places for slaughter—
But none are so sure, so snug and secure,
  As this for which now we are burning,
For 'tis noble and wise to rub the world's eyes,
  And set all the Journeymen learning.

This notable scheme, as we've all of us seen,
  To enlighten the stall and the shamble,
Is twin to a dun-coloured dull Magazine,
  The offspring of RITTER BANN CAMPBELL—
Has he wedded the Muse (I'm sure he'll excuse
  A truth which ought not to be hidden),
To publish such Banns, was the worst of all plans,
  Unless he had wished them forbidden.

This College, when formed, established, endowed,
  Will astonish each Radical's grannam,
Who may place her young fry in the midst of the crowd
  For two pounds ten-shillings per annum.
And oh, what a thing, for a lad who climbs flues,
  Or for one who picks pockets of purses,
To woo in Ionic and Attic, the Muse,
  And make quires of bad Latin verses.

Hackney coachmen from Swift shall reply, if you feel
  Annoyed at being needlessly shaken ;
And Butchers, of course, will be flippant from Steele,
  And Pig-drivers well versed in Bacon—
From Locke shall the Blacksmiths authority crave,
  And Gas-men cite Coke at discretion ;
Undertakers talk Gay as they go to the Grave,
  And Watermen Rowe, by profession.

BURDETT, who from OXFORD received the degree
  Which in Scotland procured him such laurels,
Will lecture each Tuesday at half after three,
  On manners, and marriage, and morals ;
TOM CREEVY will teach the poor Sweeps how to dance,
  LORD COCHRANE shall tutor the Sailors ;
On horseback mad Law instruct Beggars to prance,
  And FERGUSSON manage the Taylors !

PAM BROUGHAM shall teach mildness, and patience, and tact,
  And respect for the laws and his betters ;
And HUME shall instruct them to add and subtract,
  While WOOD teaches wisdom and letters.
On tactics of war civil WILSON shall speak,
  LORD SEFTON shall ground them in driving,
And MACKINTOSH shew them three days in the week
  The easiest way to be thriving.

From a College like this, what advantage must spring,
  What strides will the people be taking ;
Each cobbler will soon be as good as a KING,
  And a KING, a thing hardly worth making :
The rising of some, and the fall of the rest,
  Will bring things at last to their level ;
And just as in FRANCE, which has suffered the test,
  OLD ENGLAND will go to the Devil.

THE COCKNEY COLLEGE.
AN INVITATION TO STINKOMALEE.
TUNE—"Run, Neighbours, run."

Run, sweepers, run, 'tis now the time for lecturing,
  Ev'ry man must learned be in these wise days ;
Freedom's own island, shop-boys, recollect you're in,
  Whose native oaks we mean to graft with classic bays.
First of all discover (if you're able) where is Gower-street,
  The terræ incognitæ of Alfred-place and Store-street ;
Get safely through Carmarthen-street, escape will be a mercy t'ye,
  And on your right, at number ten, you'll see the University.
    Run, sweepers, run, 'tis now the time for lecturing,
      Ev'ry man must learned be in these wise days.

'Tis there British genius, so admirably seconded,
  Soon shall blaze all o'er the world in glory bright,
Since Reason to Freedom so elegantly beckon did,
  To come and share the pleasures of dispensing light.
Conjointly there these Goddesses apprentice boys now call ye,
  Esquired by MESSRS. CAMPBELL, GROTE, and ZACHARY MACAULAY,
To study arts and sciences most fitted to your stations, sirs,
  And raise this isle of Britain to the wisest of all nations, sirs.
    Run, sweepers, run, 'tis now the time for lecturing,
      Ev'ry man must learned be in these wise days.

The tinkers soon shall worship Pan—while all the London shavers, Sirs,
  Disdain the unread Barbari, their quondam friends ;
The cobblers, at Minerva's lap, turn sutors for her favours, Sirs,
  And leave un'tended, in their stalls, their soles and ends.
The milkmen publish scores of works on Blanco White and Paley,
  The tailors talk false quantities, and scribble fustian daily,
The pastry-cooks to Tartarus consign their ice and jellies, Sirs,
  And oyster-girls read Milton's works, or blasphemies, by Shelly, Sirs,
    Run, sweepers, run, 'tis now the time for lecturing,
      Ev'ry man must learned be in these wise days.

The postmen to Belles Lettres their attention then will turn all,
  And pot-boys study for the bar by which to live ;
The ladder-mounting bricklayers by process hodiernal
  Enjoy the Lime labor which improvements give.
Butchers turned Aruspices, shall bow to link-boy TAGES,
  And accidence be studied by the drivers of short stages ;
Mantua-makers Virgil scan, in numbers most harmonious,
  And butchers boys set down their trays to work at Suet-onius.
    Run, sweepers, run, 'tis now the time for lecturing,
      Ev'ry man must learned be in these wise days.

To know his Plata, soon will be the butler's chief ambition, Sirs,
  In Equity our coachmen versed, to drive shall cease ;
Fishmongers shall read from the Delphin large edition, Sirs,
  And poulterers on Turkey write, with plates of Greece.
Tallow-chandlers essays give on dipthongs, sure as fate, Sirs,
  And dustmen learn to venerate the ashes of the great, Sirs ;
Pickle-men discuss Saint Paul, as easy as Salt Petre, Sirs,
  While coal-heavers shall count their sacks to every kind of metre, Sirs.
    Run, sweepers, run, 'tis now the time for lecturing,
      Ev'ry man must learned be in these wise days.

When those times arrive, quite different from now, my friends,
  Reason, worth, and learning, will assert their claims,
Duchesses will knead and wash, and Dukes will hold the plough, my friends,
  Fruitless will be titles then, and all high names ;
Marquesses must clean their shoes, and Earls attend the stable, Sirs,
  Barons stir the kitchen fire, and Viscounts wait at table, sirs,
Come, then, boys—my shirtless boys, who love such gay diversity,
  No CHURCH, no KING, no "nothing else," but Gow'r-street University.
    Run, sweepers, run, 'tis now the time for lecturing,
      Ev'ry man must learned be in these wise days.

Signed, on behalf of the Privy Council of STINKOMALEE,
                                      J. A.
                                      H. B.
                                      and
                                      T. C.

49 & 50. Two of the verses ridiculing the idea of what was quickly dubbed 'the Cockney College' published in the ultra-Tory John Bull in July 1825 and January 1826, the latter by T. E. Hook. Some of the attacks on the College were mere guttersnipe outpourings of the Tory press, but these poems are relatively clever and amusing.

Pugin regarded the architecture of the College as pagan, adding acidly that it was 'in character with the intentions and principles of the institution'. The College had to put up with a good many snide remarks and attacks, especially in the crucial years between Campbell's letter in *The Times* in 1825 and the opening in 1828. The opposition was provoked partly by the apparent pretension of a joint-stock company masquerading as a university in a period of financial speculation; partly by the College's appeal to social groups excluded from the two old universities, an appeal intolerable to the Establishment; most of all, it was provoked by the rejection of all religious teaching and of compulsory religious conformity. The College soon became notorious in the works of Praed's poem as 'the radical infidel College', and more popularly and indelibly as 'the godless institution of Gower Street'.

51. A cartoon lampooning the College published at the time of the foundation in February 1826. Brougham is shown hammering at the iron bar of philosophy on the anvil of public support, while Lord Lansdowne works the bellows and representatives of the populace are made to look on in what is clearly the wrong spirit.

51

52. One of the engravings of
the College buildings given a
good deal of publicity in the late
1820s showing the wings with
their supplementary domes as
envisaged by Wilkins but never
built for lack of funds.

52

THE UNIVERSITY OF LONDON.

53. Another such engraving by
T. H. Shepherd, dedicated to the
two founders of the College.

53

THE LONDON UNIVERSITY.

TO HENRY BROUGHAM ESQ M.P. AND THOMAS CAMPBELL ESQ. TO WHOSE UNITED EXERTIONS,
LONDON IS INDEBTED FOR HER UNIVERSITY, THIS PLATE IS RESPECTFULLY INSCRIBED

Published Nov. 15, 1828. by Jones & Cᵒ Temple of the Muses, Finsbury Square, London.

54. The College as it actually appeared at the time of its opening in 1828 and for nearly fifty years afterwards.

55. Another early engraving of the building showing the back – or east front – of the College, with the Cloisters before they were glazed in.

54

55

Chapter 3
The University of London Years, 1828-36

With such a seminary in a prosperous position [*ie.* the newly proposed King's College], there will be neither motive nor excuse for any parent to inflict upon his [*sic*] offspring the disgrace of education in the infidel and godless college in Gower Street.

Standard, *19 June 1828*

It seems so short a time since the whole scheme has been planned and executed that it reminds me of Aladdin's enchanted palace which sprung up in a single night ...

Selina Macaulay in her diary, October 1828

My last account of the university ... was full of gloomy forebodings. I cannot say that, looking at the institution at large and for any permanent futurity, these are much removed. It is the opinion of many, I almost fear of most, that it contains within itself the seeds of dissolution. The expenditure has been lavish, the plans are ill-digested, and vibrating, like all things in which the Whigs have a hand, between the desire of being popular and the fear of being unfashionable, so as of course to satisfy neither class whom they seek to conciliate by cowardly half-measures. The Council are not united, and the professors as a body are openly at war with the Council.

Mrs Sarah Austin, writing to her sister, April 1830

Though the building of the Portico and the Dome was not completed until the following year, the 'University of London' began its first academic session in October 1828. Selina Macaulay, daughter of Zachary, visited it in the middle of the first term and it impressed her as 'externally and internally a noble building'. She found 'the theatres extremely spacious and so arranged that it is much easier both to see and hear the lecturer than in any other building of the same size...' 'It seems so short a

56

UNIVERSITY OF LONDON.

The MEDICAL CLASSES *will open on* Wednesday *the 1st of October.*

ANATOMY AND OPERATIVE SURGERY—GRANVILLE S. PATTISON, Esq. Daily (except Saturday), from Two to Half-past Three. Fee, First Course £4; Second Course £3.

PHYSIOLOGY—CHARLES BELL, Esq. F.R.S. Three times a week, from Eleven to Twelve. Fee, First Course £3; Second Course £2.

NATURE AND TREATMENT OF DISEASES—JOHN CONOLLY, M.D. Daily (except Saturday), from Nine to Ten. Fee, First Course £3; Second Course £3.

MIDWIFERY AND DISEASES OF WOMEN AND CHILDREN—DAVID D. DAVIS, M.D. Four times a week, from Ten to Eleven. Fee, First Course £3; Second Course £3.

CLINICAL MEDICINE—THOMAS WATSON, M.D. Physician to the Middlesex Hospital. Twice a week, from Six to Seven P.M. Fee, £4.

SURGERY AND CLINICAL SURGERY—CHARLES BELL, Esq. Surgeon to the Middlesex Hospital. Three times a week, from Six to Seven P.M. Fee, £4.

MATERIA MEDICA AND PHARMACY—ANTHONY TODD THOMSON, M.D. Daily (except Saturday), from Eight to Nine A.M. Fee, First Course £3; Second Course £3.

CHEMISTRY—EDWARD TURNER, M.D. Daily, from Ten to Eleven, commencing on the 3rd of November. Fee, First Course £4; Second Course £3.

COMPARATIVE ANATOMY—ROBERT GRANT, M.D. Three times a week, from Three to Four. Fee, £5.

MEDICAL JURISPRUDENCE—JOHN GORDON SMITH, M.D. At the conclusion of the Winter and Spring Courses.

BOTANY—JOHN LINDLEY, Esq. F.R.S. At the conclusion of the Winter and Spring Courses. Fee, £4.

DISSECTIONS AND DEMONSTRATIONS—JAMES BENNETT, Esq. Daily. Fee, First Course £3; Second Course £2.

HOSPITAL PRACTICE—Middlesex Hospital, daily, from Half-past Twelve to Half-past One. Fee for the Academical Session £12 12s.

DISPENSARY PRACTICE—University Dispensary, daily, from Half-past Twelve to Half-past One. Fee for the Academical Session £5.

The Introductory Lectures of the Medical Professors will be delivered in the following order:

Three o'clock P.M. Wednesday, 1st of October—CHARLES BELL, Esq.
————— Thursday, 2nd of October—DR. CONOLLY.
————— Friday, 3rd of October—DR. DAVIS.
————— Saturday, 4th of October—GRANVILLE S. PATTISON, Esq.
————— Monday, 6th of October—DR. A. T. THOMSON.
————— Tuesday, 7th of October—DR. WATSON.

The Medical Classes will close in May, but each Professor will give a Winter and Spring Course.

When all the Introductory Lectures of the several Medical Classes shall have been delivered, the Professors will commence their Courses at the hours above stated.

The Certificates of the Medical Professors will be received at the College of Surgeons, and at Apothecaries' Hall. The Lectures will be open to students who may not desire certificates, or who wish merely to attend single Courses.

The names of Students are entered at the University Chambers, 29, Percy Street, Bedford Square. All other particulars respecting the Medical School may be obtained by application to the Professors, or to Mr. Coates at the Chambers.

(By Order of the Council.)

THOMAS COATES, *Clerk.*

N.B. The Fee for the First Courses will be required to be paid at whatever period of the Session the Pupil may enter.

Printed by Richard Taylor, Red Lion Court, Fleet Street.

56. The full programme of medical classes offered by the College in 1828-29, its first year of operation.

time', she concluded in her diary, 'since the whole scheme has been planned and executed that it reminds me of Aladdin's enchanted palace which sprung up in a single night...'

The opening inaugural lectures were well attended by the public and were pronounced a great success. The first of them was delivered on 1 October 1828 by Charles Bell, the Professor of Surgery and the most famous member of the distinguished Medical Faculty that had been assembled. He had been educated at Edinburgh, becoming a member of the Speculative Society there, that notable group brought together in the 1790s which was to provide the London University with no fewer than five members of the original Council and three of the first professors. He conducted important research on the working of the nervous system and became a surgeon of repute at the Middlesex Hospital. John Conolly too studied medicine at Edinburgh, graduating in 1821 and subsequently practising medicine at Stratford-on-Avon, twice becoming mayor of the town. Neither Bell nor Conolly were to stay long at the College owing to the unfortunate quarrels which soon engulfed the Medical Faculty. Bell resigned in 1830, going to build up the medical school at the Middlesex and then returning to Edinburgh University. Conolly resigned in 1831, later taking charge of the Hanwell Lunatic Asylum where he introduced humane methods of treatment for the insane and pioneered revolutionary changes in this field. His pupil and son-in-law Henry Maudsley (who qualified at UCL in 1856 and became Professor of Medical Jurisprudence, 1869-80) was to be commemorated by the Maudsley Hospital.

57. Sir Charles Bell, FRS, the Professor Physiology and Surgery, who gave the first inaugural lecture in October 1828.

58. John Conolly, the Professor of the Nature and Treatment of Disease, who gave the second of the inaugural lectures.

57

58

A contemporary of Bell's at Edinburgh, Anthony Todd Thomson, became Professor of Materia Medica. He too had come to London in the first decade of the nineteenth century to make his mark in the medical profession, and also in the literary world. He conducted original research into the composition of alkaloids and iodides, and published a good deal. David D. Davis, a Glasgow graduate of Welsh origin, became Professor of Midwifery and Diseases of Women and Children. He had established himself as a successful London obstetrician, becoming a leading private teacher of the subject and pioneering many advanced methods, especially associated with obstetric forceps. He achieved some prominence by delivering the future Queen Victoria at Kensington Palace in 1819.

Robert E. Grant was appointed Professor of Comparative Anatomy at the time of the opening and he remained in this post until his death forty-six years later in 1874 as the longest survivor of the original professoriate. Throughout this period he gave five lectures a week and was believed never to have missed one. Imposing if eccentric in appearance, he invariably wore full evening dress. He was yet another Edinburgh graduate and had done important research there prior to coming to the College, especially on sponges, a genus of which is named after him. Amongst his Edinburgh pupils was Darwin, who was arguably deeply influenced by his ideas and who lived next door to UCL in the early 1840s. A friend of Cuvier as well as of Darwin, Grant remained on the fringes of the forefront of his subject. He gave his students breakfast in his house near Euston and took favoured ones on continental walking-tours,

59. Anthony Todd Thomson, Professor of Materia Medica from the opening of the College until his death in 1849.

60. Robert E. Grant, FRS, Professor of Comparative Anatomy (to which Zoology was later added) from the opening of the College until his death in 1874.

59   60

A. T. Thomson

M.D. F.L.S. G.S. Professor of Materia Medica & Therapeutics &c of General Medicine University Col. London.

Robert E Grant

M.D. YRS L.S.E. &c Professor in the Royal Inst of Great Britain in University College London.

but he did little further research. He left his valuable collection of early books on biology to the College.

The first holder of the Chair of Natural Philosophy was the Revd Dr Dionysius Lardner, an extraordinary man who has been described as making up in contemporary notoriety what he lacked in more lasting fame. He moved in the most fashionable literary and political circles, and was very successful as a popular lecturer and writer of great zest. His best-known work is the *Cabinet Cyclopaedia* which he edited in 133 volumes between 1829 and 1849. His early lectures at the College attracted a good deal of attention, but Lardner, his apparatus, his courses and his salary caused more trouble for the Council than any other topic in the opening years. He resigned in 1831 to make more money from writing and giving lectures in the USA. He subsequently eloped with the wife of a cavalry officer, becoming involved in very expensive law-suits and having to settle in Paris. He cut rather more of a dash in life than many of his academic successors.

61. David D. Davis, Professor of Midwifery from the opening of the College until his death in 1841, as portrayed in the College's bust of him.

62

61

THE EDITOR OF "THE CABINET CYCLOPEDIA".

62. The encyclopaedic Revd Dr Dionysius Lardner, FRS, Professor of Natural Philosophy and Astronomy, 1828-31, as pictured in Fraser's Magazine after his resignation.

63. A registration card for Lardner's class in the first session.

63

*64. Augustus De Morgan,
the brilliant Professor of
Mathematics, 1828-31,
and then again 1836-67,
as drawn by a student.*

64

Only 21 and just down from Cambridge, Augustus De Morgan was the youngest of the original professors when he was appointed to the Chair of Mathematics. He was to distinguish himself by resigning from this position on a matter of principle not once, but twice. For many, however, he was the outstanding figure in the first generation of the life of the College. Sir Henry Roscoe, the chemist who was a student at the College in the 1840s, called him 'one of the profoundest and subtlest thinkers of the nineteenth century'.

De Morgan taught logic and mathematics with a deft brilliance and penetration that his students found inescapably fascinating, and he exerted a captivating influence on many of them, including W. S. Jevons and Walter Bagehot. A prolific writer, who made a key contribution to the development of modern symbolic logic, he was also a leading member of the Astronomical Society and the first President of the London Mathematical Society.

He was also a great wit. When Sir George Cornewall Lewis as Chancellor of the Exchequer in the 1850s rejected a proposal for the decimalisation of the coinage on the grounds of the complexity of various schemes, De Morgan scornfully drew up a variety of proposals in which ten farthings would make a what's-its-name, ten what's-its-names a how-d'ye-call-it, and ten how-d'ye-call-its a thingeme-bob, or ten farthings a George, ten Georges a Cornewall and ten Cornewalls a Lewis.

De Morgan resigned in 1831 over the unhappy Pattison affair (see pp. 62-63). After the early death of his successor in 1836, he returned to the Chair and held it for thirty years until his second resignation in 1867. The Council's rejection of the appointment of James

Martineau as Professor of Mental Philosophy and Logic on the grounds that he was a Unitarian minister was, he argued, itself an ironical but fundamental desertion of the principles on which the College had been founded. He felt this so strongly that he refused to allow a bust or portrait of himself to be placed in the College to which he had brought such distinction.

Distinguished appointments were also made in chemistry and in botany. Yet a further Edinburgh medical graduate, Edward Turner, was appointed as the first Professor of Chemistry. He was rapidly to attain a European reputation in this subject. During his tenure of the Chair he was occupied in analytical work on the determination of atomic weights and in the writing of two textbooks, one of which, *The Elements of Chemistry*, came to be the standard work for many years. It was translated into German, and later edited by the great German chemist Liebig. Turner was also active in the Geological Society and began the teaching of geology in the College. He died at the early age of 39 in 1837.

John Lindley was the first Professor of Botany, a subject originally conceived as an adjunct to the teaching of medicine. Lindley was the son of a Norfolk horticulturalist and was not himself a graduate. Employed originally by a seed merchant, he became librarian to Sir Joseph Banks, the noted naturalist and President of the Royal Society from 1822. His greatest contribution to the subject derived from the success of his efforts to preserve the Royal Botanic Gardens in Kew in the late 1830s. His *Vegetable Kingdom* and *Introduction to Botany* enjoyed a long period as standard works. The contrast was noted between his own appearance, fresh, ruddy and hale-looking, and that of the students.

65. Edward Turner, FRS, Professor of Chemistry, 1828-37, whose bust by Butler remains in the Chemistry Department.

66. John Lindley, FRS, Professor of Botany, 1828-60.

65

66

T he most striking characteristic of the twenty-four professors who constituted the teaching body of the College when it opened in 1828 was their relative youth. All but three were aged under 40, and six were 30 or under. The second striking fact is the number of posts in subjects which had not previously been taught in English universities, or, more significantly still, in British universities, and even European ones. The chairs in the modern foreign languages and in English language and literature were all especially notable innovations.

P. F. Merlet, the original teacher of French, was not given the title of professor until 1834, but chairs in German, Italian, Spanish and English, as well as in Latin, Greek, Hebrew and Hindustani, were established from the outset. The modern languages were taught by refugees from their respective countries. German was taught by Ludwig von Mühlenfels, a progressive and independent thinker, who was appointed while passing through London on his way to join a band of fellow exiles in Mexico, having escaped from a Prussian political prison. Italian was put in the hands of Antonio Panizzi, who had escaped from a death sentence in Italy. Besides his post in the College, Panizzi took that of Assistant Librarian at the British Museum in 1831, becoming Keeper of Printed Books there in 1837 and eventually Principal Librarian in 1856. After giving up his Chair, he achieved permanent fame as virtual creator of both the library catalogue and the Reading Room at the British Museum. Spanish was handled by Antonio Alcalá Galiano, a marked man in Spain after 1832 when he moved a resolution against Ferdinand VII in the Spanish parliament and as a result was sentenced to death. A leading figure in Spanish Romantic literature, Alcalá resigned

67. The first of four of the original professors in what was to become the Faculty of Arts, all portrayed at much later stages in their unusual careers, after they had left the College: Sir Antonio Panizzi, Professor of Italian, 1828-38.

68. Antonio Alcalá Galiano, Professor of Spanish, 1828-30.

67

68

in 1830 to go to Paris, hoping to take part in the July Revolution. In 1831 von Mühlenfels also left, hoping for an improved political climate in Germany. His successors in the Chair of German were of little or no consequence for many years, while Spanish was not taught again after 1830 until the establishment of the present Department in 1964.

Thomas Dale, the first Professor of English, took his holy orders very seriously and evangelically. 'I shall invariably aim', he announced in his inaugural lecture, 'to impart moral as well as intellectual instruction...I shall esteem it my duty...to inculcate lessons of virtue.' After two years of grappling with this task, he departed to devote himself to the ministry, becoming vicar of St Bride's, Fleet Street, and later of St Pancras. Between 1836 and 1839 he was also to find what was doubtless a more receptive audience for his inculcation of lessons of virtue as the first Professor of English at King's College, London.

George Long, the original professor of Greek, was a more significant figure. He had been recruited from Trinity College, Cambridge, to be the founding Professor of Ancient Languages at the University of Virginia. He returned to England to take the Chair of Greek, but then resigned over the Pattison affair in 1831 and worked full-time for the Society for the Diffusion of Useful Knowledge as editor of the *Quarterly Journal of Education* and then of the famous twenty-nine-volume *Penny Cyclopaedia*. He was to return to UCL as Professor of Latin for four years in the 1840s, but left again to combine school-teaching in Brighton with his literary and scholarly work.

69. The Revd Thomas Dale, Professor of English, 1828-30.

70. George Long, Professor of Greek, 1828-31, and later Professor of Latin, 1842-46.

69

70

The study of the workings of society was naturally not to be ignored in a College so influenced by utilitarian thought. In law and in economics distinguished appointments were made at the outset. Law was taken to be an important subject of study from the very beginning and the College can fairly claim to have inaugurated the systematic university study of law. To the Chair of Jurisprudence John Austin was appointed in July 1827; he then spent a year in Bonn preparing his lectures while mixing with the great German scholars and jurists there. Austin was recognised as a powerful intellect, and his deep learning and original thought duly impressed the students (including John Stuart Mill). But he completed very little in his lifetime, not even managing the preparation of his lectures for publication, a task his wife had to finish after his death in 1859. After the demand for the law classes had apparently fallen away, Austin left the College, becoming first a member of the Criminal Law Commission, later conducting an inquiry into the state of Malta and subsequently living in Germany and France. The other law professor, Andrew Amos, also held very popular and well-attended classes for the first sessions, but also left after enrolment collapsed. A successful barrister, he had earlier been Shelley's only friend at Eton and was later a county court judge and a professor at Cambridge. His son, Sheldon Amos, was Professor of Jurisprudence at the College, 1869-78, and

71

71. The bust of Andrew Amos, Professor of English Law, 1828-34, presented by his former students and still kept in the Laws Faculty.

72

72. The certificate of appointment of John Austin as Professor of Jurisprudence, a post he was to hold until 1835.

his grandson, Sir Maurice Sheldon Amos, was Quain Professor of Comparative Law, 1932-37.

In economics the same story is repeated of high hopes unrealised despite an outstanding appointment. J. R. McCulloch was the first professional economist in the sense of one who made his living from the subject as journalist, author and teacher. An Edinburgh man, he was appointed to the Chair of Political Economy after coming to London to give the lectures established as an independent memorial to David Ricardo. McCulloch soon embarked on a prolonged dispute about his salary, eventually refusing to lecture after 1835 unless the Council agreed to guarantee it at a higher level than the fees from the small number of students who attended. In 1837 his Chair was declared vacant.

Notable among the original appointments was that of F. A. Rosen, who brought the best of German scholarship to the College introducing notions basic to comparative philology. Professor of Oriental Literature at 22, he was later Professor of Sanskrit for the two years before his early death in 1837. Teaching of various Oriental languages continued until 1917 when they were transferred to the new institution that became the School of Oriental and African Studies.

74

73

73. J. R. McCulloch, Professor of Political Economy, 1828-37, painted clasping respectfully a copy of Adam Smith's Wealth of Nations.

74. The elegant bust of Friedrich August Rosen, Professor of Oriental Literature until 1831 and then of Sanskrit, 1835-37. He also worked for the British Museum where this bust remains today.

75

75. The most idyllic of the
early prints of the College,
again showing the wings as
Wilkins planned them, but
as they never were.

The three years of hopeful expectation prior to the opening gave way after 1828 to three years fraught with many problems and wasteful quarrels. The only sources of finance were, first, what could be raised through shares or donations as capital and secondly, what the fees of the students brought in as income. The capital was splendidly but unwisely used up by the cost of the site and the buildings. 'The expenditure has been lavish,' wrote John Austin's wife in 1830, 'the plans are ill-digested, and vibrating, like all things in which the Whigs have a hand, between the desire of being popular and the fear of being unfashionable...' Professorial dependence on a proportion of the fees meant, when fewer students than expected enrolled, that their incomes were unacceptably low, and the Council's guarantees of at least £300 a year were hard to meet. The grievances of the teachers were compounded by their not having any formal status as a body nor any say in the running of the College, but also by the attitude of the Warden.

The first appointment made by the Council had been that of Leonard Horner as Warden in May 1827. Horner came, like so many of the others, from Edinburgh, where he was regarded as 'one of the most useful citizens that Edinburgh ever possessed'. He was the founder of the School of Arts there in 1821, now Heriot-Watt University, and was an energetic Secretary of the Geological Society in London from 1810. From the start, however, he took a high-handed view of his new office. The generous salary of £1,200 a year on which he had insisted was itself a source of irritation to the professors, and Horner's continual petty interference in their work proved increasingly objectionable.

Matters came to a head in 1830-31 over the complicated issues raised by the criticisms against Granville Sharp Pattison, the Professor of Anatomy. The medical students were provoked by what they saw as Pattison's incompetence both as an anatomist and as a teacher (when he did turn up to lecture, he did so in hunting pink) and their opinions were supported by Charles Bell. Horner's clumsy attempts to sack Pattison, however, led to the case being

Dr Gordon Smith
27 Oct 1830

76

P380

Wednesday. Oct. 27. 1830.

Sir,

Understanding that Dr Thomson, senior, is giving out that I am insane, I think it appropriate to inform you that he said the same thing of you, at a meeting of the Professors, last year.

Your obedient servant

Gordon Smith

L. Horner Esq

76. Evidence that life in the College was no idyll: a letter addressed to the Warden at the start of the third session by J. Gordon Smith, Professor of Medical Jurisprudence, 1829-32, one of the first of the professors to become an alcoholic and perhaps the only one to die in a debtor's prison.

77. The focus of many of the early quarrels: Leonard Horner, FRS (1785-1864), the first and only Warden, 1827-31.

77

taken up by the other aggrieved professors as a stick to beat Horner with.

The issue gathered, as such disputes do, many bitter subtleties. It led to the first student demonstration, in 1830, and eventually caused the resignations not only of Bell and Conolly from the Medical Faculty, but, following the dismissal of Pattison, of De Morgan, Long and Rosen too. In the end Horner himself was forced to resign and the office of Warden was abolished, being replaced by a Secretary at £200. Horner had a distinguished career later as the first Factory Inspector. The Pattison affair had many consequences; one of them was that the professors were organised into a Senate and into Faculties; another was that the College was to manage without a full-time head for the rest of the century.

KINGS COLLEGE VERSUS LONDON UNIVERSITY
or Which is the Weightiest

78

78. *A cartoon portraying the initial antagonism
between the College and the rival King's College
founded in 1828: a clutch of bloated bishops,
including the Archbishop of Canterbury and the
Revd Dr George D'Oyly, with the added weight
of Money and Interest, are pitted against the
founders of University College, including Brougham
(waving the broom) and Bentham (clad in dressing
gown), supported by Sense and Science.*

Lying behind the financial difficulties of the early years was the problem of student numbers. There had been talk of providing for 2,000 students; at least 1,100 were deemed necessary in order to balance the books in the first year: in fact, 641 materialised in 1828-29, and only about 630 in the following year. Thereafter they fluctuated rather, and did not begin to increase substantially until the 1870s. It took over eighty years to reach the projected 2,000 (see the graph on p. 161).

If imitation implies success, however, the College achieved it before the doors were opened. An Establishment rival in the form of King's College began at a meeting in June 1828 chaired by the Duke of Wellington and attended by no less than three archbishops, seven bishops and 'the principal nobility'. The prime founder was the Revd Dr George D'Oyly, the Rector of Lambeth, who had been much disturbed by the exclusion of religious teaching from the curriculum of a University of London. D'Oyly believed that the Church of England 'presents Christianity in its most pure and perfect form', and that the interests of the Church and the State combined to demand a new institution with different principles to those adopted in Gower Street. With the backing he naturally received, there was no difficulty in obtaining a charter in 1829. A new wing was built to Somerset House in the Strand and by October 1831 a second institution of higher education was opened in London. A healthy rivalry has been maintained between the two colleges ever since.

79. The first entries in the register of students for the opening session in 1828: they represent the youthful offspring of some illustrious names in the history of the College.

79

80

80. A late nineteenth-century photograph of the Botanical Theatre, one of the four main lecture theatres in the semi-circular projections at the rear of the College, showing it a little more drab perhaps, but not substantially different from its original appearance.

81. A Certificate of Honours as awarded in the early years.

The system of education established at the College was based upon instruction by means of lectures and upon written examinations. This was a deliberate departure from the method of the older English universities; it was modelled on the practice of Scotland and of Germany. The early years saw an enormous amount of lecturing taking place. The naturalist and Registrar of the University, W. B. Carpenter, as a student in the early 1830s attended no less than thirty-five lectures a week. There was some bleak justification for Coleridge's contemptuous reference to the College as a 'lecture-bazaar'.

Initially no degrees were offered. There was in 1830 a proposal to award the cumbersome degree of M. Med et Chir. U. L., but the absence of a royal charter was generally held to deny degree-

81

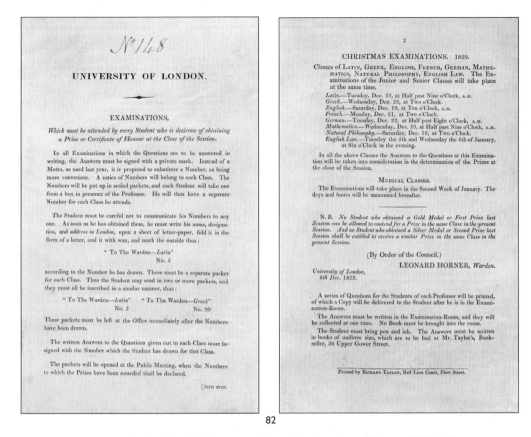

giving powers to a body that had no outside authority for calling itself a university. Instead Certificates of Honours were presented in connection with each course, and a General Certificate was obtainable after three years of following an agreed programme of study. Fees were payable for each separate course of lectures. The average cost for a student nominated by a proprietor (such students were admitted at a lower rate) was approximately £22 7s. 6d. per annum, an amount it would have taken a coachman, say, a year to earn. The College was thus well beyond the means of the working class.

82. The elaborate regulations for what seem to have been the first examinations, held at Christmas 1829.

83. Both sides of a gold medal as awarded to the best student in every subject.

84

84. The playground of
University College School
as drawn by the German-
born artist George Scharf,
published as an engraving
in 1833. Scharf's son –
later Sir George Scharf, the
first director of the National
Portrait Gallery – was a
pupil at the School.

A school was established in connection with the College in 1830, and from the start it prospered at a time when the College was not otherwise growing. Opened in a Gower Street house with eighty boys in the first term, a year later the School had 249 boys and accommodation had to be found within the main building. After 1832 in an unforeseen way the School came to take up a good deal of space in the College, particularly in the area originally intended for the Great Hall and the rooms below it. Thomas Hewitt Key and Henry Malden, Professors of Latin and Greek, were put in joint charge of the School once its success was evident.

Key, very versatile in his interests, had been the first Professor of Mathematics at the University of Virginia, and in 1842 gave up the Chair of Latin at UCL for that of Comparative Grammar – the first such chair in England, though his scholarship in this field was not beyond question; he combined this post with that of Headmaster until the day of his death in 1875. He was a great and vigorous teacher, while Malden was the more careful and urbane scholar. Malden gave up the joint headship in 1842, though he continued to teach the Sixth until 1868.

85

86

85. Thomas Hewitt Key, FRS, Professor of Latin, 1828-42, and of Comparative Grammar, 1842-75, and also Headmaster of the School from 1831 to 1875, as painted by Langlois.

86. Henry Malden, Professor of Greek, 1831-76, and Joint Headmaster of the School with Key between 1831 and 1842, as shown on the medal established in his memory for a third-year student with a creditable knowledge of Greek. It was found difficult to award it in some years until W. P. Ker devised the ruling: 'Any knowledge of Greek is creditable'.

Other professors also taught at the School, which quickly built up a considerable reputation for religious tolerance, a broad curriculum and a sympathetic relationship between teacher and pupil. It was one of the earliest schools to attempt to dissociate education and flogging.

The first Librarian of the College was the Revd Dr F. A. Cox (see p. 32), the original Secretary of the Council. By the beginning of 1829 he had judiciously built up a collection of some 6,500 volumes. A year later there were 9,027 volumes. 'The Council would gladly have announced a larger addition', recorded the Annual Report for 1830, 'but prudential considerations have limited the purchases.' The books were housed in what was called the Small Library at the southern end of the building, since funds were inadequate for the proposed Great Library. A further economy in 1831 was to dispense with the services of the Librarian: there was to be no proper successor until 1871, the Library being left in the charge of an assistant and sometimes simply of a beadle. Less than £50 altogether was spent on books in the poverty-stricken four years 1832-35, and the average annual expenditure for the forty-three years from 1832 to 1875 was a mere £51.

In this period, growth was therefore heavily dependent on donations and bequests. Some 4,000 books came from Jeremy Bentham

87

UNIVERSITY OF LONDON.

Nº 98.

REGULATIONS for the LIBRARY.

I. *Perfect silence must be maintained.*

II. If any Gentleman wishes for a Book, he must write the title on a slip of paper, and give it to the Assistant in attendance, for the Librarian.

III. When a Gentleman has finished reading a Book, he must return it to the Assistant in attendance.

IV. If Gentlemen wish to make Extracts, they must not place their paper *on* a Book in writing the extract.

V. The Library is accessible from *Ten* in the Morning until *Four* in the Afternoon.

(By Order of the Council.)

F. A. COX,
LIBRARIAN.

87. The earliest Library Regulations issued soon after the opening of the Library in January 1829.

in 1833, and Joseph Hume's large collection of tracts followed in 1855. An impressive number of collections were left by professors of the College, the earliest really notable one being that left by J. T. Graves in 1870. Despite being Professor of Jurisprudence and later a Poor Law Inspector, Graves formed a valuable library of over 14,000 items chiefly devoted to early mathematics. His sister married Leopold von Ranke, the founder of modern historical method, and he was a forebear of Robert Graves. He once compiled a list of 2,862 anagrams on the name of Augustus De Morgan in English, Latin, French and German.

The 1830s saw retrenchment on other fronts besides that of the Library. No initial appointment had been made in history, and the Chair was not filled until 1830, and then only briefly and inadequately by a retired headmaster. There was no regular history teaching until after 1834. One of the few developments of the period, other than the School and the Hospital, was in geography, though as it turned out even this was abortive. In 1833 Alexander Maconochie, Secretary of the newly-founded Royal Geographical Society, was made the first Professor of Geography in the College – and the first in Britain. A retired naval captain, he left in 1836 to go to administer Van Diemen's Land and to investigate penal conditions. No successor was appointed, and geography was not revived at the College until 1903.

88. Capt Alexander Maconochie, RN, the first Professor of Geography, 1833-36.

89. J. T. Graves, FRS, Professor of Jurisprudence, 1839-43.

88

89

90. A hospital had been regarded by the Medical Faculty from the beginning as an essential part of the College, but for some years they had to put up with the limited facilities offered by the University Dispensary in Upper Gower Street. Plans for the building of the 'North London Hospital' on the unused part of the College site on the other side of Gower Street were accepted in 1832, and the foundation stone was laid in May 1833 by the Duke of Somerset, FRS, President of the Royal Institution and the then Chairman of the Council of the College. George Scharf was present and recorded the occasion in a sketch.

90

William Sharpey's active tenure of his Chair for nearly forty years earned him the title of the father of modern physiology in Britain. Before being appointed in 1836, he had been trained at Edinburgh and had studied at the French and German universities where physiology was much more highly developed than it was in Britain before his own lifetime. He was a thorough and inspiring teacher. He hardly ever showed an experiment or piece of apparatus in classes, but he was one of the first to introduce the microscope for practical illustration of his teaching, having a table especially constructed for this purpose. He exerted a considerable influence through his students, who came to dominate the subject (see pp. 110-11), and through being for twenty years after 1853 a powerful and effective Secretary of the Royal Society.

Sharpey's Chair was nominally in anatomy as well as physiology, but anatomy was primarily in other hands. After Charles Bell's resignation it was taught by two brothers – Jones Quain, Sharpey's predecessor as Professor of Anatomy and Physiology, and Richard Quain, Demonstrator, 1831-32, then Professor of Anatomy, 1831-50, and later surgeon at the Hospital, Professor of Clinical Surgery, 1850-66, and President of the Royal College of Surgeons. He is remembered as founder of the Quain chairs and for presenting the law library of his half-brother, Sir John Richard Quain, a judge and himself a former student of the College. Many of Bell's preserved anatomical and pathological specimens were acquired by the College before his resignation as the beginnings of the Anatomy Museum (see p. 111); some are still in use for teaching purposes at the Medical School.

The first stage of the Hospital was opened in November 1834 with beds for 130 patients. It was built for less than £7,600, much more cheaply than the College itself: 'all architectural decorations', it was plainly stated, 'have for the sake of economy been studiously excluded'. The building was financed entirely through public appeals at a time when the College was seriously in debt. The intimate connection with the College was recognised in 1837 when its name was changed to 'University College Hospital'. A southern extension was added in 1841 and a northern one in 1846.

Much of the early success of the new Hospital was due to John Elliotson, Conolly's

91

92

93. A drawing by George Scharf of the Hospital soon after its completion, showing the gate maintained across the part of Gower Street owned by the College. The roadway was eventually sold in 1892 to St Pancras for the large sum of £15,000.

93

successor in 1831 with the title of Professor of the Theory and Practice of Medicine. Elliotson was exceedingly popular as a teacher and was a practitioner of great energy and originality. He was a pioneer of the stethoscope and he introduced the use of quinine for malaria. With the best of scientific intentions, however, he got involved in the earliest of the scandals arising from the Victorian mesmerism craze. The two Okey sisters threw hystero-epileptic fits and were put into mesmeric trances before large and fashionable audiences, attracting much attention, including that of Charles Dickens. The College found it all rather embarrassing, even before the *Lancet* exposed the sisters as fakes. Elliotson had to make an untimely resignation.

94

94. John Elliotson, FRS, the advanced but controversial Professor of Medicine, 1831-39.

95

95. A watercolour picture of
the College from Old Gower
Mews (the site of Foster Court)
painted by George Sidney
Shepherd in 1835. Behind
the dome can be seen the
uncompleted Great Hall, later
destroyed by fire. The picture
was bought by the College in
1988.

Chapter 4
The Years of Men, 1836-78

That His Majesty's Ministers, in consequence of the Address of the House of Commons on the 26th day of March last … having devised a plan for conferring Academical Degrees more comprehensive and efficient than that contemplated by such Address, by extending to all other duly qualified Colleges for education equal facilities for obtaining Degrees, including those in Medicine. This Meeting, confiding in the sufficiency of the Board of Examiners to be constituted by the Government, and satisfied that this Institution has nothing to fear from competition with any other body, recommend to the Council gratefully to accept the Collegiate Charter offered.

Resolution carried unanimously at the Annual General Meeting of the
Proprietors of the University of London, 22 February 1836

… in those years [mid-1840s, when Richard Hutton and Walter Bagehot were students together at UCL] London was a place with plenty of intellectual stimulus in it for young men, while in University College itself there was quite enough vivacious and original teaching to make that stimulus available to the full. It is sometimes said that it needs the quiet of a country town remote from the capital, to foster the love of genuine study in young men. But of this, at least, I am sure, that Gower Street, and Oxford Street, and the New Road, and the dreary chain of squares from Euston to Bloomsbury, were the scenes of discussions as eager and abstract as ever were the sedate cloisters or the flowery river-meadows of Cambridge or Oxford.

R. H. Hutton's memoir of Bagehot prefaced to his edition of
Bagehot's Literary Studies *(1878)*

Had some ices; danced; had supper at ½ past 1; danced a country dance etc.; took a cab to Walshe's [where he lived] at ½ past 3; read, etc., went to bed. Got up at 20m to 8; had breakfast; attended Prof. De Morgan's lecture on Mathematics till 20m past 10; wrote in my Sermon book for an hour; put some plants into my book of Botanical Specimens; attended Prof. Malden's lecture on Greek till 20m to 2; arranged my plants; had dinner; Tom Graham called and chatted until 3; dressed; … attended Prof. Potter's lecture on Natural Philosophy till 5, and Dr. Lindley's examination on Botany till quarter to 6; had a parcel from home, unpacked it; … dried plants until 8; Dr. Scratchley came to tea; finished dressing; took a cab at 20m past 9 to Mr. Grahame's; had some coffee, had ices; quadrilled and waltzed; had supper: Fine day.

F. J. Furnivall's diary for 13 May 1842, recording 24 hours
from midnight to midnight in the life of a student

96

96. The examination in
July 1842 for matriculation
in the new degree-giving
University of London.

97. The Royal Charter
granted to the College in
1836.

On 28 November 1836 a Royal Charter was at length granted by the Whig government which included, in Lord Lansdowne and Lord John Russell, two of the members of the College's founding Council. The opposition of Oxford and Cambridge to the award of degrees to non-members of the established Church was overcome; so too was that of the various hospital medical schools in London to the exclusive power of awarding medical degrees. These problems, and that of the existence of King's College, were solved by establishing an entirely new body as the 'University of London'. The College gave up this, its original title, taking that of University College, a style first suggested in the medical press in 1833, though a possibly misleading one in that it suggests an Oxbridge rather than a continental or a Scottish model. Later the same day, another

97

Charter was granted to the new University of London, empowering it to award degrees in Arts, Laws and Medicine to students of both UCL and King's, besides such other institutions as might be approved later on. It was a sensible compromise, but the separation of teaching and examining stored up great difficulties for the future.

Engineering was one of the first victims of the College's financial insecurity. John Millington had been announced as professor of the subject in 1827, but he resigned before the opening when the Council refused to guarantee him an adequate income. Not until 1841 was a chair of Civil Engineering established, the first of its kind in the country. The period of intensive railway building had started, and the first professor, C. B. Vignoles, was a leading railway engineer and inventor of the 'Vignoles rail'. He came to UCL having lost £80,000 in shares while Chief Engineer on the Sheffield and Manchester Railway. He was later responsible for the construction of railways in many parts of the world, especially in Russia, where he built the Dnieper suspension bridge at Kiev, the largest of its kind in the world.

Two distinguished figures in other fields of engineering were appointed to new chairs in 1847. Both came from near Manchester, where they had sat at the feet of John Dalton and the inquiring scientific community there; neither was a successful teacher. Eaton Hodgkinson, who had started out as a pawnbroker in Salford, became the first Professor of Mechanical Engineering. He invented an important new type of cast-iron girder, the forerunner of the modern I-beam, and worked with Stephenson on the Menai bridge.

Bennet Woodcroft worked originally in his family textile firm, but made a range of ingenious inventions and became a consulting engineer. His great work was the creation of the modern Patent Office, to which he devoted himself after resigning the Chair of Machinery in 1851. The valuable collection of mechanical models, donated by the Society of Arts in order to form a Machinery Museum in the College, found their way, without apparent authority, to the Patent Office Museum and later to the Science Museum.

98. Bennet Woodcroft, FRS, who between 1847 and 1851 enjoyed the distinctive title of Professor of Machinery.

99. Charles Blacker Vignoles, FRS, the first Professor of Civil Engineering, 1841-45.

98

99

In 1846, Lord Brougham was obliged to say that his anticipations of success for the College twenty years previously had not been realised. Yet while the impoverished 1830s had seen major developments in the School and the Hospital, the barely better endowed 1840s saw the first new buildings for the College itself in the shape of the new General Library and the new Chemistry Laboratory. The latter, the first purpose-built teaching laboratory for chemistry in the country, was a particularly important innovation.

Turner's successor as Professor of Chemistry in 1836 was Thomas Graham, a chemist of real distinction. 'If along the great highroad of Chemistry', one of his own successors stated later, 'temples were erected to the memory of the master minds who moulded and guided the science forward into the unknown future, one of the greatest of these would be to the memory of Thomas Graham.' Educated at both Glasgow and Edinburgh, he worked on the fundamental problems of the ultimate particles of matter and the diffusion of gases, formulating the earliest modern understanding of these questions. He was one of the founders and the first President of the Chemical Society in 1841. He also started the teaching of chemistry through the practical system of personal experiment by the student. Liebig's pioneering laboratory at Giessen was earlier (it was opened in 1826), but Graham introduced the modern method in this country. It led in 1845 to the founding of a chair in Practical Chemistry and to the building of the Birkbeck Laboratory.

Opened in January 1846, the new Laboratory was partly financed by money raised to commemorate George Birkbeck's services to the widening provision of education. With bench accommodation

100. The Birkbeck Laboratory, the College's first teaching laboratory for chemistry, as pictured in the Illustrated London News soon after its opening in 1846. It was subsequently used by the Department of Botany and latterly Physics until its demolition in 1968.

100

for twenty-four students, each place with gas and water laid on, it was pronounced 'the most perfect of its class in the kingdom' by the *Illustrated London News*. George Fownes, the newly-appointed Professor of Practical Chemistry, had studied under Liebig in Germany, and had a number of advanced features incorporated in the design. Fownes published some papers on fermentation and a *Manual of Chemistry* that was to go through eleven editions, but he died young in 1849. The beginnings of practical chemistry were developed by his more famous successor Alexander Williamson (see p. 104). When Fownes died, the *Lancet* said the College 'could ill afford to lose so good a man', and declared that his death 'seems to second the efforts which intrigue had so successfully commenced for the destruction of this once flourishing institution'. It was a premature judgement.

The Birkbeck Laboratory was designed by Thomas L. Donaldson, the Professor of Architecture since 1841, and architecture must find its place alongside engineering and practical chemistry as the significant developments of the 1840s. The Chair of Architecture was the first to be founded in a university, and Donaldson, who held it until 1865, was an established architect of repute, as well as an outstanding draughtsman and lecturer. He played a leading part in the foundation of the Royal Institute of British Architects, becoming known as the father of the architectural profession in Britain.

101. Thomas Graham, FRS, Professor of Chemistry, 1836-55, and later Master of the Mint, where he was responsible for the change from copper to bronze coinage.

102. George Fownes, FRS, Professor of Practical Chemistry, 1845-49.

101

102

An important addition to the life of the College in 1849 was the opening of University Hall in Gordon Square, intended to 'provide for students … the accommodation and social advantages of college residence'. The Hall was built by the Unitarians in commemoration of the Dissenters' Chapels Act of 1844, 'the first recognition by the legislature', as an inscription on an interior wall originally proclaimed, 'of the principle of unlimited religious liberty'. It was also to be a place where theology, excluded of course from the College, could be taught, 'disavowing all denominational distinctions…'. The first Principal was the highly eccentric F. W. Newman, the brother of Cardinal Newman and Long's successor in the Chair of Latin. He resigned before the opening and was succeeded by Arthur Hugh Clough, the poet, who for three years held the Chair of English. Clough had resigned his Oxford fellowship out of religious scruple, but found himself unhappy both at the College and at the Hall, and he too soon resigned. Later distinguished principals included E. S. Beesly and Henry Morley (see pp. 132 and 103). From 1853, the building was shared with Manchester New College, an institution which had its origin in the well-known dissenting academy at Warrington in the eighteenth century, but which migrated to London to be close to

103. University Hall, the present Dr Williams's Library, designed by Donaldson as the first hall of residence for the College, at the time of its opening in 1849.

103

104

UCL. In 1889 it moved on again, this time to Oxford and, under rather odd circumstances, the Hall was then lost to the College and the lease sold to Dr Williams' Library. In 1949 the College acquired the freehold, but the lease does not expire until 2850. The rear annexe, built while Henry Morley was Principal and subsequently named after him, has since 1930 been in the possession of the College, and is occupied by the School of Library, Archive and Information Studies.

104. The General Library, also designed by Donaldson and now named after him, built in 1849 with the aid of a bequest from Jonathan Brundrett on the site of the unfinished original Great Hall which had been destroyed by fire in 1836.

105. Thomas L. Donaldson, the College's first Professor of Architecture, 1841-65, as shown on the medal established in his honour by the Royal Institute of British Architects, of which he was a founder.

105

At University College Hospital in 1846, Robert Liston performed the first operation under anaesthetic conducted in Europe, an event which marked one of the most striking advances in the history of surgery. Present as a student on that occasion was Joseph Lister, who was later to revolutionise surgery through his work on infection and antisepsis. Both developments made an enormous contribution to the reduction of human suffering.

Robert Liston was brought from the Royal Infirmary at Edinburgh to be one of the first surgeons at the Hospital when it opened in 1834, and Professor of Clinical Surgery at the College. He was remarkable for his dexterity while operating at a time when speed was the only relief that could be afforded to the patient. It was said the gleam of his knife was followed so instantaneously by the sound of sawing as to make the two actions appear simultaneous. He could amputate a leg in 20 seconds. He began the era of anaesthetics for major surgery in Britain on 21 December 1846, after hearing of the first use of ether by a dentist two months previously in the Massachusetts General Hospital; ether was again used successfully by James Robinson, a dentist attached to the Royal Free Hospital, on 19 December operating in Gower Street; and, after hurried consultations over the weekend, Liston used the new technique for an amputation two days later. The glass for administering the ether during the leg amputation was devised by

106. Robert Liston, Professor of Clinical Surgery, 1835-47, the first surgeon to perform an operation under anaesthetic in this country in December 1846 at University College Hospital.

107. A replica of the original apparatus used on that occasion for administering the ether, from the collection of the Wellcome Institute of the History of Medicine.

107

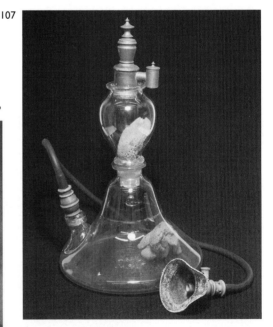

106

William Squire, a 21-year-old medical student. After the experience of the Okey mesmerism fiasco, any new attempt at avoiding pain at UCL was regarded with suspicion, but news of the success spread speedily and the innovation was rapidly adopted. 'This Yankee dodge', Liston had announced to the watching students, 'beats mesmerism hollow.'

Joseph Lister was appointed a house surgeon in 1851 after he had taken his BA at the College, but before he had graduated in medicine. In 1853 he left for Scotland, serving as a surgeon in the Infirmaries of Edinburgh and Glasgow and as a professor in both those universities in turn, thus beginning to repay a little of the College's considerable northern debt. It was at Glasgow that he made his revolutionary discovery of the startling effect of the antiseptic treatment of wounds, reported to the BMA in 1867. He was inexcusably passed over for a chair at UCL, but later returned to London to bring distinction to King's College. In 1897 he became one of the first academics to be raised to the peerage.

Despite these clear signs of potential in the Faculty of Medicine, domestic quarrels continued to characterise the place, a particularly memorable one being that in 1848 over Liston's successor. James Syme was so horrified at the 'spirit of dispeace in the College' that after a tenure of only five months he packed up and went back to Edinburgh.

108. The old wooden operating table used in UCH in the early decades.

109. The College's plaque in commemoration of Lord Lister, OM, a student between 1844 and 1852, later President of the Royal Society and famous for the development of antiseptic treatment.

108

109

JOSEPH LISTER MDCCCXXVII–MCMXII
STUDENT ARTS AND MEDICINE MDCCCXLIII–
-MDCCCLII FELLOW MDCCCLXI CREATED
BARON LISTER OF LYME REGIS MDCCCXCVII
AWARDED THE ORDER OF MERIT MCMII

To record the deeds of the professors in the first decades of the College's existence is easier than to portray the lives of the students. Their dominant feature was that they were too few to start with, and that they got fewer. The 630 of 1829-30 was just exceeded in the peak of the late 1830s after the building of the Hospital, but then went no higher and by 1864-65 fell below 400. This was despite the age limit being set as low as 15 (though some of the earliest students were even younger) and despite there being no entrance requirements whatsoever. Even after the establishment of University degrees the matriculation exam was taken following entry into the College; the degrees were first examined for in 1839 after a two-year course. Since the students were so young, so few and all male, it is not surpising that activities other than lecture-going were, by modern standards, limited.

Student societies, however, quickly sprang up, mostly of an earnest Victorian character, but the medical students soon took on many of their later characteristics. 'As far as

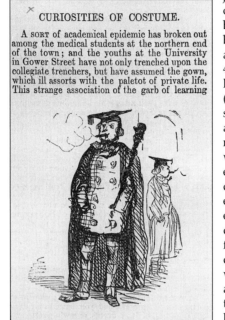

CURIOSITIES OF COSTUME.

A SORT of academical epidemic has broken out among the medical students at the northern end of the town; and the youths at the University in Gower Street have not only trenched upon the collegiate trenchers, but have assumed the gown, which ill assorts with the paletot of private life. This strange association of the garb of learning

with the habits of the medical students as they live, produces a curious effect; and the neighbourhood of Gower Street has been accordingly startled by the appearance that the combination presents.

We have not heard by what authority the assumption of the toga has taken place among the youths of Gower Street; and indeed it requires no less a person than old GOWER himself to come forth and explain the mystery.

110

111

110. A be-gowned but dissipated medical student as portrayed by Punch *in 1847.*

111. The distribution of prizes in the Faculty of Medicine as portrayed in the Pictorial Times *in 1843.*

vulgarity goes', said *Punch* in 1846, 'the concern in Gower Street may vie with the older establishments of the Cam and the Isis.' In 1837 *Punch* drew attention to the medical students who were reported as having assumed the wearing of gowns: 'This strange association of the garb of learning with the habits of the medical students as they live, produces a curious effect…'

J. J. Sylvester was one of the first students to be expelled (for threatening another student with a refectory knife), but he returned as a professor in 1837. In the meantime he had been placed as Second Wrangler at Cambridge, though as a Jew he could not take his degree there. One of the great mathematicians of the century, he became an inspiring but baffling teacher. After four years he left for the University of Virginia, beginning to balance the College's account with that university. However, he did not stay long in Virginia either, returning to England to follow the profession of actuary and ending up as a professor at Oxford.

112

113

112. The title page of a College note-book kept while a student by Walter Bagehot, later author of the classic English Constitution (1867) and editor of the Economist.

113. J. J. Sylvester, FRS, Professor of Natural Philosophy, 1837-41.

'Persons respectably dressed', noted a London guide-book in 1834, 'are allowed to see the interior of the University every day.' There would have been little to be seen, however, apart from the dignity of Wilkins's building itself, though after 1837 there was also Westmacott's statue of Locke. But from 1851 there was the large collection of casts and reliefs by the distinguished sculptor and artist, John Flaxman, on display in what was established as the Flaxman Gallery. Flaxman, who died in 1826, had no connection with the College himself. The Gallery was the work of Henry Crabb Robinson.

Crabb Robinson was an extraordinary figure who lived to be 91 in 1867, the friend of Goethe, Schiller, Herder, Hegel, Charles Lamb, Wordsworth, Coleridge and Blake, and of a good many students at UCL for some thirty years. Having studied at Jena and been a correspondent for *The Times* in the Napoleonic Wars, he worked as

114

114. Henry Crabb Robinson, the long-lived diarist and conversationalist who devoted himself to the College for over thirty years after his retirement.

115

115. A drawing of a charioteer: many of Flaxman's drawings were purchased after Maria Denman's death and originally displayed in a room associated with the Gallery. They now form part of the College's notable Art Collection.

116. An invitation to the opening of the Flaxman Gallery in 1851.

a barrister before retiring in 1828. In that year he bought a share in the College 'as a sort of debt to the cause of civil and religious liberty', and in his absence was elected to the Council in 1835. 'Old Crabb' devoted much thought and effort to the problems of the college throughout the rest of his life, and, as a Unitarian, was particularly associated with University Hall of which he was a leading founder. His breakfast parties became an institution. 'There was little to gratify the unintellectual part of man', recalled Bagehot. 'Your host, just as you were sitting down to breakfast, found he had forgotten to make the tea, then he could not find his keys, then he rang the bell to have them searched for; but long before the servant came he had gone off into "Schiller-Goethe" and could not in the least remember what he wanted. The more astute of his guests used to breakfast before they came...'

He regarded as his most memorable act the creation of the Flaxman Gallery, constructed between the Portico and the new General Library added by Donaldson in 1849. Into the Gallery were put the works of Flaxman presented by Maria Denman, Flaxman's sister-in-law and adopted daughter, who had got into financial difficulties until Crabb Robinson came to her aid.

When the Gallery was redecorated in 1922, Tonks produced the large painting that included Crabb Robinson as well as Bentham amongst the 'founders' of the college (see p. 26). This painting was originally placed high above the casts under the dome, but, for some years after the war, was instead conspicuously hung in the North Cloisters. Then, in 1986, simultaneously with a rest-oration of the casts, it was put back in its original place in the Flaxman Gallery.

In September 1994, the plaster model for the sculpture of St Michael overcoming Satan, which had been on loan to the Victoria and Albert Museum since 1973, was restored

116

INSTRUCTION.

The Committee of Subscribers to the fund for preserving the

WORKS OF FLAXMAN.

request the honor of the company of
Sir Wm Heny Maule Knt.
and friends to a private view
of the **Flaxman Hall,** *on Wednesday*
the 30 *April* *or Saturday*
the 3ʳᵈ *May* *between*
One and five o'clock.

University College, London.
26 April 1851

H. C. Robinson.
Treasurer.

117

117. The Flaxman Gallery,
as it appeared in the
nineteenth century.

118. The Flaxman Gallery
as it appears now.

to its original position in the centre of the Flaxman Gallery, where it stands today. The decision to revert to the original Victorian scheme for the whole gallery was not altogether an uncontroversial one, because one of the most elegant features of Albert Richardson's restoration after the war-time bombing (see below, pp. 212-13)

118

had been an opening through which those in the gallery could look down on passers-by in the octagon below, while those in the octagon could look up into the gallery and the dome above. Successive librarians, however, were convinced that those in the gallery not only looked down, but also threw down the Library's books, so that closing the gap became a major security objective.

119. One of the models by John Flaxman in the College's possession, which now form part of the Flaxman Gallery as reconstructed after the bomb damage in which many of his works were destroyed: the model for the monument to Lord North, Prime Minister, 1770-82, at Wroxton in Oxfordshire.

119

Richard Potter marked a low point in the teaching of science. Although he did conduct experiments, it was in the terms of eighteenth-century optical theory and, as a teacher, he was notoriously weak. 'The apparatus', one student later recalled, 'was as worn out as the professor. It never did what it was expected to do. Magnetic force, for example, would be demonstrated experimentally by holding a needle to what might once have been a magnet, but had ceased to attract, while the professor said, "You see it wants a little helping, gentlemen".'

A Chair in Geology had been planned from the very beginning of the College, but no appointment was made and professors of other subjects offered the teaching until 1841. Thomas Webster then accepted the Chair, but though very distinguished he had done his best work far earlier. A. C. Ramsey, who succeeded him in 1847, was a survey officer with the Geological Survey and a far more successful professor, but he resigned owing to pressure of other work after four years. Thus John Morris, who stayed from 1853 until 1877, was the first to build any tradition in the subject; it was he who started field-work; the geological museum was founded as a result of gifts in 1855; and the Chair itself was partly endowed under the will of Morris's friend James Yates (see p. 142) who also left a collection of specimens to the museum.

George Grote had been, at 33, the youngest member of the original Council, though his connection with the College had been severed abruptly over the appointment of a minister of religion, J. Hoppus, to the Chair of Philosophy in 1830. It was only resumed in 1849 when he was re-elected to the Council. In the meantime the young banker and MP had published the early volumes of his *History of Greece* and so became one of the most famous liberal scholars in Europe, far more distinguished than most of the professors. He now played a leading role in the reform both of the University

120. Richard Potter, Professor of Natural Philosophy, 1843-65.

121. John Morris, Professor of Geology, 1853-77.

120

121

122. Medical students in
1865, one of the earliest
photographs of a College
group (see p. 106 for the
earliest known photograph).

123. The terra-cotta bust of
George Grote now displayed
in the Housman Room.

122

(of which he was Vice-Chancellor from 1862 to 1871) and of the
College, where he became Treasurer in 1860 and then President on
the death of Brougham in 1868.

The University's reform of 1858 was far from popular with many
of the College's professors. It opened University examinations to all
comers and thus reduced still further the control of the teachers over
the examinations; it also left the University of London without any
teaching functions, a situation which was to lead to progressively
more rigorous protest as the century went on. However, the same
reform brought a major step forward, through the introduction

123

of degrees specifically in science; science
courses had previously simply been part of
the Faculty of Arts. The College's own constitution was in turn reformed in 1869 by Act
of Parliament. The main purpose of the Act
was the abolition of the system of proprietors
and share-holders, which had become dis-
used and discredited over the years. The
proprietors were replaced by Governors, who
had the right of nominating their successors,
and Life Governors, who were appointed by
the Council.

Grote's final act of generosity to the College,
on his death in 1871, was the endowment of
the Chair of Philosophy of Mind and Logic; the
conditions were characteristic of his principles:
'If therefore any such Minister [of religion]
should at any time or times be appointed by
the Council to the Professorship of Mind and
Logic ... I direct that no payment should be
made to him out of the present endowment.'
It was the same issue over which he had
resigned as a member of the Council in 1830.

124

124. A drawing of the College showing the new South Wing constructed for the School between 1869 and 1876, as it appeared soon after completion.

125. A photograph of the South Wing housing University College School.

Whether or not Grote was responsible for the revival, there can be no doubt that the late sixties and early seventies gave clear signs of new-found energy in the College. New benefactors were attracted and new building was undertaken. So far, only the central block had been built and Wilkins's plans for north and south wings had seen no realisation except in the early prints. The School, which had from the beginning proved one of the more successful elements of the enterprise, was occupying a considerable part of the building. The Council reported in 1866 that every room was in constant use and that the School could not be confined within the area allocated to it. Worse, space which the School had long been allowed to use was now needed for science

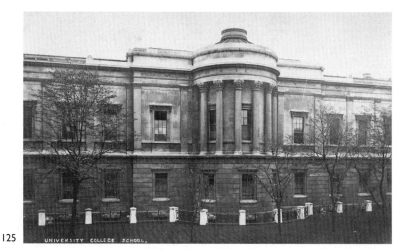

125

teaching, while the School itself was looking for better facilities for its own physics and chemistry classes.

The answer came from Samuel Sharpe, a notable and wealthy Egyptologist and Unitarian translator of the Bible, who became a member of the Council in 1866. He proposed that the South Wing should be built as soon as possible and gave £1,000 to open the building fund, and later another £5,000. The new wing, designed to harmonise with Wilkins's building, was the work of Hayter Lewis, the successor to Donaldson in the Chair of Architecture. It was opened in three stages in 1869, 1873 and 1876. The School gradually moved into its new premises and the space vacated was re-allocated for College use. The Library took over more of the first floor, sharing the new space with Arts, which moved upstairs from the ground floor. This in turn created room for a new Hygiene Laboratory after the creation of the Department of Hygiene and Public Health in 1869.

126

127

126. University College School's device, with its spray of oak and the motto Paulatim, 'Little by little'.

127. The Headmaster's Room in the South Wing, now part of the Registry.

128. The Monitor's Room in the South Wing.

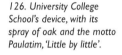

128

The next development again began with a gift. Felix Slade was a famous London collector, especially of Venetian glass; his collections form a distinguished part of the British Museum. He died in 1868 and left endowments for three professorships in Fine Art, at Oxford, Cambridge and London. Ruskin was appointed in Oxford, Digby Wyatt in Cambridge, but at UCL it was decided to take the opportunity to raise further funds and establish a new School of Fine Art for the teaching of professional artists. Further Slade money helped with the project and also set up Slade Exhibitions and Scholarships for proficient students. These benefactions were received in 1870; another building fund was opened and Hayter Lewis again prepared plans this time for the North Wing. The first section was completed very promptly and the new department opened in October 1871.

The Slade was an immediate success and had 220 students by 1875; but its expansion then had to be checked for lack of space. The first Professor was Edward Poynter, who had some experience of the French schools and announced in his opening address the principles the Slade was to follow: 'The superiority of foreign artists … is undoubtedly due to a habit in the schools of thoroughly following out a course of study from the living model…' It was therefore he who set the Slade tradition of working from living models, though his own very academic work was totally remote from later developments.

The completion of the North Wing needed another appeal in 1878; this was launched in conjunction with the celebration of the College's Jubilee, at which the foundation stone of the extension

129. Earl Granville as Chancellor of the University of London laying the foundation stone of the North Wing on the occasion of the Jubilee Festival in 1878.

129

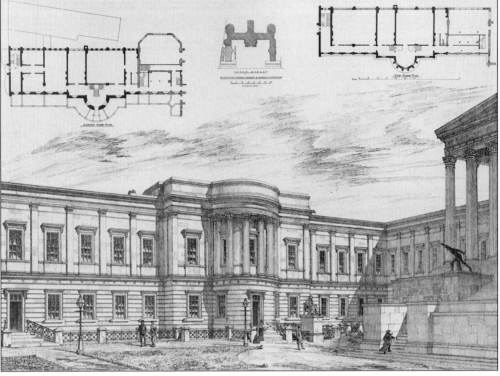

130

was laid and an ambitious statement of the College's requirements issued. Completed by 1881, the Slade occupied the first floor and some of the ground floor, Physiology the top floor and Chemistry the basement, while Zoology moved into the first stage of the building, which the Slade had just left. The twelve years between 1869 and 1881 had seen both the North and South Wings added to the college, but not fully paid for; the College had had to borrow money and its debts became progressively greater.

130. The North Wing shortly before its completion as illustrated in Building News in 1880, showing the stages of the building.

131

131. Felix Slade, whose name is commemorated by the School of Fine Art established through his benefaction.

Chapter 5
The Years of Women and Men, 1878-1904

I need not say how strongly I feel that it is the business of U.C. to be boldly first in recognising fully any new and real want of the time.

Henry Morley, writing to the Secretary of the College
about the admission of women, 14 June 1872

I shall look back during my remaining years with pride at having been one of a body of men such as those we have in this College; for I know nothing more truly honourable and noble than to work in the earnest and disinterested manner in which my colleagues as a body have always worked for the advancement of learning and for the cultivation and development of the highest faculties of the human mind. It might be difficult to find any such band of men as those who have worked in this College under circumstances so little favourable to their exertions. When this College is viewed not merely for what it has done, but for the proportion between what the men in it have done and the encouragement given to them from without, I think it must be felt that they deserve very unusual and very exceptional credit for their labours.

A. W. Williamson in his retirement speech on 16 June 1887
after thirty-eight years as Professor of Chemistry

Housman's remarks were so caustic as to paralyse the female section of his class. But what, I think, hurt them more was that, having reduced Miss Brown, Miss Jones and Miss Robinson to tears, Housman professed, when he met them next week, not to know which was Miss Brown, which Miss Jones and which Miss Robinson.

R. W. Chambers recalling A. E. Housman's teaching
as Professor of Latin in the 1890s in his
Centenary lecture, 2 May 1927

Edward Poynter, the first Slade Professor, had maintained from the time of his appointment that women could and should be taught in the same classes as the men – '…except of course those for the nude model' – and the Slade went on to play a key part in the introduction of women to College life. The *Annual Report* noted with satisfaction as early as 1872 that 'Professor Poynter and his Assistants report that not the slightest inconvenience has arisen from having classes composed of ladies and gentlemen, and the officers of the College are not aware that objections have ever been made by any of the students to this combined instruction'.

The movement for admitting women to the College began with the creation in 1868 of the London Ladies Educational Association, an independent body which organised classes for women and to which UCL professors lectured, the first to do so being Henry Morley and Carey Foster. It may have been the intention from the beginning that this should lead to the opening of regular classes to women students, but the process was very gradual: at first, the women's classes took place off the College's premises; they then moved into College, but the Association not the College was the responsible agent. Finally, it became too much trouble to hold classes separately; the Professor of Political Economy was the first to weaken and lecture to a mixed class. The University opened its degrees to women and by 1878 the Association could be wound up and women students were at last admitted on the same footing as men. Hale Bellot called this the most revolutionary development in the history of the College.

In 1882, a hall of residence known as College Hall was opened for women. Carey Foster and Henry Morley again played a leading role. A year later Rosa Morison, one of the administrators of the new Hall, and a strong

132

133

134. Henry Morley, the indefatigable Professor of English, 1865-89, and one of the leading figures in all developments of the College in the late nineteenth century.

134

supporter of women's suffrage, became the 'Lady Superintendent of Women Students' until her death in 1912, when her successor took the less pioneering title 'Tutor to Women Students'.

The hero — as opposed to the heroines — of this story was Henry Morley who was indeed one of the most energetic and sympathetic College figures of this period. He had come to UCL from King's as Professor of English in 1865, with a reputation already established by his *English Writers*, a massive survey of English language and literature. Apart from up to twenty hours a week of teaching in College, he lectured generously for Ladies' Educational Associations all over the country, for schools and for the Royal Institution. In 1882 he became Principal of University Hall and was the founder in 1884 of the University College Society, the forerunner of both the Union and the Old Students' Association. As editor of *Morley's Universal Library*, he pioneered cheap reprints of the classics. His nickname, Professor More-and-Morley, was hard-earned. There is no denying the success of his classes or the devotion he inspired in his pupils, but it has to be remembered how isolated his success was in the Faculty of Arts in these years. The greatest advances in the late nineteenth century were almost all to be in Science and Engineering.

The dominant figure in science in the mid-century was Alexander Williamson. He succeeded Fownes in the Chair of Practical Chemistry in 1849, and united both chairs in the subject from 1855 until 1887. He suffered great physical disabilities, being paralysed in one arm, blind in his right eye and myopic in his left. When he came to UCL, he was already in touch with the leading continental centres of research and theory; he was a professed follower of Auguste Comte, and had studied with Liebig at Giessen. The accepted theory of etherification at the time was that ether was formed from alcohol by the loss of water. Williamson was able to show that the relationship had rather to be one of substitution than of the addition or loss of water; i.e., he postulated a process of continuous atomic exchange, in which the atoms and molecules were conceived of as in motion rather than static. It was a masterly piece of research and made Williamson's reputation when presented to the British Association in 1850.

His period of productive research then came to an end. He became instead a considerable College figure, and was largely responsible for the introduction of separate science degrees in the University and for the creation of the College Faculty of Science in 1870. He also built up his foreign connections and was for many years Foreign Secretary of the Royal Society.

135. The first of many suggestions for 'filling the gap' after the completion of both the wings, as presented in Building News in 1881, showing also a plan of the chemistry laboratory built for Williamson.

135

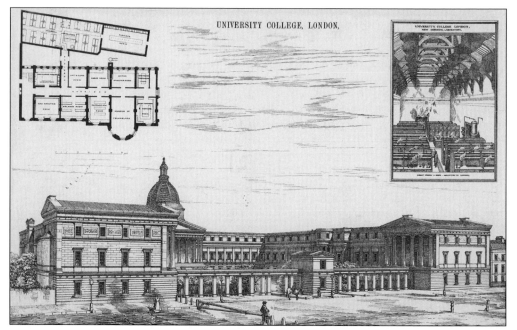

UNIVERSITY COLLEGE, LONDON,

136

136. *Alexander Williamson,*
FRS, Professor of Chemistry,
1849-87.

137

137. The five Japanese noblemen
who first came to London in
1863, four of whom stayed to
study at University College. They
are from left to right; Bunta Inoue,
Endo Kinsuke, Nomura Yakichi,
Yozo Yamao and Ito Hirubumi.
Apart from the importance of the
individuals shown, the photograph
is interesting in itself as the
earliest to show any group of
University College students.

Williamson in his later years acted as host to some of the earliest Japanese students ever to reach the West, in the period before foreign travel from Japan was legalised. The very first of these students reached London in July 1863 and stayed in Williamson's house as well as registering for his classes. All five later played important parts in the development of the new Japan after the Meiji restoration of 1868 and one of them, Ito Hirobume, eventually rose to be Prime Minister. He and Bunta Inoue (who seems never to have registered for courses) returned after a year, but the three others stayed longer and were still studying when a second group of thirteen students arrived from Kagoshima, where the importance of their visit is still recognised in the form of a monument.

The flow of students from Japan continued throughout the century and into the twentieth, one of the most influential being Joji Sakurai, who studied with Williamson from 1876 to 1881, and who later became the originator of scientific research in Japanese universities. His achievements were recognised by the College in 1937, when he became the first foreign Fellow of the College.

Not so recognised by the College was another student of the period, Ernest Satow, who had been a University College student in 1859-61, and became the first Englishman to speak and write Japanese and who also played an essential role in establishing contacts between Japan and the West. Only in 1989 was Satow's importance belatedly acknowledged by the creation of a Satow Chair in Japanese Law.

In fact, all these many early connections between UCL and the opening up of Japan to Western culture were largely forgotten after the 1940s; in the 1980s, however, visits were exchanged to mark the importance of UCL's role in Japan's relationship with the west.

138. Each of the students of the Satsuma class, who came to University College in 1865, appears on this monument in Kagoshima.

139. Sir Ernest Satow (1843-1929), a University College student who graduated in 1861, as presented in a Spy cartoon.

138

139

140. G. Carey Foster, FRS, the effective creator of the Department of Physics as Professor between 1865 and 1898, and subsequently the first Principal of the College, 1900-04.

141. The Carey Foster Laboratory opened in 1893, with All Saints' church, later the Great Hall, behind it, showing also the semi-circular lecture theatre and the General Library as Donaldson built it.

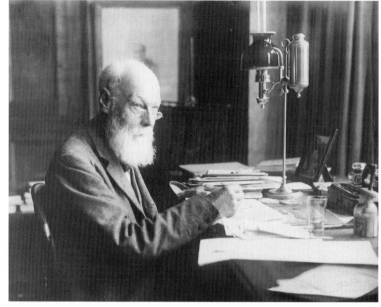

140

Richard Potter's work in what had been called 'natural philosophy' was shared after he retired in 1865 between T. A. Hirst and Carey Foster as Professors of Mathematical and Experimental Physics respectively. In 1867, Hirst succeeded De Morgan in Mathematics and Carey Foster became Professor of what was now called Physics. His great achievement was the introduction of the systematic teaching of experimental physics to students. The original 'Physical Laboratory' was created by clearing out the level space at the top of the seating in one of the semi-circular lecture theatres. Before this, the professor certainly had

141

some equipment, but the teaching had been by means of lectures and demonstrations. Now for the first time experimental teaching, as in Chemistry, was offered to the individual student. Here again, UCL was the pioneer of new methods in England. The example was to be followed in many other science and engineering subjects in the College in the subsequent years. Despite this early start, the facilities for physics remained very restricted until 1893, when the new laboratories named after Carey Foster were opened at the back of the main block. They remained in use until they were destroyed by bombing in 1940. Their site has still not been fully redeveloped (but see p. 13).

Carey Foster himself was remembered as a modest man, who published relatively little. He is now chiefly remembered for the 'Carey Foster Bridge', a very much more accurate variation of the Wheatstone Bridge. But he was a great influence as a teacher and organiser who laid the basis on which subsequent achievements in physics have been built. His last service to the College was to be as first Principal, after his retirement as Professor, an office created in 1900 and held by him for four demanding years.

142

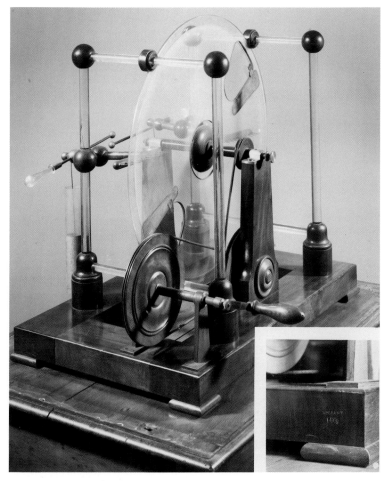

142. Holtz's Electric Machine, constructed in the Department of Physics in 1869 by William Grant, a mechanic of outstanding ability, Carey Foster's long-serving assistant, his name appearing on the base.

Physics was a pioneer in adopting modern teaching methods, but it was really only Physiology that rivalled the distinction of Chemistry in its contribution to nineteenth-century scientific knowledge. Pupils of Sharpey dominated the subject and began to colonise other universities and found new departments. Michael Foster became Professor of Practical Physiology while Sharpey still held his Chair in 1869. In that same year, he and T. H. Huxley gave the first practical courses ever offered in biology; in 1870, Foster went to establish physiology as a subject in Cambridge and was succeeded at UCL by Burdon Sanderson. In 1874, when Sharpey retired, Burdon Sanderson combined both chairs until he in turn left to establish physiology, this time at Oxford, in 1883. Then a third of Sharpey's pupils took over the chair – E. A. Schäfer, later Sir Edward Sharpey-Schafer, a name he somewhat confusingly took in honour of his teacher. These men virtually created physiology as a research subject in this country.

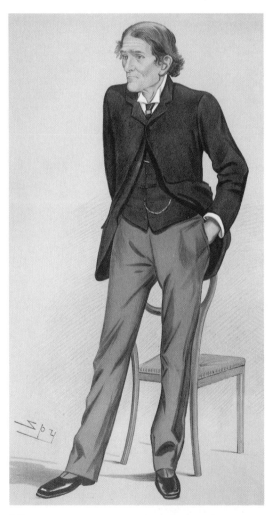

143. The Spy cartoon of Sir John Burdon Sanderson, FRS, Sharpey's successor in the Chair of Physiology.

143

Burdon Sanderson's years at UCL saw a transformation of the whole position. In 1871 physiology – with some pressure from T. H. Huxley as external examiner – became a compulsory subject for all medical students, and laboratory facilities then had to be expanded to deal with the extra numbers. In 1873, the Chair received its own endowment from T. J. Phillips Jodrell, a wealthy eccentric, so that Burdon Sanderson became the first Jodrell Professor.

A landmark was the creation of the Physiological Society. Its first meeting was in Burdon Sanderson's house and it retained close connections with the College. Originally brought into existence by way of self-defence against the active anti-vivisectionist movement of the 1870s, it subsequently became a link between physiologists working in different parts of the country and a clearing-house for ideas and research. Burdon Sanderson's own research was on problems of cardiac function and in particular the contraction of the heart and all the accompanying phenomena. This was to be a major research area in the Department for many years. But perhaps his most significant contribution lay in the introduction of experiment as a central part of the student's education and in the development of the laboratory facilities which this required. By the time he left, the new accommodation for Physiology at the top of the North Wing was open. His actual teaching was less distinguished; he was notoriously absent-minded and far from lucid as a lecturer. A

144

144. Sir Edward Sharpey-Schafer, FRS, Burdon Sanderson's successor as Jodrell Professor of Physiology, 1883-99, as stylishly portrayed on the prize medal established in his memory.

145. A late nineteenth-century view of the Anatomy Museum, an important part of the teaching of medicine at the time.

pupil looking back in 1905 recalled that his eccentricities 'invested what he did with something of the same charm that the conjuror arouses in juvenile spectators, and we were in a state of suppressed excitement based on the uncertainty as to what Dr Burdon Sanderson might do next'.

145

Zoology too found a major research scholar as its professor in 1874 and it too received an endowment from Jodrell, though sadly the donor became insane before he could complete the making of the gift, so that the Masters in Lunacy had to act on his behalf in a complex legal situation. E. Ray Lankester was only 27 when he took the chair, having previously been a Fellow of Exeter College, Oxford. Lankester was a large man, with a massive

146

146. Sir Ray Lankester, FRS, Professor of Zoology and Comparative Anatomy, 1874-91, shown by Spy in genial discourse with a hornbill, overheard by a fossil fish cephalaspis. 'His religion', said Vanity Fair, 'is the worship of all sorts of winged and finny freaks.'

frame, a mobile expressive face, a booming voice and an impetuous temperament – 'a veritable swashbuckler amongst professors'. He was a dominating figure in his subject, editing the major zoological journal of the period for fifty years and placing his pupils in many of the chairs in the subject at home and in the Empire. He wrote prolifically on a wide range of subjects including fossil fishes, molluscs and arthropods, and in his later years on prehistory and the early history of man.

Soon after his appointment, Lankester introduced practical work into the zoology courses. With the exception of Huxley's exper-imental courses, this was yet again an innovation for a British university. It was increasingly becoming a standard part of a science undergraduate's education to receive laboratory experience as an integral part of his course. The practical classes were in this case so successful that in 1879 a laboratory assistant, H. Jessop, was appointed to prepare experiments; his work was pioneering in the running of a zoological laboratory and he was a notable College figure for many years.

147. The very fine drawings on the blackboard and on posters used by Lankester in his lectures: some were inherited from Grant, some done by Lankester himself and some were the work of Edwin Goodrich, a young student at the Slade who was later to occupy Lankester's Chair of Zoology at Oxford.

147

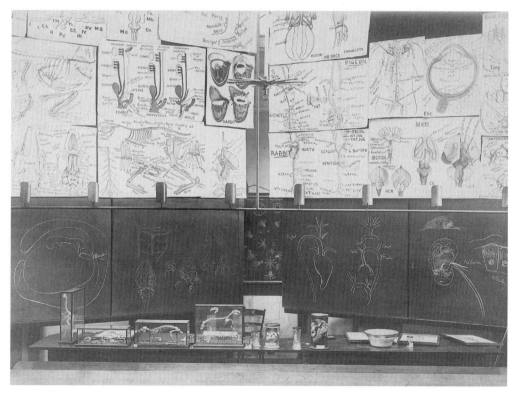

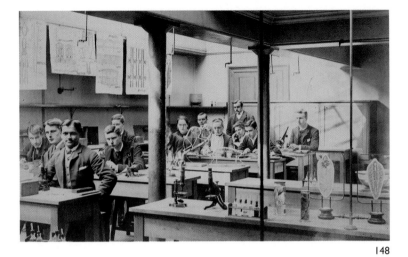

148

148. The students
attending one of
Lankester's courses in
1887.

149. The Comparative
Anatomy Lecture Theatre in
the first stage of the North
Wing vacated by the Slade
after 1881.

In 1891, Lankester returned to Oxford and was succeeded by W. F. R. Weldon, who in fact was to succeed him again at Oxford ten years later when Lankester was appointed as Director of the Natural History Museum. Weldon was one of the first men to introduce quantitative methods into zoology and together with Galton and Pearson (see pp. 128-29) created a new branch of the subject known as biometrics, the statistical study of animals. Weldon's own research, especially on shrimps, was designed to test the theory of natural selection by carefully devised statistical analyses of inherited characteristics.

149

150

151

150. W. F. R. Weldon, FRS, Jodrell Professor of Zoology and Comparative Anatomy, 1891-99, whose widow in 1936 left money to establish the Chair of Biometrics in his memory.

151. The Zoology Museum in the 1880s, with many of the exhibits which are still part of what is now the Grant Museum of Zoology and Comparative Anatomy in the Department of Biology.

152

153

152. Daniel Oliver, FRS,
Professor of Botany,
1860-88.

153. Daniel Oliver's son
and successor, Francis Wall
Oliver, FRS, Quain Professor
of Botany, 1890-1929.

154. The first Botany
Laboratory, as it was
in 1891 in the North
Cloisters (looking towards
the, now closed, cloakroom).

154

Three Professors of Botany spanned the whole first century of the College's existence. Daniel Oliver succeeded Lindley, one of the original professors, in 1860, and in 1888 he was in turn succeeded by Francis Oliver, his son, first as lecturer (at 24) for two probationary years, and then as professor for thirty-nine years until 1929. Both Olivers made notable contributions to their subject and advances in its teaching.

Daniel Oliver worked for thirty years primarily as Keeper of the Herbarium at Kew Gardens when it was the world's botanical Mecca. He helped form an incomparable systematic collection of the plants of all continents. He lived at Kew and for twenty-eight years gave his lectures in College every morning during the summer terms at 8 o'clock, which meant being woken by the Gardens night-constable rapping on his window at 5 a.m. He regularly brought with him six different specimens for each of the students to examine. The subject took a major step forward in 1880 with the establishment of its first laboratory in the narrow former Microscope Room in the North Cloisters. Botany became no longer simply a subsidiary subject for medical students, one in which they could often see little point, but a scientific discipline in its own right. Soon after the young Oliver succeeded his father, he put a plan requiring further accommodation to Sir John Erichsen, the then President of the College, who opened the interview and closed the matter with: 'Mr Oliver, you are a very young man and not the only professor in the College.'

F. W. Oliver began field courses in botany, related especially to his interest in the vegetation of maritime habitats. The pioneer expedition was to the Norfolk Broads in

1903, followed by the first of a series of Edwardian summer visits to Bouche d'Erquy on the coast of Brittany. After 1910 the field courses found a settled home at Blakeney Point in that part of Norfolk which is perhaps the finest stretch of marshland coast in Britain. Oliver was instrumental in having the area preserved by the National Trust so that students could, as he said, 'come face to face with the operations of Nature in its most dynamic form'. A series of Blakeney Point publications followed, and Oliver's approach to the changing relations of habitat and vegetation had a very significant effect on the development of the subject in Britain. Ecology has remained an important interest of the botanists of the College, and Blakeney Point is still in regular use for field trips by undergraduate and postgraduate students of the Department of Biology. Since 1960, there has been a postgraduate Diploma in Conservation (later an MSc course) set up as a result of a joint initiative with the Nature Conservancy. Ecology and conservation were thus matters of concern at UCL long before they became vogue words in the 1970s and after.

155. The Old Lifeboat House at Blakeney Point.

156. Soil investigations being conducted at Bouche d'Erquy in 1904, by, amongst others, the young Marie Stopes (see p. 150).

156. Soil investigations being conducted at Bouche d'Erquy in 1904, by, amongst others, the young Marie Stopes (see p. 150).

157. The Laboratory at Blakeney Point, Norfolk, built in 1913 for the Department of Botany, now part of the Department of Biology.

155

157

156

158. Sir Alexander Kennedy, FRS, Professor of Mechanical Engineering, 1874-89, as drawn by one of his students.

159. A torsion testing machine, built by Kennedy himself, which had been installed in the original Engineering Laboratory housed in the space now occupied by the Lower Refectory.

158

159

L ike Lankester, Alexander Kennedy came to University College in 1874 when he was 27. He stayed fifteen years and then left to start a new career. His achievements in the meantime give him a fair claim to be considered the creator of modern engineering education. At the moment of his arrival, engineering at the College was in some trouble, both his predecessors having left after short stays for better paid posts. The *Annual Report* of 1874 acrimoniously commented on Kennedy's predecessor's resignation to go to one of the new provincial university colleges, that it 'furnishes an additional illustration of the unequal competition with state-aided institutions to which this wholly self-supporting college is exposed, and which from time to time robs it of able teachers, to the detriment of its usefulness and prosperity'. Despite the low salary (under £200), Kennedy's immediate contribution was to provide new teaching methods and approaches by providing translations of up-to-date foreign research.

More significantly, he followed the lead of Carey Foster in establishing laboratory work as a fundamental part of undergraduate education. By the time of the Jubilee in 1878, the College had firmly adopted his line and the formation of a new Engineering

160. The Drawing Office on the top floor of the Engineering building long desired by Kennedy, soon after its eventual construction in 1893.

161. The single-storey part of this building along the Gower Street frontage of the College, before the second storey was added in 1922.

160

Laboratory – the term itself being new – was one of the objectives of the Appeal. Space was provided in the main building and, with a small grant and much improvisation, the pioneering laboratory which was to serve until 1893 was established. Kennedy was versatile and restless: he left College in 1889 to found a highly successful firm of electrical consultants – Kennedy and Donkin. In his later years, he wrote on mountaineering and on archaeology; he was knighted and much honoured. It is a measure of his impact on University College that he left three chairs where he had found one: in 1883, a separate appointment was made to the Chair of Civil Engineering and Kennedy limited himself to Mechanical Technology. In 1885 came a completely new and very important departure – Electrical Technology.

161

162

*162. Sir Ambrose Fleming,
FRS, Professor of Electrical
Engineering for forty-
five years from 1885, as
painted by Sir William
Orpen.*

Ambrose Fleming was the first Professor of Electrical Engineering, holding the post between 1885 and 1926. He was
born in Lancaster in 1849, but educated at UCS and UCL,
where he studied physics under Carey Foster and mathematics
under De Morgan. He had taught science in schools and at
University College, Nottingham, before being offered the new
Chair established by Kennedy which he was to hold until he retired
at 77; he lived on to be 95.

It is clear that his teaching duties were not over-onerous; for many
years he gave one lecture a week on Fridays at 11 o'clock. This gave

him plenty of time for wide public lecturing, and for profitable service as scientific consultant to Marconi. It was this connection that led to Fleming's most celebrated achievements. The plans for the first long-distance wireless station in the world at Poldhu in Cornwall, were, he later claimed, drawn on the lecture-table of the Electrical Engineering Department. His key discovery, made in 1904, was the thermionic valve, a revolutionary new technique for receiving high-frequency electro-magnetic waves, which made radio possible and marked the birth of modern electronics. Fleming realised that use could be made of an effect noted by Edison that, if a metal plate is introduced into an ordinary evacuated carbon filament electric lamp, current will flow in only one direction. From this clue, he developed a bulb which would act in relation to electric current as a valve acts in a water-pipe. The system was improved later by others, but Fleming had made the fundamental breakthrough.

The equipment Fleming found when he took his Chair was 'a blackboard and a piece of chalk'. The situation improved slowly, but in 1891 yet another appeal initiated a new building to accommodate the developments in both Mechanical and Electrical Engineering. This is the building (shown above p. 119), still used by some Engineering departments, facing onto Gower street at right angles to the South Wing, beginning the enclosure of the Front Quadrangle. For lack of resources, only a part of the upper storeys could be built, some of the ground floor being left with a temporary roof.

163

164

Original Fleming Valves. 1904

163. The thermionic valve as invented by Fleming at UCL, one of the most important inventions of the twentieth century, now on display in the Department of Electronic and Electrical Engineering.

164. The original versions of the thermionic valve, with Fleming's own caption.

Nothing worried the Victorians more than their drains and, in this as in other respects, the College was responsive to the needs of society. Hygiene was at first taught as part of medical jurisprudence, though its most famous teacher, Edmund Parkes – 'the father of hygienic science' – was in fact Professor of Clinical Medicine from 1848 to 1860, before he left to become Professor of Hygiene at the Army Medical School. In 1869 the Council decided, since 'the subject has become so extensive in its developments and applications', to appoint a Professor of Hygiene and Public Health. W. H. Corfield, one of the leading authorities in the field, held the Chair for thirty-four years, simultaneously holding posts as a Medical Officer of Health and running a large consulting practice. In 1875 he opened the first laboratory in London for the practical teaching of hygiene; this was on the ground floor of the main building where it was to remain until 1908.

When Sir Edwin Chadwick died at the age of 90, he left a large sum in trust 'for the improvement of sanitation'. Chadwick had been Jeremy Bentham's secretary in his last years and, as a leading

165

167

166

disciple, played a combative, if not truculent, part in the struggle to achieve satisfactory public health and sanitary conditions. A large collection of his papers is kept in the Library. It was because of the Benthamite connection and the presence of the teaching of hygiene in the College that Chadwick's trustees chose UCL as the home of a new course of instruction for young men likely to become municipal engineers. Both the new Chair of Municipal Engineering and the existing one of Hygiene became Chadwick Chairs.

168

By a somewhat curious arrangement, the new Chair was first occupied by Chadwick's son Osbert, the chairman of the trustees: he drew no salary and performed his duties vicariously, though he did organise the syll-abus and the courses, and did this admirably. The Department of Hygiene was moved to the top floor of the South Wing when the Boys' School moved out, but then medical hygiene left the College entirely in 1929, when it became a major part of the new School of Hygiene and Tropical Medicine. Municipal hygiene, however, was retained in Engineering at UCL. Major research activity in the Dep-artment dates from 1930 when a new Chadwick Laboratory was opened thanks to the continued support of the Chadwick Trust. Municipal Engineering and Hygiene remained as a separate Department until 1947, when it was merged with Civil Engineering.

169

170

168. The Chadwick medal, still awarded for the study of public health, in commemoration of Sir Edwin Chadwick.

169. The apparatus of an early experiment in sewage treatment in the Chadwick Laboratory of Municipal Engineering established in the 1890s.

170. The Hygiene Laboratory of 1908 in the South Wing.

William Ramsay came to University College in 1887 from University College, Bristol, where he had been both Professor of Chemistry and Principal. He had already completed distinguished research, had travelled widely, and made personal contact with most leading contemporary scientists. The research that was to make his name famous was undertaken at UCL. The physicist Lord Rayleigh discovered that the density of the element nitrogen obtained from the atmosphere was always greater than that of nitrogen produced from its chemical compounds. With Rayleigh's consent, Ramsay set out to provide an explanation. Using the fact that nitrogen is taken up by heated magnesium, he established that the progressive removal of nitrogen from air concentrated in the residue an unknown gas heavier than nitrogen.

The result was the discovery of a chemically inert gas which he called argon (the Greek for 'idle'). Furthermore, Ramsay realised

171

171. Sir William Ramsay, FRS, Professor of Chemistry, 1887-1913, photographed in his laboratory in the basement of the North Wing.

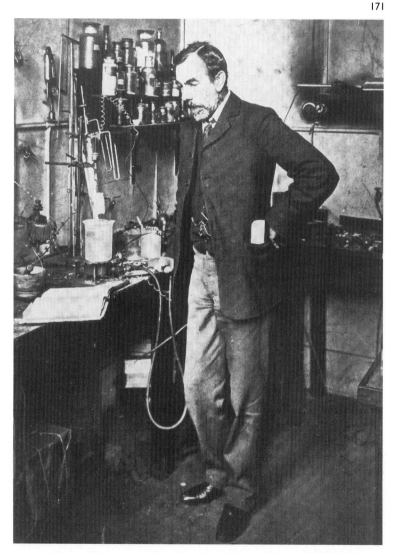

172

that if there was to be one inert gas then there ought to be a whole group of such gases filling a gap in the periodic table of the elements. In rapid succession between 1895 and 1900 he established the existence of terrestrial helium (the presence of helium had already been detected in the sun's chromosphere during the eclipse of 1868), as well as of neon, xenon and krypton. His successes brought swift recognition; he was knighted in 1902 and received the Nobel Prize together with Rayleigh in 1904.

173

172. This cartoon by Henry Tonks, shows Ramsay receiving the news that he has been awarded the Nobel Prize. It has recently been presented to UCL by Mrs Charlotte Gere and her family; she is the daughter of C.O.G. Douie, who was Secretary of the College, 1927-38 (see p. 196); it was originally given by Tonks to Gregory Foster and later by Foster to Douie as a wedding present. It is now safe in the Strang Print Room.

173. The Nobel Prize awarded to Ramsay in 1904 for his discovery of the inert gases.

Ramsay's great discoveries were made in the North Wing basement laboratories that had been built for Williamson in 1881. Williamson had evidently inspired little activity in his last years and a good deal of the space then allocated had not in fact been used. Ramsay's staff at first consisted of two assistants who had, of course, to be paid out of the professor's fees. Later he was able to appoint a student demonstrator. There was no money available for research expenses and indeed Ramsay paid for his own scientific work very largely out of his own consultancies. The Department of Chemistry expanded rapidly from this slender foundation.

In the early nineties, the whole laboratory was fitted with working benches and extra space in the basement cleared out. In 1902 a second Chair, in Organic Chemistry, was established and filled by J. Norman Collie, who had been one of the two assistants when Ramsay first came to London. Student numbers increased year by year; Ramsay was closely involved with their instruction and toured the laboratory twice a day, at least in the early years. He and his wife also established personal relations with students and had groups of them to dinner regularly through the winter. He was also a notable public figure. Before coming to UCL, he had been a leader of the movement to obtain government support for the universities and university colleges, a campaign which led to the first Treasury grant and the origins of the University Grants Committee in 1889. He worked for some years in connection with the Royal Commission on the Disposal of Sewage, and was a leading advocate of the reform of the University of London. He was honoured throughout the world.

Norman Collie, Ramsay's professorial colleague, was involved in his days as an assistant with the development of X-ray photography. In 1882 he had gone to Würzburg in Germany to do his PhD (a degree then not yet introduced into this country), and happened to be there again in 1895 when Röntgen accidentally discovered the remarkable

174. The working benches in the Chemistry Laboratory in the North Wing as in Ramsay's day.

175. The Department of Chemistry in 1899, one of the earliest surviving departmental photographs, with Ramsay standing in the centre.

174

175

properties of what he called X-rays. Two months later, in February 1896, Collie was back in London and was responsible for taking the first X-ray photograph used for clinical purposes in this country. The subject was a patient at University College Hospital who had a broken needle in her thumb. The use of X-rays for medical diagnosis and for treatment was rapidly taken up after this signal example of co-operation between scientific research and medicine in the College. Within a few years the Hospital had an expanding radiography department.

Collie went on to work with Ramsay on the inert gases and later co-operated in the pioneering work on the 'emanations' of radium, later to be called 'radon', and the decomposition of this into helium. Here they were unquestionably working on the fringes of the understanding of atomic structure, though the most dramatic discoveries were to be made in Cambridge some years later and through different techniques.

176

176. J. Norman Collie, FRS, Professor of Organic Chemistry, 1902-28, as photographed in his laboratory for the Sphere in 1921.

177. The first X-ray photographs used in Britain for clinical purposes taken by Collie in 1896 and preserved in the Chemistry Department. They show a broken needle in the thumb of a patient at University College Hospital.

177

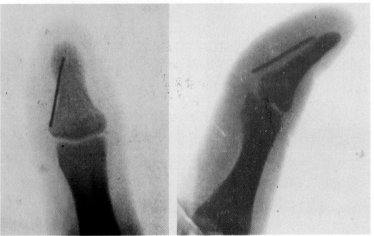

178

K arl Pearson was one of the dominating figures in the academic history of the College, with interests and enthusiasms ranging across politics, literature, law and science. Of the beginnings of his long and productive association with UCL, he characteristically said: 'Professor Beesly, just because I had lectured to revolutionary clubs, Professor Croom Robertson, just because I had written on Maimonides in his journal *Mind*, Professor Alexander Williamson, just because I had published a memoir on atoms, and Professor Henry Morley, just because I had attended and criticised lectures of his on the Lake Poets, pressed me to be a candidate for the Chair of Mathematics!' It was Alexander Kennedy who finally persuaded him to forsake the law and take the Chair of Applied Maths in 1884.

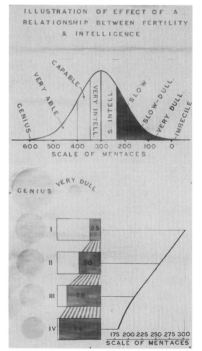

179

180

In the 1890s he became more and more interested in applied statistics and the correlation of biological and sociological data. He was captivated by Francis Galton's *Natural Inheritance* (1889) and the beginnings of 'eugenics' based on the conviction that the ideas of Darwin – Galton's cousin – might be applied purposively to improve the human race. In 1901, Pearson, Galton and Weldon founded *Biometrika*, and in 1903 the Drapers' Company funded a new Biometrics Laboratory for Pearson. Soon afterwards Galton founded the Eugenics Laboratory in a Gower Street house, and after his death in 1911 Pearson came to have charge of both laboratories as Galton Professor. An enormous output of research continued on many aspects of intelligence, craniometry, heredity and 'questions of the day and of the fray'. There was a good deal of fray. Originally housed in the South Wing, after 1920 the work moved into the Bartlett Building, appropriately renamed the Pearson Building in 1980, before the death of his son, Egon Pearson (see p. 230).

181

181. *Francis Galton, the creator of 'eugenics' and founder of the Galton Laboratory – one of the pictures in the massive biography 'K. P.' wrote of him.*

182

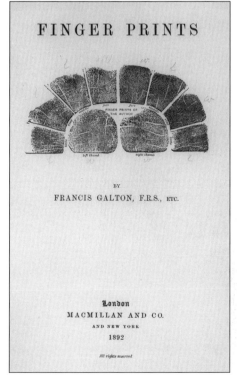

FINGER PRINTS

BY

FRANCIS GALTON, F.R.S., ETC.

London
MACMILLAN AND CO.
AND NEW YORK
1892

All rights reserved

182. *Galton's finger-prints, as appearing on the title-page of the pioneering book on the subject he published in 1892.*

183. *Galton's pocket recorder of anthropometric information, as displayed in the Galton Collection, housed since 1968 in Wolfson House across the Euston Road and now in the Department of Biology, of which the Galton Laboratory has formed part since 1996.*

183

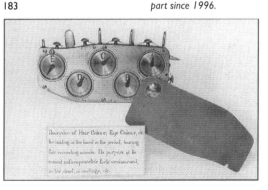

The Revd T. G. Bonney succeeded Morris as Professor of Geology in 1877 and remained for almost twenty-five years. He came from St John's College, Cambridge, retaining his Fellowship there and originally continuing to teach and live in Cambridge, while commuting to London. Bonney was a vigorous and respected teacher, though the Department remained a small one; he published prolifically and authoritatively, specialising in the study of rocks and in the geology of the Alps. Throughout his years at UCL, Bonney remained a part-time professor; he was a very active Secretary of the British Association for five years and in the nineties found lucrative employment writing for a London newspaper.

W. K. Clifford in his brief tenure of the Chair of Applied Mathematics left an enduring impression of quite exceptional abilities. A brilliant mathematician and an original thinker on the philosophy of mathematics, he was one of the pioneers of the conception of non-Euclidian space. His lectures were given with a minimum of preparation beforehand and from the briefest notes. 'The worst of these examinations', he once said, 'is that you have to think what to ask the fellows before you come in, whereas, when you lecture you need not think at all.' His health soon deteriorated and he died of 'pulmonary disease' in 1879 when he was 33. T. H. Huxley regarded his death as one of the greatest losses to science in his time.

184. Revd T. G. Bonney, FRS, Professor of Geology and Mineralogy, 1877-1901.

185. W. K. Clifford, FRS, Professor of Applied Mathematics, 1870-79.

184

185

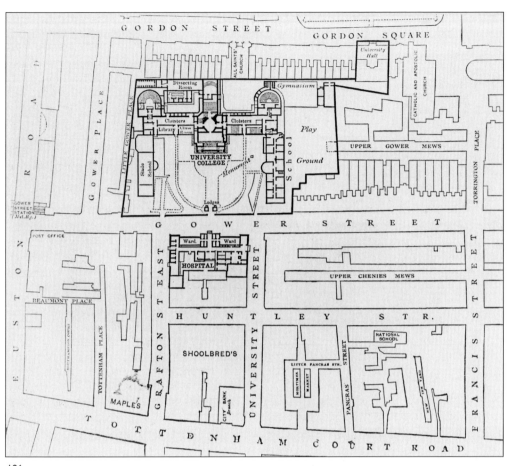

186

187

186. A plan of the College as it was in 1887. By this time, both wings had been built, but the South Wing was still housing the School, the fourth side of the Quadrangle was open except for the old lodges, and there was still no development outside the Quadrangle itself.

187. A view of the Front Quad from Gower Street c.1880.

188. E. S. Beesly, Professor of History, 1860-93.

189. G. Croom Robertson, Professor of Philosophy, 1867-92, the first Grote Professor.

190. W. Stanley Jevons, FRS, Professor of Political Economy, 1875-81.

188

It is paradoxical that the College's weakest subjects in the nineteenth century were those in which a Benthamite foundation might have been expected to be most creative – history, law, philosophy and economics. The problem resulted from a shortage of students and money, rather than of talented teachers. E. S. Beesly, for instance, Professor of History for over thirty years, was an important figure outside the College. He was a follower and translator of Comte, an active socialist and one of the first British academics to be in touch with the Labour movement, indeed with Marx and the First International. *Punch* honoured him with the nickname 'Professor Beastly'. Crabb Robinson lamented that 'Beesly is going to a meeting of bricklayers and says they conduct business better than scholars'; a serious attempt to sack him in 1867 was narrowly diverted by Grote. His commitment to his classes, however, was minimal; he used to 'come into his lecture room at 2 o'clock every Thursday, give us one lecture on Ancient History, one on Modern History, put on his comforter and hat; walk out; and that was all we saw of him till next week'.

Philosophy by contrast found a devoted and inspiring teacher in Croom Robertson, despite the bitterness which attended his original appointment (see pp. 56-57). Intellectually active, and editor of *Mind* for its first sixteen years, he was a trenchant critic of the existing degree examining system. In Political Economy too a distinguished professor had little impact.

189

190

W. Stanley Jevons was a former student of both UCS and UCL, where he had developed his scientific interests; they led him to his pioneering application of quantitative and statistical techniques to economics. Jevons was the first to apply the modern concept of 'utility' in economics. But he found lecturing a great strain and, as his health deteriorated, gave the Chair up after six years. Neither he nor his successor H. S. Foxwell made any significant progress towards the creation of a school of economics at UCL and the foundation of LSE in 1895 was a conscious reaction to the failure of the College to develop the social sciences.

191

191. An unmistakable failure even on his own view ('I could not help feeling I was scarcely a success') was the Revd A. J. Church, Professor of Latin, 1880-89. His cousin, Sir John Seeley, Regius Professor of Modern History at Cambridge, who had himself held the Chair of Latin in the 1860s, tried to dissuade him from putting in for it since 'as a Christian' he would find his position uneasy at UCL. He certainly met with student protest. The first signatory of the petition against Church's classes was later to become the College's first Provost.

In 1876 the Dante scholar H. C. Barlow died leaving the College his library, his papers relating to Dante and a fund for the endowment of public lectures on the Divine Comedy. The foundation played a significant part in the development of Dante studies in this country, and it also provided some small (£30) relief for the professor of the day, Antonio Farinelli. He held the lectureship from 1880 to 1886 and, as his letter clearly shows, was deeply offended when replaced by the most distinguished Dante scholar of the day, Edward Moore. Farinelli's protests were not quite unavailing, since the College was able to make him a small

192

192. A letter from Antonio Farinelli, Professor of Italian, 1880-95, addressed in 1887 to Carey Foster which rather pointedly draws attention to the financial position of many professors at the time. It was discovered in a second-hand book bought in 1977.

193. Another letter written ten years later to the College by A. J. Butler, Professor of Italian, 1898-1910, succinctly drawing attention again to the problems of professorial pay as well as those of teaching languages.

193

grant from the Quain fund in 1887. A. J. Butler, who took the Chair of Italian in 1898, was the first Englishman to hold it after a succession of Italians; a distinguished scholar, he took it strictly as a part-time job and with certain reservations, as his letter shows.

The difficulties of the Arts Faculty in this period are illuminated by these two letters. Payment to the professors was still being made, with the exception of a few endowments, on the basis of the number of students who attended their classes. If the class was small, the professor starved. Apart from those who succeeded in attracting large classes and the famous scientists who could supplement their incomes by consultancies, University College professors were effectively part-timers who had to earn their living when not giving their lectures. One improvement had been made in 1868, when a 'Retired Professors Fund' was created for the first time through the generosity of Samuel Sharpe; but the situation over salaries remained unsatisfactory.

194. Alphonse Legros, Slade Professor of Fine Art, 1875-93, photographed at work.

194

The Slade was one part of the Faculty of Arts which proved a great success; it went from strength to strength. Its second professor, Alphonse Legros, came from the world of Paris, and the heart of the realist movement. However, if he came as a new influence in 1876, he fairly soon lost touch with the latest developments in Paris and became an increasingly isolated figure, speaking little English and teaching mostly by demonstration; but the School prospered and expanded in his years, and amongst his pupils were William Rothenstein and Frederick Brown, who succeeded him in 1893 and who admired him as a teacher. All the same, it is said that as Legros left the college for the last time, he muttered 'Vingt ans perdus'. The College still possesses and prizes a splendid collection of Legros' etchings; as an artist, he seems as yet much under-rated, though he is now receiving his share of the reviving interest in realism.

195

195. The assembled Slade School photographed in the late 1890s; Brown is just discernable amidst the hats of the Slade ladies.

196. Frederick Brown, Slade Professor, 1892-1918.

The first significant and influential period of the Slade's history was when Brown was professor and Henry Tonks and Wilson Steer his assistants. It was Brown who discovered Steer's talent as an artist and he who persuaded Tonks to leave his job as a demonstrator in anatomy in a London hospital and join the Slade. The three men were friends and all members of the New English Art Club, the focal point of the most adventurous English artists in the nineties. At first, they introduced the ideas of the Impressionists and later developed their own reaction to them. At this stage the Slade was the mediator of the new Parisian methods and ideas; the students who passed through between 1894 and 1914 were to play a leading role in all the new currents in English art up to the 1930s.

The greatest strength of the Slade tradition lay in the variety of talent and technique that it fostered. Brown and Tonks stood for a sort of Impressionism, putting great emphasis on the individuality of the natural object and the artist's response to it; but, not very consistently, they taught a strongly academic tradition, derived from the Old Masters and emphasising structure and proportion in drawing above all else. This core tradition influenced artists as widely different as Augustus John, William Orpen, David Bomberg, Stanley Spencer and Wyndham Lewis.

196

197

198

*197. Wilson Steer, OM,
Assistant from 1892
and Assistant Professor,
1922-30.*

*198. Henry Tonks, Assistant
from 1893 and Slade
Professor, 1918-30, the
third of the great teachers
at the Slade in one of its
most influential periods.*

*199. The Slade picnic in
1899. Seated on the horse
are, from the left, William
Orpen, Augustus John,
Gwen John and, with his
foot on the shaft, Albert
Rutherston. In the wagon
are William Rothenstein
and his wife, the parents
of Sir John Rothenstein,
later himself a research
student at the College and
subsequently Director of
the Tate Gallery.*

199

200

200. Augustus John's Moses and the Brazen Serpent won the Slade Prize for 1898 and now hangs in the Housman Room. Ambitious but extremely derivative, it shows little sign of his later style.

201. Augustus John, OM, a Slade student from 1894 to 1898 and hence one of the earliest of Brown's successful pupils. His legendary talent and iconoclastic life-style made him the very stereotype of the bohemian artist, but he had great influence both on his own and on succeeding generations of Slade students.

201

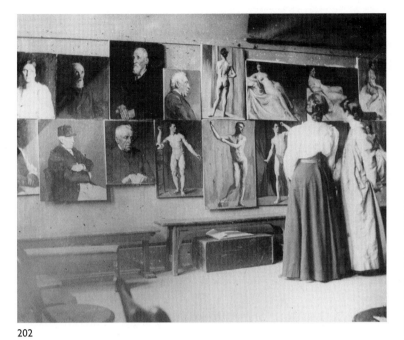

202

202. A display of life paintings in the Slade, c. 1906.

203. Stanley Spencer's The Nativity which won the Slade Prize in 1912, now in the Housman Room. Spencer had spent four years at the Slade, but this work shows how independently he developed and how mature his style, now so familiar, already was as a student.

203

Brown and Tonks were soon left behind by events; they reacted with hostility to the whole Post-Impressionist invasion. Sickert and the Fitzroy circle represented the antithesis of the Slade, but Slade-trained artists like Wyndham Lewis and Edward Wadsworth were in the forefront of new movements. 'What a brood I have raised up' was the austere Tonk's remark about his aberrant pupils. The memories of a contemporary student, Lilian Lancaster, give a vivid picture of one moment in this story of alienation. She and her friend had studied with Sickert and then joined the Slade's classes in 1908 – 'serving God and Mammon', said Sickert. 'It is not surprising that this new way of painting caused something of a sensation among the Slade students … We used to peep through the crack of the door in the rests and saw a number of students crowding round our paintings examining them with great interest, and one day, when I came back to my work, I found "Stipple be damned" scrawled in charcoal in a corner of my canvas.' Miss Lancaster and her friend were discreetly asked to leave at the end of the session.

204

205

204. Wyndham Lewis, a Slade student from 1898 to 1901, later the leader of the extreme avant garde in London.

205. Slade ladies painting in the early years of the twentieth century.

206

207

208

206. The Slade picnic, c. 1912, showing Professor Brown (back row, third from right) and many students who later became famous: David Bomberg, on Brown's right; Dora Carrington, left of front row; C. R. W. Nevinson, on her left; Mark Gertler, on his left; Edward Wadsworth, in his bow tie and white hat; Stanley Spencer, second from right. Isolated from the others by position and dress, on the extreme left, is Isaac Rosenberg, later one of the most individual voices among the poets of the First World War; he was killed on patrol in 1918.

207 & 208. Two more scenes from the famous picnics, one showing Professor Brown with a sandwich.

The first Professor of Classical Archaeology was Charles Newton, a distinguished excavator and one of the founders of the Hellenic Society. He was also Keeper of Classical Antiquities in the British Museum, a post he combined with the professorship. His appointment in 1880 coincided with the height of the aesthetic movement and of the vogue for Greek art, so the new professor's opening lectures on this topic were a sensational success; the fashionable crowds in the Botanical Theatre were led by Oscar Wilde and Lily Langtry. 'But Newton', remarked one of his successors 'never lectured down to his audiences ... and the attendance soon fell to a normal level'. Five years later, the College received an endowment for the Chair. The benefactor was James Yates, an antiquarian and collector who had taken an interest in the College from its foundation – and indeed even earlier, for he had written on the need for a new university in 1826, before he heard of the plans of Campbell and Brougham. When he died in 1871, his will left endowments for Geology and Archaeology, the money to be paid on the death of his wife. Yates's intention had been to regulate the behaviour of his new professor by rules and regulations. 'Another prohibition on which I would insist is that

209

210

the Professor should not smoke tobacco, nor distinguish himself by moustachios, beard or whiskers. He should be a gentleman in manners and appearances and set a good example to his pupils in this and all other things.'

Fortunately, Yates never completed the drafting of these rules and regulations; on these grounds, however, his wife tried to dispute the bequests. There was prolonged litigation on the point and College only eventually won the case in the House of Lords. Newton's successor, R. S. Poole, was again a part-time professor, holding a British Museum post as Keeper of Coins. It was E. A. Gardner, the Yates Professor from 1896 to 1929, who was the first to organise the Yates Archaeological Library and set up a working Department.

211

211. Sir Flinders Petrie, FRS, FBA, the Egyptologist for whom a chair was endowed in 1892, photographed in 1921 with exhibits in the College's remarkable Egyptological collection which he built up.

Another bequest started the Department of Egyptology. Miss Amelia Edwards, a novelist and explorer, founded a chair in the subject specifically for W. M. Flinders Petrie. It was her wish that the professor should spend his winters excavating in Egypt; the Department has stood at the centre of the British archaeological effort in Egypt ever since. Petrie's great achievement was to establish the archaeological chronology of Egypt, by collecting and analysing the whole material culture of Egypt, where previous scholars had mostly devoted themselves to art or inscriptions. His collections were eventually acquired by the College and illustrate the long history of Egypt in all its aspects.

Another notable member of the Department in its early days was Margaret Murray, who taught Egyptian hieroglyphics and history at the College for the best part of fifty years, before becoming in her old age a highly controversial figure in the historiography of witchcraft. When over 100, she published memoirs which included entertaining, though wildly inaccurate, memories of UCL in the late nineteenth century, including an account of her own part in the formation of a women's common room. Following the desegregation of the senior common rooms in 1969, the former women's common room was re-named the Margaret Murray Room; the name survived until 1989, when the room became the office of the Director of Finance and Planning. Today, it houses the office of the Graduate School.

212. Henry Wallis's romantic painting of Petrie excavating at Thebes.

A second great age for the Department began with the appointment of W. B. Emery as Professor in 1951. His digs in Saqqara, the necropolis of Memphis, led to the discovery of the sacred ibises,

212

UC 14786

213

213. A find from the Petrie
Collection: a relief from
Koptos of Sesostris I
(c. 1971-50 BC) conducting
a ceremonial dance before
the ithyphallic fertility god
Min.

214. Another find from the
Petrie Collection: a portrait
of a woman from Hawara
(third or fourth century AD).

falcons, baboons and the mothers of the Apis bull.
Emery's excavations have been extended by his
successors, H. S. Smith, who worked on the temple
complexes of the gods Anubis and Bastet, and G. T.
Martin, who discovered the tombs of the General
Horemheb and of Tutankhamun's treasurer, Maya.
Work at Memphis, including extensive survey and
excavation work in the great city itself, and at the
North Saqqara necropolis are still continuing today,
while the Department became part of the Institute of
Archaeology in 1993 (see p. 16).

215

214

215. Margaret Murray,
Petrie's assistant for many
years, receiving an address
from the Professorial Board
on her 100th birthday in
1963.

216. A. E. Housman, Professor of Latin, 1892-1911, author of A Shropshire Lad. This drawing by Francis Dodd hangs in the Housman Room, the senior common room so called in his honour.

217. The College's portrait of W. P. Ker, FBA, Professor of English, 1889-1922, by Wilson Steer. It is said that the intense quality of the portrait arises from the strong mutual antipathy of artist and sitter.

The real revival in Arts began with the appointment within a few years of three remarkable scholars: W. P. Ker in 1889, A. E. Housman in 1892 and Arthur Platt in 1894. All three played their full part not only in the intellectual but also in the social life of the College and were much in demand as speakers in an age of debates and dinners. Ker, Henry Morley's successor, was to be Professor of English for over thirty years. He published little at first, but his later writings on medieval literature were to have a wide influence. His pupils found him an awe-inspiring figure, full of erudition and of a disconcerting sour wit. Of the three men, Ker was the politician. He was one of the creators of the honours school of English in the University; and, at the end of his career, he initiated Scandinavian Studies in the College, acting as the first Director of what remained for a long time a unique Department. He was famous for his silences. After his *Dark Ages* was published, Mrs J. R. Green expressed her appreciation of it to him. Ker gazed at her, but said nothing, and did not help the conversation, till she stopped in some embarrassment. After a long pause, he said, 'Go on; I like it'.

Arthur Platt, the Professor of Greek, was very different. He was remembered as the creator of the common-room life of the academic staff, at first using his own private room as a meeting place after lunch: 'there he sat for more than a quarter of a century, instructing Chemists in the Humanities and teaching Zoologists wisdom', wrote a colleague – an Arts colleague, of course. He inspired affection in all, including the animals at the Zoo; even the giraffe, a contemporary student recalled, would bend its long neck down and rub its head on Platt's bald pate.

The most famous of the three is, of course, Housman. He had had a chequered early career, having obtained a first in Mods at Oxford, but then failed in Greats. For ten unhappy years he worked at the Patent Office, though for the latter five he was publishing a series of remarkable papers on classical literature. It is one of UCL's

216

217

claims to glory to have brought him back into the university world and, when he left after seventeen years, it was to the Latin Chair at Cambridge. His main work was limited in scope to the exposition and textual criticism of Latin poetry – he produced three editions of unsurpassed quality. He struck contemporaries in College as austere and reserved, though all his letters to Platt were destroyed by Mrs Platt after her husband's death as 'too Rabelaisian'. He must have seemed, then as now, a tissue of inconsistencies. There was kindliness beneath the cold exterior, especially towards young people; but he attacked other scholars with extraordinary ferocity. He was a poet – *A Shropshire Lad* was published during his years at UCL – who would write nothing about the beauty of ancient poetry, and devoted thirty years to elucidating the text of a writer for whom he felt little sympathy.

218

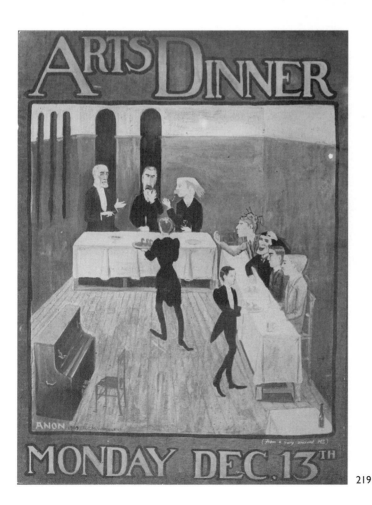

219

218. J. Arthur Platt, Professor of Greek, 1894-1925.

219. Cartoon of an Arts Dinner in 1909, showing Ker, Housman and Platt, all regular speakers, and 'students crowded to hear them'. The cartoon was the work of R. E. M. Wheeler, a prominent student of the time who attended Housman's lectures; later, as Sir Mortimer, he was to be a famous pioneer both as scientific archaeologist and as academic television personality.

220. The medical staff of UCH in 1897; in the middle are Chirstopher Heath, the surgeon and Professor of Clinical Surgery, 1875-1900, and Sir Victor Horsley, FRS, Heath's successor, 1900-07.

221. Sydney Ringer, FRS, who entered the College as a student in 1854 and stayed for the rest of his life, serving as a professor in the Faculty of Medicine between 1862 and 1900. He invented 'Ringer's Solution', due to a fortunate accident on the part of a technician.

222. Sir William Jenner, FRS, a professor in the Faculty of Medicine from 1849 to 1879, as sketched by Sir Henry Thompson in 1850.

220

In the second half of the nineteenth century, the Faculty of Medicine was less rent by quarrels and its teaching came to be regarded as unequalled. It had some outstanding professors. Three became baronets: Sir William Jenner, Physician to Queen Victoria and the undisputed leader of the profession at the height of his career; Sir John Erichsen, Danish by origin, Surgeon Extraordinary to the Queen, whose *Science and Art of Surgery* long shaped the teaching of the subject; and Sir Henry Thompson, Assistant Surgeon at UCL from 1856 and Professor of Clinical Surgery, 1865-75, a man of very wide interests, founder of the Cremation Society and of Golders Green Crematorium. Christopher Heath was the last of the great surgeons of the old style: he took to Listerian surgery only under protest, operating in an old frock-coat, turning green, which hung on a hook outside the theatre.

The Hospital itself was by no means as modern as it needed to be, and in 1896 Sir John Blundell Maple, the furnishing shop millionaire, offered £100,000 for its re-building. Alfred Waterhouse's design for the new Hospital was arresting, though its red-brick and terracotta Renaissance style was not to everyone's taste; but it was practical in its diagonal cruciform plan from the point of view of ventilation and drainage. In the end it cost £200,000, but Maple generously paid it all.

221

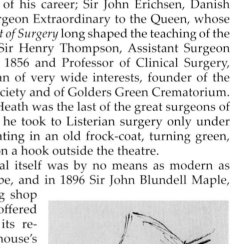

222

223

224

223. Sir John Erichsen, FRS, another leading figure in late nineteenth-century medicine. He was Professor of Surgery from 1850 to 1877, and President of the College from 1887 to 1896.

224. The bust of Sir John Blundell Maple who financed the complete rebuilding of the Hospital between 1898 and 1906.

225

225. The old Hospital seen across the tennis court in front of the College.

226. The new Hospital at the time of its opening in 1906. Since 2000, the building, lavishly refurbished and re-christened as the Cruciform Building, has been the home of the Wolfson Institute for Biomedical Research (see p. 280).

226

227. *Marie Stopes in sensuous pose while a lecturer at the College. A notorious figure in the social revolution which sought to free women from the miseries of sexual ignorance and haphazard reproduction, Marie Stopes managed to take her First in botany in 1902 after only two years at the College, and her PhD at Munich after only two years more. She returned to UCL in 1911 as lecturer in palaeobotany under F.W. Oliver, holding this post until after Married Love was published in 1918, following which she sought a wider stage.*

228. *Sir George Thane, Professor of Anatomy for forty-two years of blameless service to the College between 1877 and 1919, commemorated by the naming of the medical sciences library after him. He was best known outside the College for his editions of Quain's Anatomy, originally written by two of his predecessors in the chair.*

A great sensation for several years in the first decade of the twentieth century was the 'Brown Dog Affair'. It all began in May 1903 when Stephen Coleridge (a leading anti-vivisectionist of the day) made a widely-reported speech to the National Anti-Vivisection Society accusing William Bayliss, a teacher at UCL since 1888, of having carried out cruel and illegal experiments on a dog without anaesthetic in the Physiology Laboratory at the College. He had given a lecture showing an experiment involving a dog, which was already anaesthetised for research on pancreatitis and diabetes being carried out by Ernest Starling, the Professor of Physiology. The lecture was attended by two Swedish ladies, active in the anti-vivisectionist cause, and their very garbled account was the basis of Coleridge's absurd charges against the College: 'into its dark portals there passes a never-ending procession of helpless dumb creatures … into a scene of nameless horror…' Sir Victor Horsley, the UCH Surgeon, and Starling, encouraged the wealthy Bayliss to bring a libel case, and amid much publicity, he won it. It was clearly established that the dog had been humanely treated and that the experiments were necessary and legal; Bayliss won £2,000 damages which he at once donated to the College for the furtherance of physiological research.

The matter, already a *cause célèbre*, did not end there. The anti-vivisectionists arranged for a statue of the 'Brown Dog' – as the Press had named the creature – to be mounted on a drinking fountain in Battersea. This was put up in 1906. With its insulting inscription referring to the laboratories of UCL, it was naturally found offensive in a College justly proud of the various pioneering laboratories it had built up during the previous generation. The students especially rose to the provocation, and in 1907 there was an attempt

227

228

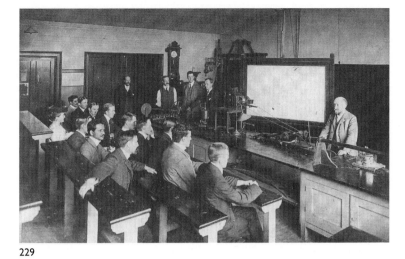

229

229. The photograph
of the reconstruction of
Bayliss's lecture used in the
famous 1903 libel case.
Bayliss – later Sir William
Bayliss, FRS, Professor of
General Physiology, 1912-
24 – is on the right, with
Professor Ernest Starling
and Sir Henry Dale on
the left.

230. A postcard issued
by the National Anti-
Vivisection Society showing
the Brown Dog Statue at
Battersea.

231. A press photograph of
the police guarding the site
of the Brown Dog statue

to knock the statue down which resulted in ten medical students
being fined. Marches, bonfires and other riotous demonstrations
ensued, as well as a vigorous correspondence in *The Times* and the
British Medical Journal. Eventually in 1910, while the College was
still taking legal advice, Battersea Council had the statue removed,
though the site was for some time
afterwards guarded by the police.
The outcome of the affair, so far as
the anti-vivisectionists were concerned, was a loss of credibility,
while according to the Secretary
of the College at the time, Walter
Seton, this was the first time that the
students of different colleges of the
reconstituted University had united
in support of a common cause.

230

231

This is a picture of the Memorial erected at Battersea to the Brown Dog vivisected
in the laboratories of University College, London, in 1902-1903.

The evidence of the vivi-
sectors themselves, in the trial of
Bayliss *v.* Coleridge, proved that
a deep wound was made in the
body of the dog in December,
and a duct in its inside was tied
up so as to deprive it of the
proper use of one of its internal
organs. The wound was then
sewn up and the dog having
recovered from anæsthetics it
was kept in a cage from
December to February. Then
a fresh wound was made in its
body to ascertain whether the
tying of the duct had produced
inflammation or not. This was
done under anæsthetics, then
the dog, with this wound
clamped together with iron
forceps, was handed over to

another vivisector, who fastened
it down to a board and made
another severe wound in its
neck, exposing a gland; he fixed
little pipes to the end of its
arteries, he attached electrodes
to its dissected-out nerves, he
put a tube into its severed wind-
pipe which was connected
under the floor to an automatic
pump in another room, in the
charge of a laboratory boy,
supplying artificial respiration
of anæsthetics, on which
apparatus depended the dog's
insensibility. After about an
hour on that board the dog was
finally handed over to a third
operator, who killed it.

Men and women of England,
how long shall these things be ?

THE NATIONAL ANTI-VIVISECTION SOCIETY, 92, VICTORIA STREET LONDON S.W.

Students had long been forming societies for literary, scientific and debating purposes, and from 1858 there was a Reading Room Society. The Union, and hence a coherent structure for clubs and sports activities, grew out of the University College Society founded by Henry Morley in 1884 and open to teachers and students, past and present. In 1890, a separate Old Students' Association was founded and three years later the Union emerged to take over the UC Society's responsibilities for current students and for sports facilities.

The step did not at first arouse the enthusiasm of the College authorities. It was preceded by radical agitation, particularly about the inadequacies of the sports grounds and bureaucratic obstructions by the College Office. A brief but spectacular contribution was made by *The Privateer*, a journal edited by E. V. Lucas, which began and ended in 1892-93. Towards the end of 1892, a committee chaired by Edward Schäfer, the Professor of Physiology, put a proposal up to the Council for a 'combined athletic and social union'. By June of the following year, the Council had not given its consent but at a student meeting a constitution was adopted and a provisional committee set up. The Council then gave its retrospective blessing and from this point on the new Union seems to have received full support from the College. It was given control of three student rooms and began its first session in October 1893, with Schäfer as its first – rather reluctant – President. Not until 1903 was there a student President.

For the seventieth anniversary of the College in 1897, the Union proposed a number of celebrations which became the first Foundation Week. Besides the sports, a concert in the Botanical Theatre, a Union dance in the Holborn Restaurant, there was the first Oration: given by G. Vivian Poore, one of the Professors of Medicine, it was a lively and well-received survey of the history of the College. Foundation Week remained a regular feature of the College for many years.

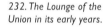

232. The Lounge of the Union in its early years.

232

233

233. One of the earliest team photographs owned
by the Union: the UCL Cricket Club First XI in 1906
– seated on the ground to the right is E. N. da C.
Andrade, later Professor of Physics (see p. 231).

234. Another early Union photograph: the Joint
College and Hospital Hockey Club in 1906-07
– seated in the middle, as President, is Sir Victor
234   Horsley, the famous neurosurgeon.

235. The Union's crest, with
the College motto: 'let them
all come and receive the
rewards their merit earns'.

236. Phineas Maclino, the
College mascot.

Another event significant in the College's history, if on a rather different plane, was reported in March 1900 in the *University College Gazette*, which had been revived in 1895 as the Union's record of events. 'The students then filed into Gower Street, and marched round the Hospital to the tune of nothing in particular admirably rendered by the bugles and penny whistles. A Scott's Emulsion van which happened to drive into the quadrangle at this moment was filled to overflowing, and escorted round the neighbouring streets by numbers of those who didn't succeed in getting in. The sound of an adjacent piano-organ was the signal for a further expedition, and both the organ and its unwilling owner were gently propelled through the College gates ... An exploring party in Tottenham Court Road seized the famous Highlander, and placed him in the post of honour on the Portico – he was soon joined by a representative of the Army, who had been carried to the College on the shoulders of an enthusiastic crowd.' There followed a procession to the West End in a large festooned cart lent by Sir Blundell Maple, a rendition of 'Rule Britannia' outside the War Office and finally a bonfire in the Front Quad.

The occasion for the rejoicing was the relief of Ladysmith by Sir Redvers Buller during the Boer War. The 'famous Highlander' was Phineas Maclino, a large wooden tobacconist's sign, who stood outside Catesby's in Tottenham Court Road. From this occasion onwards, he was repeatedly commandeered for rags, riots and celebrations. In the course of time, Phineas came to be a resident of UCL, if a somewhat erratic one, as the College mascot. He has frequently been the victim of raiding parties from other institutions, but is now in the Union's safe-keeping, sprucely re-painted by Slade students in the mid-1980s, and proudly displayed in the Academical Bar.

235

236

237

238

237-241. A number of snap-shots showing the commandeering of Phineas on Ladysmith night in 1900, and the patriotic scenes leading up to the bonfire in the Front Quad which were enthusiastically undertaken by the students and by the boys from the School.

239

240

241

The College's situation at the end of the nineteenth century was far from secure. Building developments had led to a debt of £30,000 which the College had no way of paying off. The salaries of professors were in general inadequate and they had no proper means at all of financing their research. Moreover, the administration of the College had not succeeded in keeping pace with its expansion, though the College was in fact on the verge of a great leap forward in terms of student numbers, buildings and research. Meanwhile, University reform had been under discussion for many years and this was to affect UCL's development in a radical way. From the 1880s there was a strong campaign to promote a 'Teaching University', examining still being the University of London's only function. The solution arrived at in 1898, after two Royal Commissions and innumerable set-backs, was that an organic connection should be established between the teaching College

and the degree-giving body. The teachers were given representation on University committees and on Boards of Studies set up to control the various subject areas, while the students were to be required to complete courses of study in the colleges if they were to take 'internal' degrees. UCL wanted to go further than this. It proposed that the College and all its assets

242

242. The only known photograph of the Council Room as it was in the late nineteenth century.

243. The General Office as established in 1908, when the old Office was allocated to the Provost, who had previously made do with the Council Room when not otherwise in use.

244. The College Servants' Association on one of the earliest annual outings in the 1890s.

243

244

245

should be vested in the University and that all its activities should be carried out under the University's authority. Eventually, after the Drapers' Company paid off virtually all the College's debts, this plan was given effect by the University College (Transfer) Act of 1905.

245. An unfulfilled proposal for the College frontage, published in 1894 by T. Roger Smith, the Professor of Architecture.

246. The cover of the UCL Union Magazine which succeeded the UC Gazette in 1904.

246

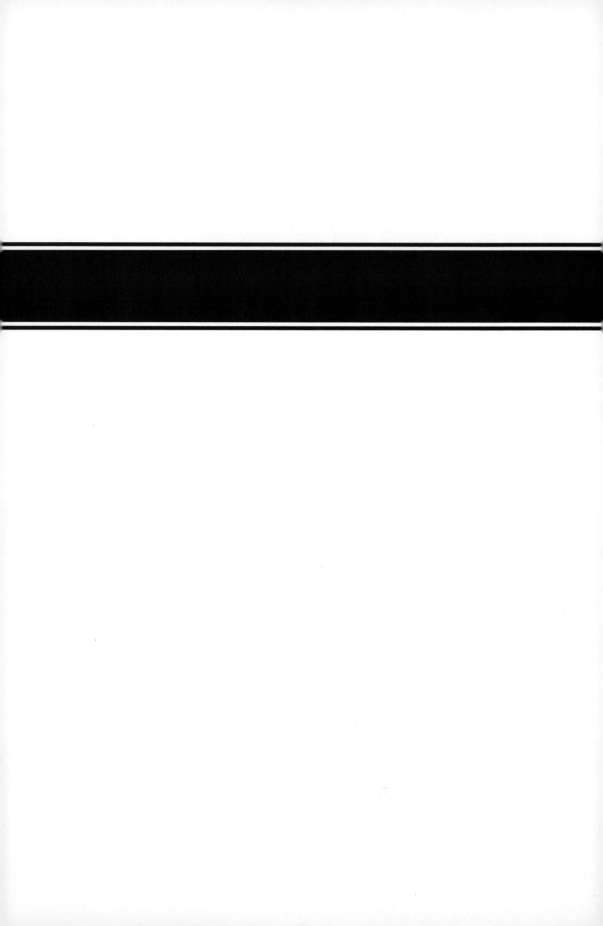

Chapter 6
The Gregory Foster Years, 1904-29

Foster! Foster!
Gregory Foster!
Gower Street!
Gower Street!
U.C.L. L. L.
U.C.L.

The College chant, The UCL Student's Song Book
(1st ed., 1926; 4th ed., 1946)

[Sir Gregory Foster's] appointment came at a difficult time. The university of London had at last become a true university instead of a glorified examining body. The colleges and schools had as yet but little sense of unity and co-operation. There were jealousies and rivalries among them, while there was continued friction between the external and the internal sides of the university. Foster during his long term of office (1904-1929) steered the college with wisdom, vigilance, and courage through all these difficulties. Many important new departments of study were established; the college buildings were increased threefold; and the number of students was trebled. It would be difficult to overrate the part which he played in this important development. He may well be regarded as the second founder of the college.

H. E. Butler writing in the Dictionary
of National Biography Supplement *(1949)*

Both before and after my time, University College lay under the strong hand of Sir Gregory Foster, provost. Foster was an imposing figure of a man, with a sultry countenance and a Socratic forehead that concealed little in the way of academic understanding but a great capacity for administrative push. His ambition was to make University College bigger and wealthier every day and in every way. Alas, he succeeded. He never paused to think that he was nailing down and forcibly feeding a perfectly good goose with the sole object of putting more and more fatted liver on the market. He never reflected that 'It is not growing like a tree in bulk doth make a man better be'. There were many things on which he did not reflect, for his was not a reflective nature.

Sir Mortimer Wheeler, Still Digging *(1955)*

247. Orpen's portrait of
Sir Gregory Foster, who
was the first Provost, 1906-
29, having already been
Secretary of the College,
1900-04, and Principal,
1904-06.

The first Provost of UCL was Sir Gregory Foster. Since the ill-starred days of Leonard Horner as Warden, the College had only had the formal leadership of the President, who chaired the Council, while another member of the Council acted as chairman of the Senate. In 1900 it was decided that there should once more be a salaried head, with the title of Principal, who was to chair

247

248

248. Walter W. Seton in his office as Secretary of the College, 1904-27. Like Sir Gregory Foster, he devoted himself to the College in its period of transformation.

249. A graph of student numbers during the first century of UCL's existence, showing the rapid expansion of the Gregory Foster years, despite the interruption of the First World War

the Senate and act as the professors' link with the Council. Carey Foster held the post for four years, in which some of the toughest problems were faced, and was then succeeded by the man who had been Secretary since 1900, Gregory Foster (no relation), while W. W. Seton took over the secretaryship. These two men were to guide the College for a long period of substantial change and development. Gregory Foster had been a UCL student in the eighties (see p. 133), becoming a teacher at UCS and then an assistant in the English Department in the 1890s, and third President of the Union in 1896. His title was changed from Principal to Provost in 1906, evidently to avoid confusion with the Principal of the newly reconstituted University of London.

Seton was an even younger man: he had come to UCL on his seventeenth birthday and was only twenty-two when he became Secretary. He too had strong academic interests, particularly in Scottish History and in Franciscan studies. Seton was a dour, hard-working Scot, with a somewhat underdeveloped sense of humour, while Foster was a very popular figure, at least with the students. He insisted on interviewing personally all of them at the beginning of each session throughout his Provostship, an increasingly time-consuming exercise which repaid itself in terms of the regard in which he was held. Gregory Foster was very largely responsible for founding the twentieth – as distinct from the nineteenth – century College.

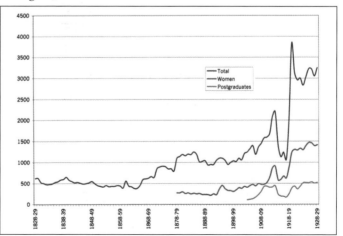

249

250. The new Medical School being built; it was ready for opening in 1907.

251. The crest of the Medical School, with Currie symbolised by a ship, Sir Blundell Maple by maple-leaves and medicine by the snake.

250

251

The decision to 'incorporate' the College fully into the University meant the separation of two elements of the College – the Advanced Medical School and the Boys' School. Both had therefore to be found new premises away from the College. For this purpose the Faculty of Medicine had to be split, the College retaining the pre-clinical teaching and the new 'University College Hospital Medical School' taking over the advanced courses in surgery and medicine. A site and a building were needed. The site was provided opposite the College on the corner of Huntley Street in 1903 through an anonymous gift. The building was presented wholly by Sir Donald Currie, the founder of the Castle Steamship Company and one of the richest men in England, who gave well over £100,000 to the project. He had had no previous connection with the College or with the area, but his life had been saved by a doctor from UCH. The College, after thanking Sir Donald for his gift, passed a vote of thanks to Dr Batty Shaw 'for having so successfully interested Sir Donald Currie in the Scheme ...'.

The Boys' School was to move a great deal further away, to the site in Frognal, Hampstead, which it still occupies today. Money was again raised by an appeal and the School was re-founded as an independent body. The leave-taking on 25 July 1907 was a solemn affair; '... the School, headed by the Cadet Corps, marched into the College quadrangle, formed three sides of a hollow square, facing the great steps and portico, where a chair had been placed for the Provost, Dr T. Gregory Foster. The Head-Master, supported by Beadle and Sergeant, advanced into the Square, and

252

253

252. Sir Donald Currie,
the wealthy shipowner who
financed the new Medical
School building, now
eccentrically re-named the
Rockefeller Building.

253. Eric Gill's design for
the seal of the College
Transfer Commissioners
appointed under the 1905
Act of Parliament.

254. The new building for
University College School
at Hampstead, soon after
its opening by Edward VII
in 1907.

when the Provost had taken his seat above, read the valedictory address before giving up formally the keys of the School building'. Moving speeches were made about the maintenance of intimate links between School and College, hopes which have found little fulfilment in the years since.

The formal act of incorporation took effect on 1 January 1907. From now on, the College was to be controlled by a Committee of the Senate of the University; the College Senate became the Professorial Board and the College itself ceased to have a separate legal existence from the University.

254

255. R. W. Chambers, FBA,
Librarian 1901-22, the
creator of the modern
College Library, who later
succeeded Ker as Quain
Professor of English
Language and Literature,
1922-41.

256. The Science Library
as created by Chambers to
the north of the Flaxman
Gallery on the first floor of
the main building.

It is ironical that it was exactly seventy years later, in 1977, that the College completed the lengthy and expensive business of undoing the effects of incorporation. In 1907 it had been an act of faith in the new order, but only King's followed the lead and the University became instead a federation of independent colleges, so that UCL and KCL found themselves in an increasingly anomalous situation. In 1977, the College became once more an independent corporation, with a new Royal Charter. The short-term effects of the constitutional change of 1907, however, were unquestionably beneficial.

The departure of the School and of the Medical School enabled a major reorganisation of accommodation to take place. Geology took most of the first floor of the South Wing and began a considerable expansion under E. J. Garwood, who had succeeded Bonney in 1901 and who was the first full-time Professor. Extra space was provided for Electrical Engineering and Applied Mathematics while the Eugenics Laboratory was moved into College from 88 Gower Street. Philosophy was also housed in the South Wing, with the Psychological Laboratory adjoining it.

Perhaps the chief beneficiary was the Library, whose reorganisation is one of the great success stories of the period. When R. W. Chambers was appointed Librarian in 1901, he inherited a rich but disorganised domain, largely consisting of bequests and gifts, many of them very valuable and many having been the collections of the professors themselves. But there had been years of neglect: from 1831 to 1871, there was no proper Librarian; there was a printed catalogue, thanks to the generosity of Samuel Sharpe and the efforts of Adrian Wheeler as Librarian between 1871 and 1901, but there was no card-index to facilitate the cataloguing of accessions, no space to store them and no administrative structure.

Chambers had been a pupil of Ker and was to succeed Gregory Foster as Assistant Professor in 1904; later he was to succeed Ker himself as Quain Professor in 1922. He took over as Librarian to face great problems, not least a profound controversy between those who wished to see the Library develop a single centralised organisation and those who preferred subject libraries

255

256

257

258

under the professor's own control and hence available for teaching use within the department. Chambers fought from the beginning for the integrity of the Library and the solution adopted conceded his main point; the books were to remain under the Library's control, but be kept in separate though linked rooms, as far as possible one for each main subject. With this plan in mind, the Library was able to use the 1907 reorganisation to the best effect: the area to the south of the Flaxman Gallery became a series of linked Arts libraries, while the area to the north – the old Anatomy Museum – became the College's first coherent Science Library.

A most distinguished accession in 1906 was the library of Frederick Mocatta, the wealthy collector and philanthropist, who left his collection of Jewish books and antiquities to the Jewish Historical Society. They arranged, as a memorial to him, that a library, a museum and a room for the meetings of the Society should be provided by the college: in return, UCL became the permanent home of one of the most important Jewish libraries in Britain.

257. The old Mocatta Library, destroyed in 1940.

258. The bronze plaque of Frederick Mocatta in the Library.

259 & 260. Two parts of the new Geology Department, set up in the South Wing vacated by the School in 1907 – the Mineral and Rock Room and the Geological Museum.

259

260

The years after incorporation saw significant steps towards the establishment of sustained research programmes of the type that was to become increasingly familiar in the twentieth century. Ernest Starling as Jodrell Professor of Physiology played a major role. A medic from Guy's, he had been working with William Bayliss (his brother-in-law) for some years before coming to UCL in 1899. Their collaboration was at first directed to the functioning of the heart and to the analysis of cardiac failure. Then in 1902 they turned to work on intestinal function and rapidly made startling discoveries, leading to the principle of hormonal control mechanisms; they were the first to establish that messages were conveyed by chemical agents, transported in the bloodstream, and Starling himself introduced the word 'hormone' in 1905.

Starling conceived and brought to birth the plans for a new medical complex at UCL involving Anatomy and Pharmacology as well as Physiology, intending to transform both medical education and research in London. The first stage, the Institute of Physiology – a title little to the taste of the Provost, who feared secession – was built in 1909 on what had been the Boys' School playground.

In 1912, through the generosity of Andrew Carnegie, the second stage was added for Pharmacology. Starling went on to evolve a general theory of the regulation of the heart-beat (Starling's law of the heart). His experiences in the First World War left him bitterly convinced of the sheer ignorance of the British ruling classes and he campaigned vigorously for basic educational reforms with a scientific curriculum. He resigned the Jodrell Chair in 1923, but remained in UCL as a Royal Society Professor. He died, ironically enough of a heart attack, at sea off Jamaica in 1927.

261. The Institute of Physiology, built on the former University College School playground, soon after its opening in 1909.

261

262. The College's portrait of Ernest Starling, FRS, Jodrell Professor of Physiology, 1899-1923 and Foulerton Research Professor, 1923-27.

263

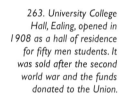

264

*263. University College
Hall, Ealing, opened in
1908 as a hall of residence
for fifty men students. It
was sold after the second
world war and the funds
donated to the Union.*

*264. A view of Perivale,
the sports ground opened
in 1908 and used by the
College until the 1940s.*

*265-267. Three Homeric
tableaux from the Bazaar
and Fete of 1909: from
the top, 'Death and Sleep
with the body of Memnon',
'Nausicaa playing ball with
her Maidens' and 'Penelope
at her loom discovered by
the Suitors'. In the first,
Death is played by E.
A. Gardner, Professor of
Archaeology, 1896-1929,
and in the third, one of
the suitors is Mortimer
Wheeler.*

Before 1897 the College had no playing-fields of its own and teams had to rent pitches in Regent's Park or Primrose Hill, the area where many of the students were accommodated. From 1897 to 1906 the new Union rented a ground at Acton, but by 1905 this had proved too small and 15½ acres were bought at Perivale, which was to be the centre of athletic activities until after the second world war. The Perivale ground was formally opened in June 1908. By this time the Women's Union Society was also looking for a sports ground. It had come into existence owing largely to the efforts of Rosa Morison (see p. 102), who had persuaded the College to provide a Reading Room for women students in the eighties and who became the first President of the new Union when it was set up in 1897. Like the Men's, the Women's Union was responsible amongst other things for athletic facilities and so a ground for the women too became a priority. The problem was solved by buying another 7½ acres adjacent to the men's ground at Perivale. The cost of the two together was £3,600; including equipment and drainage, the requirement of the two Unions by 1909 was £7,000. Fund-raising activities, therefore, took up a good deal of student time in the following years. The great Bazaar and Fête of 1909 lasted for three days, occupying the Front Quadrangle and large parts of the College buildings as well. The programme included a fair, dances, concerts, demonstrations, exhibitions and scenes from Shakespeare, as well as Indian and Homeric tableaux. The whole affair was a great success, raising more than a third of the sum needed.

As early as 1912, there was talk of amalgamating the two Unions, a project which in fact had to wait over forty years. The

265   266   267

proposal was roundly denounced in the *Union Magazine* for June 1912, which expressed the hope that 'this futile chatter and the exaggeration with which it is embroidered will cease; as it may endanger the present cordial relation which exist between the two Union Societies'. These pre-war years did, however, see a major development in the provision of accommodation for men students. This had been gravely deficient since 1889, when the old University Hall was acquired by the Trustees of Dr Williams's Library. A committee was set up with Seton as its secretary and Sir William Ramsay as treasurer, to acquire land in Ealing, about a quarter of an hour's walk from the new athletic ground. It was opened in 1908 with room for fifty students, and extended in the 1920s. Walter Seton continued to take a great interest in the new Hall and was its Warden from 1912 to 1922.

The years before the first world war saw a vigorous continuation of building activity assisted by benefactions. In 1911 Sir Herbert Bartlett, a building contractor, provided practical support to the proposal that the Departments of Architecture at King's and UCL should be merged, by donating £30,000 for the necessary building. The benefaction was also intended to provide for the accommodation needed by Karl Pearson's department; the whole building would provide a north-west frontage onto Gower Street. Almost complete by the outbreak of war, it was first used as a temporary war-time hospital under the management of UCH.

268. A view of the scene in the Front Quad during the Bazaar and Fête in July 1909.

269. The set built by F. M. Simpson, the Professor of Architecture, in one of the old semi-circular lecture theatres, as used in 1907 for the production of the Greek plays which were a feature of the years about the turn of the century.

270. The programme of events at the three-day Bazaar and Fête of 1909.

268

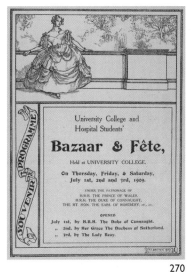

270

269

271

271. Stafford Cripps, the Union's President for 1910-11, later, as Sir Stafford, the austerity Chancellor of the Exchequer in 1947-50; he made his name by elegant but economic furnishing of the Union's rooms.

272. An advertisement from the first Students' Handbook, published for 1913-14.

273. The original Bartlett School (now the Pearson Building) being built just before the war.

274. Sir Herbert Bartlett, whose generosity made the building possible and whose name is borne today by the School of Architecture and Planning in Wates House, where his bust remains.

The Gower Hotel

EUSTON SQUARE STATION, N.W.

Luncheons, 12 to 3 - - - 1/6
Special Student's Luncheon 1/-
Afternoon Tea - - - - **6d.**
Dinners, 6 to 8 - - 1/6 and 2/-

MEALS À LA CARTE
From 7.30 a.m. to 10.30 p.m.
SUNDAYS INCLUDED.

Bedroom, Breakfast, Bath, & Attendance,
From **4/-**
Special *En Pension* Terms

BILLIARDS

Inclusive Terms from £2 2s. per week.

Telegrams :   *Telephone :*
" *Proximity, London.*"   No. 466 North.

272

274

273

275

275. The new chemistry Laboratories facing onto Gower Place, first opened in 1915; since 1983, the building has housed the Sandoz Institute (now the Novartis Institute) for Medical Research, associated with the Department of Pharmacology (see p. 255).

276. A cartoon inspired by a remark of F. G. Donnan, FRS, Professor of Chemistry, 1913-37: 'The lifeblood of England is sulphuric acid.'

The other major benefaction on the eve of the first world war provided expanded accommodation for the work of the Department of Chemistry. Sir William Ramsay's successor as Professor of Chemistry was F. G. Donnan, a disting-uished physical chemist, who had first come to UCL to work in Ramsay's lab-oratory in 1898, and subsequently held posts in Dublin and Liverpool before his return in 1913. He is now best remembered for the 'Donnan membrane equilibrium', concerned with the transport of ions and molecules across the living cell. By the time he took over the Department, the building of the new laboratories, facing Gower Place and extending the College site northwards, was already well advanced. Much of the money was given in 1911 by Sir Ralph Forster, whose bust remains in the entrance hall; a closing order was obtained for Little Gower Place in 1912 and the impressive building, designed by Simpson, was in use, though not finished, by 1915.

276

277. The College's work continued during the war, though the number of students declined sharply (see p. 161). A high proportion never returned; no fewer than 301 members or former members were the College's contribution to 'the lost generation'. Here Armistice Day is being commemorated in the Front Quad in November 1922, by the memorial inscription placed in front of the Portico; the Roll of Honour was read out by the Provost and the Dean of the Medical School, and the Librarian received the first volume of the War Memorial Album. In the background can be seen the addition to the College buildings opened in 1920 by Lord Addison, the first Minister of Health, after its use as a war-time hospital annexe; Sir Herbert Bartlett by then had been revealed as the donor, and his name was given to the new School of Architecture.

278. The first man to win the VC twice – Arthur Martin-Leake, a graduate of the Faculty of Medicine: he won it first in the Transvaal during the Boer War in 1902 and then again in France in 1914.

277

278

279

279. A cartoon from the University College Union Magazine of 1915, showing the way to post-war fashions.

280. A view of the South Cloisters between the two world wars, showing along the wall the photographs of those who died in 1914-18. The South Cloister suffered severely in the Second World War (see p. 211), and in Richardson's post-war reconstruction the pillars down the centre were not replaced. The Marmor Homericum, which can be seen at the far end, survived the bombing in the Second World War; it had been presented by George Grote in 1865, at the time when the Cloisters were glazed. An unusual creation out of pieces of marble by the Baron Triqueti, it shows scenes from the works of Homer.

280

281

281. The College Christmas and New Year card for 1915-16 sent jointly by the Provost and the President of the Union to all members of the College serving in the forces.

282

282. An aerial photograph
of the College and its
vicinity taken in about
1920 before motor traffic
had begun to make
much impact. It shows
the empty site in Gower
Street cleared ready for
the construction of the
Anatomy building designed
by Simpson himself and
opened in 1923. This
photograph also contains
the only view known to
have survived the bombing
in 1940 of the Carey
Foster Laboratory
(see also p. 108).

Between the 1890s and the 1920s, the expansion in the College's activities was matched by striking developments in the buildings. (Compare the plan opposite with that on p. 131.) First the Front Quadrangle was closed in by the new buildings added to the North and South Wings and fronting on to Gower Street – Engineering, Architecture and Statistics. Secondly, Physics, Chemistry, Phys-iology, Pharmacology and Anatomy began the process whereby the larger science departments moved out of the original building into more generous quarters on the periphery, leaving the main building for the most part to the Library, administration and the Arts. After westward and northward moves up to the 1920s, further expansion was to be eastward and southward (compare also with the plan on p. 207).

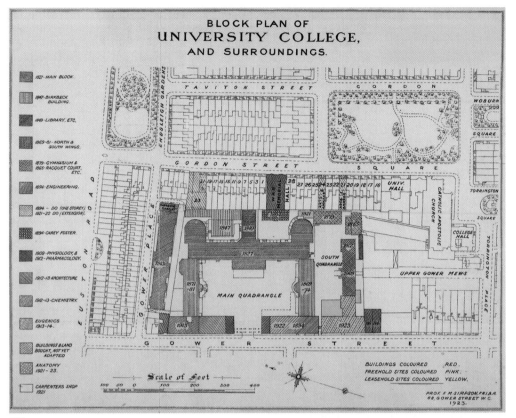

283

In 1905-07, the two distinctive round observatories were built on the lawns of the Front Quad. These additions were partly the initiative of Karl Pearson, and partly of M. T. M. Ormsby, later Professor of Municipal Engineering, whose interest was in their relevance to surveying courses as well as astronomy. The Chadwick Trustees largely paid for one, and the Drapers' Company largely for the other. They remained in use up to the Second World War, serving subsequently for the storing of garden tools, the teaching of classics, and as an office for the manager of the College branch of the NatWest. They are currently devoted to 'Grounds Maintenance'.

283. A plan of the College prepared by F. M. Simpson in 1923, after his term as Professor of Architecture; it shows the distribution of departments shortly before the Centenary, but is rather inconsistent in its dating of the various buildings.

The third stage of Starling's plans for medical sciences achieved completion with the opening of the Anatomy Building in 1923. This was funded by the Rockefeller Foundation as an expression of American friendship towards the British Empire. The £370,000 given was the College's largest benefaction up to that time. The building adjoins a further extension to the Institute of Physiology and faces the Medical School across Gower Street; all these buildings are physically linked, with the intention of encouraging the correlation of their activities, even the Medical School being connected by a tunnel under Gower Street.

In 1923 also, Anatomy was strengthened by the transfer of Histology and Embryology from Physiology; 'paradoxical as it may appear', wrote Sir Grafton Elliot Smith, Thane's successor as Professor of Anatomy, 'the reforming zeal of Professor Sharpey at this College seventy years ago had as one of its ultimate results the crippling of anatomical effort in England...' Anatomy had become very largely a descriptive science and by restoring to it the study of the nervous system from its development and growth to its degeneration, Elliot Smith laid the foundation of a tradition of research on the brain and the lower nervous system that continues to produce striking experimental results. He is also remembered for his diffusionist anthropological theories on the development

284

285

of culture, theories that in their extreme form led to the view that all culture was ultimately derived from Ancient Egypt. Whatever the value of his theories, Elliot Smith made UCL a centre for both physical and cultural anthropology and the current Department of Anthropology descends from his work. Another branch of study that owes its origins to the growth of Anatomy in the 1920s is the History of Medicine, still very active as a sub-department, latterly as the Wellcome Unit for the History of Medicine.

In Physiology, Starling's successor when he gave up the Jodrell Chair was A. V. Hill, who soon after his arrival received the Nobel Prize for his work on the energy cycle associated with the contraction of muscles. He held the Chair for only three years, but remained at UCL until his retirement in 1951 as a Royal Society Research Professor. This relieved him of responsibility for teaching and he developed a very influential research unit within Physiology, which worked on problems in the physics of muscle and nerve function and which after his retirement became the Department of Biophysics. Hill was a public man, serving on many national and international bodies; he was also MP for the University of Cambridge during the war and President of the British Association in 1952. Charles Lovatt Evans succeeded Hill when he gave up the Jodrell Chair in 1926; he had for many years worked with Starling on the functioning of the heart and he continued the tradition of research in this area.

286. A.V. Hill, CH, FRS, Jodrell Professor of Physiology, 1923-26, and Foulerton Research Professor, 1926-51, being chaired by students in 1923 outside the Institute of Physiology in celebration of his Nobel Prize; wearing the white coat is Sir Alan Parkes, FRS, as a young researcher, who virtually lived in College for eight years, producing twenty papers a year, snatching sleep in a seminar room; he was rewarded with the FRS at thirty-two.

287. The monument to Sir Charles Lovatt Evans, FRS, erected in the entrance to the Institute.

286

287

In the new Physiology building of 1909, there was already provision for 'chemical physiology', thanks to R. H. A. Plimmer, Assistant Professor and later Reader in what was a new subject. He was succeeded in 1919 by J. C. Drummond, who became the first Professor of Biochemistry in 1922; predictably enough, the new Chair was funded by the Rockefeller Foundation. The Professor of Pharmacology, A. J. Clark, with unprecedented generosity for a Head of Department, gave up some space to the new unit, and Pharmacology did not return to its 1912 boundaries until 1960, when Biochemistry moved on.

Drummond's interests lay in nutrition and especially in vitamins, in the analysis, identification and even naming of which he played a notable part. He always sustained a broad range of interests, which extended later to practical questions of nutrition policy and to the history of diet on which subject he published *The Englishman's*

Food in 1939. He was most successful in making his unit exercise an influence out of all proportion to its size. During the second world war, he became Scientific Adviser to the Ministry of Food and, after it, resigned his Chair to become Director of Research for Boots. He, his wife and their daughter were murdered while camping in France in 1952, a sensational and unsolved crime.

Biochemistry was restored after the war-time chaos by Sir Frank Young, who created the independent Department in the subject. Between 1958 and 1961, it moved into its new quarters in the Biological Sciences building, by which time it was offering undergraduate

288

289

as well as postgraduate courses. The developing interests of the Department were recognised in 1990 when its name was changed to 'Biochemistry and Molecular Biology'.

A research school of physics in the sense in which it would be understood today, does not go back earlier than the twenties and owes its origin to Sir William Bragg and to his successors A. W. Porter, Professor of Physics, 1924-28, and E. N. da C. Andrade (see p. 231). Bragg graduated from Cambridge in 1884 and soon afterwards went to Australia where he held the Chair of Mathematics and Physics in Adelaide. He came back to Leeds in 1909 and moved to the Quain Chair at UCL in 1915. In the same year he received the Nobel Prize for Physics, jointly with his son, later Sir Lawrence Bragg. He had been quite unusual in starting serious research relatively late in his career. He was already in his forties when, in 1904, he began to be fascinated by the work then being done in the areas of radioactivity and X-rays. In particular, he and his son succeeded in establishing a technique for studying the arrangement of atoms in a crystal by the use of X-rays. This was basic work which helped to lay the foundations for the science of crystallography. Amongst Bragg's research students in this period at UCL was Kathleen Lonsdale, later to be Professor of Crystallography in the Department of Chemistry (see *000.*).

L. N. G. Filon was of French origin; he came to UCL as a student and became a faithful pupil of M. G. M. Hill and Karl Pearson. He became a Lecturer in Pure Mathematics in 1903, but worked on the theory of stresses and, after Pearson moved over to Eugenics, Filon succeeded him in the Chair of Applied Mathematics, which he held until 1937. He became progressively more of a figure in academic administration, acting as the first Director of the Mill Hill Observatory in 1929, becoming Vice-Chancellor of the University in 1933, and serving as Vice-President of the Royal Society in 1935-37.

290. Micaiah J. M. Hill, FRS, Professor of Mathematics, 1884-1924, Vice-Chancellor of the University of London, 1909-11, photographed at his desk for the Sphere *in 1921.*

291. L. N. G. Filon, FRS, Professor of Applied Mathematics, 1912-37, Vice-Chancellor of the University of London, 1933-35, photographed in the Senior Common Room.

290

291

292

One of the most prolonged research projects the College had seen was the work pioneered by Filon together with E. G. Coker on photo-elasticity between 1909 and 1934 and the resumed programme of research undertaken by their successors after the war. In 1909 Coker was head of the Engineering Department at Finsbury Technical College and Filon still a lecturer in Pure Mathematics at UCL. Filon had worked on elasticity in connection with the bending of beams and he was much impressed by a paper of which Coker was joint author which suggested that the use of xylonite models would allow the stresses in engineering components to be studied by optical techniques. Filon supplied the theory, Coker the practical application. In 1912 Filon, as Professor of Applied Mathematics, obtained his own laboratory; two years later, Coker became a Professor at UCL, and Head of the Department of Civil and Mechanical Engineering for twenty years, so that he too set up a photo-elastic laboratory, which worked in parallel – sometimes uneasily – with Filon's.

293

294. Excavation in progress in 1921 for the Hydraulics Laboratory built alongside the Engineering building underneath part of the Front Quad.

295. The assembled staff and students of Engineering, a separate Faculty since 1908, photographed during the first world war, amongst them a number of the College's most distinguished scientists who then provided teaching for Engineering students; they include Sir William Ramsay, Sir William Bragg and Karl Pearson.

Their joint publication *Treatise on Photo-elasticity* (1931) was the most authoritative account of the subject possible at that date. Coker, however, failed to convince industry of the viability of his new methods and when he retired in 1934 his laboratory was virtually abandoned and, on the outbreak of war, completely dismantled. After the war, new advances in the technique made in the USA, together with a new interest in British industry, caused the programme to be resumed; Coker's laboratory was reconstructed, and a new research group created under H. J. Jessop.

295

Two fundamental changes affected the Faculty of Arts in the years after incorporation into the University: the rise of the 'honours' degree, which enabled the students to specialise, and the proper funding of salaries, which enabled the professors to become full-time. The teaching of history especially was revolutionised. From 1896 the honours degree in the subject was available, and from 1905 the 'internal' honours degree in the reorganised University. The moving spirit in the ensuing trans-formation was not F. C. Montague, Beesly's successor in the Chair of History, 1893-1927, 'a tolerant rationalist and a blameless epicurean', but the redoubtable Tudor historian A. F. Pollard. In 1903 there was a vacancy in the Chair of Constitutional Law and History and the two outstanding candidates were Pollard and W. S. (later Sir William) Holdsworth. The appointing committee hit on the idea of splitting the Chair into two and taking them both: 'why not?', suggested the presiding genius; 'there is no stipend for either, and it will cost the College no more to have two chairs than one'.

Pollard had worked in the 1890s as Assistant Editor of the *Dictionary of National Biography*, and his involvement in that great exercise in scholarly co-operative organisation proved formative. It provided the model for his postgraduate seminar and the germ of the Institute of Historical Research, which he founded in 1921. He was also the architect of two other important developments in the subject: he created the School of History, which survives today as the only major example of co-operation in teaching between most of the colleges of the University of London, and, at a meeting in UCL in 1906, he founded the Historical Association as a forum for the teachers of the expanding subject. Ten years later, Pollard became first editor of its journal, *History*. For many years from 1950, two years after his death, Pollard was commemorated, in a

296   297

way that would have shocked him, in the *Pollardian*, an irreverent journal of the History students.

The study of German was placed on a firm academic footing by Robert Priebsch, the correct but kind Austrian who held the chair of German for thirty-three years from 1898. Priebsch was a medievalist with a consuming passion for manuscripts; his great published work was a catalogue of German manuscripts in England. In building up a notable Department of German, Priebsch was considerably aided by John G. Robertson, a modernist, who between 1903 and 1933 held a chair of German shared with Bedford College, and who also succeeded W. P. Ker as Director of Scandinavian Studies.

A conspicuous figure in Anglo-Italian life was Antonio Cippico, a writer and journalist who became a teacher of Italian before the first world war and Professor of Italian in 1918. A fervent and poetic Italian patriot, he was one of the earliest apostles of the Fascist movement and founder of the Fascio of London, becoming a senator after Mussolini's march on Rome in 1922. For a few years he combined his public duties in Rome with his teaching in London, but resigned in 1925 to become Italian delegate to the League of Nations.

Most of the teachers of Law, if distinguished, were transient figures in College, devoting themselves to their own professional careers. A more consistent presence, over the forty-two years for which he was in post, was A. F. Murison, Professor of Roman Law from 1884 to 1925. A Scottish schoolmaster turned barrister, he set himself the enormous task of collating the codices of the text of the *Institutes* of Justinian distributed all over the libraries of Europe. He mastered every European language, except Turkish, but never finished his undertaking; his voluminous transcripts and notes remain in the Library, untouched since his death in 1934. Murison was obliged to support himself by vast quantities of miscellaneous lecturing, examining, translating and journalism. For the first thirty years of the tenure of his Chair he claimed he was paid no more than £30 per annum. Only after 1912 was the old system phased out by which the unendowed professors were paid 5s. in the guinea out of the students' fees. H. F. Jolowicz, Murison's successor in 1931, was guaranteed £800 per annum. This trend was to have profound effects on the nature and structure of academic life.

298. A. F. Murison, Professor of Roman Law, 1884-1925, and of Jurisprudence, 1901-25, photographed as Dean of the Faculty of Law in 1921.

299. Antonio Cippico, Professor of Italian, 1918-25, as shown on the medal established in his honour, itself a fine period-piece.

298

299

300

300 & 301. Scenes from the great age of rags.

The great age of rags spanned the period between the two world wars. It began before 1914, as can be seen from the jollifications on Ladysmith night in 1900 involving the capture of Phineas (see p.155). In the heyday of rags there were some great set-piece battles with King's, the target being Reggie, their lion mascot, the weapons including flour, sprays of water, mud, deception, furniture vans and debagging. Annual bonfires were a great institution too, until the Provost announced in 1952 that 'much to his regret he cannot sanction a bonfire in the Main Quadrangle this year'. The era of indulging in such escapades had begun to fade, and the original pressing need to raise money in this way had passed.

301

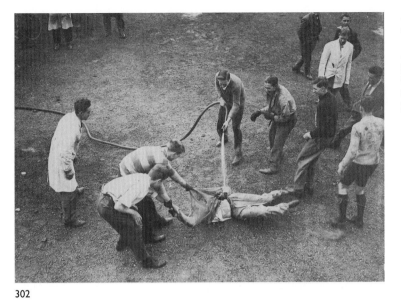

302. Scene from the great age of rags.

303. Phineas, the College's great symbol on such occasions, being borne triumphantly out of the front gates in 1932.

302

303

304. The front Quad in November 1927 during one of the greatest of the battles against the students of King's College.

304

*305. The cover of the Rag
Magazine produced on the
occasion of the celebration
of the College's Centenary
in 1927.*

*306. Some undergraduettes
flourishing the Centenary
Rag Magazine for sale.*

The Centenary of the College was celebrated in some style in June 1927. It was inaugurated by the visit of King George V and Queen Mary and included – inevitably – a new Appeal for funds, as well as the opening of the Great Hall, the receiving of delegates from universities throughout the world, a series of lectures, a variety of exhibitions and dinners, and a service of thanksgiving in Westminster Abbey. The Students' Union quite reasonably objected to the sectarian nature of this last celebration, but the Centenary as a whole was found an agreeable exercise in self-congratulation. The King made an interesting and uncharacteristically controversial point in his speech, one that the press reported as producing cheers of an enthusiasm that broke royal protocol. 'The State', he said, 'now aids University Institutions on a scale which, to your founders, would have seemed impossible, but there are limits to public assistance. Moreover there is some danger to our national ideas of University freedom in too great reliance upon State grants.'

G. K. Chesterton, a former student, was in more characteristic mood for his lecture a few days later. 'It was at the Slade School', he claimed, 'that I discovered that I should never be an artist; it was at the lectures of Professor A. E. Housman that I discovered that I should never be a scholar; and it was at the lectures of Professor W. P. Ker that I discovered that I should never be a literary man.

305

306

The warning, alas! fell on heedless ears, and I still attempted the practice of writing, which, let me tell you in the name of the whole Slade School, is very much easier than the practice of drawing and painting.' He went on, with perhaps a touch of exaggeration, to claim that the Centenary was in fact that of the opening of the modern world (see p. 9).

307

307. King George V and Queen Mary in procession through the Front Quad after their official visit to the College in June 1927.

308

309

308 & 309. The King and Queen descending the Portico steps and processing to tea on the Front Lawn on the occasion of their Centenary visit.

310

311

310. The King with Sir Gregory Foster, the Provost (on his right), and Sir William Beveridge, Director of the LSE and Vice-Chancellor of the University of London at the time (on his left); Lord Chelmsford, Chairman of the College Committee, 1922-32, with the Queen. The royal party went on to visit the exhibition in the Slade, where the King expressed his distaste for Cubism to Tonks, who was able to assure him he would 'find none here'.

311. The 208 delegates from other universities being photographed on the steps of the Portico.

312. H. Hale Bellot, author of the definitive Centenary history of the College, first Commonwealth Fund Professor of American History, 1930-55, and Vice-Chancellor of the University of London, 1951-53.

313. Another well-remembered historian: Norman H. Baynes, FBA, Dean of the Faculty of Arts at the time of the Centenary, Professor of Byzantine History, 1931-42.

312

313

The College had never had a Great Hall since the abandoning of the one originally planned by Wilkins and it was decided to remedy this by a suitable conversion of All Saints' Church built by Donaldson in 1846 at the rear of the College. The building was in a dilapidated state when the College bought it in 1914. After the war it was agreed that it should also serve as a war memorial to the 301 members of the College who had been killed. The reconstruction was finely undertaken by A. E. Richardson, the Professor of Architecture, and the opening

314

314. Hanslip Fletcher's drawing of the Great Hall as designed by Richardson.

315. The dedication of the new Great Hall by Prince Arthur of Connaught in June 1927 as a memorial to the dead of the first world war. It was entirely destroyed in the Second.

315

316

316. The Gustave Tuck Theatre as it then was, before destruction in the Second World War.

317. The Exhibition Gallery being opened by Lord and Lady Duveen in 1930, with Professor Sir John Rose Bradford, FRS, Chairman of the College Committee, 1932-35, in attendance, and some of the Rembrandt etchings in the background. After the war, the room was used for other purposes, but in 1981, thanks to the persuasive powers of Professor John White, it was restored to its original use; it was, however, renamed the Strang Print Room, in memory of Lord Strang, a distinguished diplomat and Chairman of the College Committee, 1963-71.

constituted a major part of the Centenary celebrations. The Appeal was less successful. The aim was to raise £500,000 but such was the difficulty in deciding how it should be spent that the centenary had to be postponed from February 1926 to June 1927. Then, as it turned out, the time chosen was one of deepening economic depression, and by July 1930 less than half the expected total had been raised, and the Appeal was closed.

One success resulting from the appeal was the benefaction of Gustave Tuck, Treasurer and President of the Jewish Historical Society, for the rebuilding of the Mocatta Library and the provision of a new lecture theatre. Much of the Mocatta collection was destroyed in the Second World War, but the renewed library is now once again an important resource for the activities of the Department of Hebrew and Jewish Studies and for all students of Judaism.

In the week of the Centenary celebrations, it was finally settled that the University of London should acquire a central headquarters site, to the south of UCL, after its years in Burlington House and in South Kensington. After complicated negotiations involving the Duke of Bedford, the government, Beveridge and the Rockefeller Foundation, the scene was set for Senate House to rear its head in Bloomsbury.

317

318

318. The bronze plaque erected in the Library to Gustave Tuck in 1932.

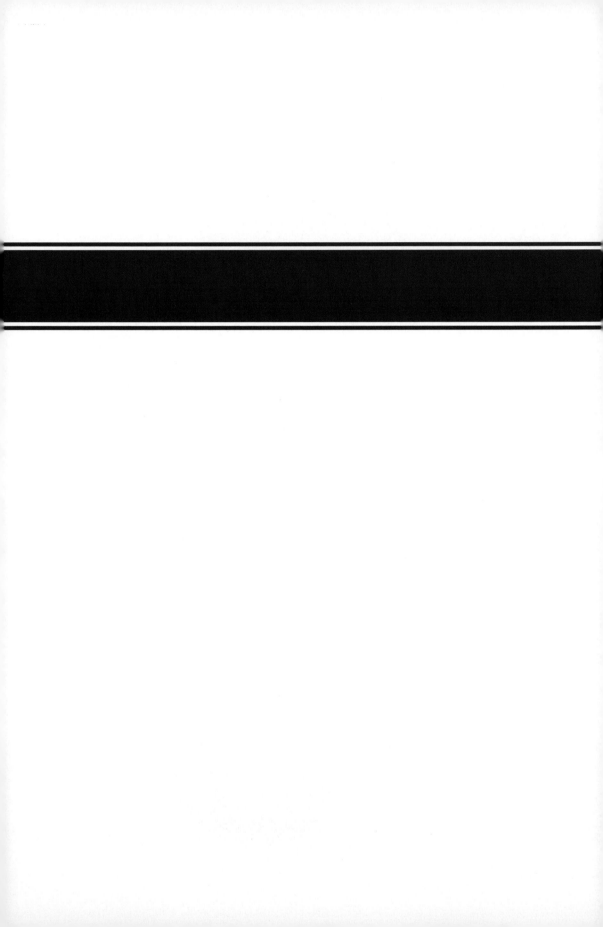

Chapter 7
The Years of Peace and War, 1929-51

[Hugh Gaitskell and I] were both junior lecturers at University College, and towards the end of the first term of 1930 we found ourselves sitting opposite each other at the annual dinner of the Professors' Dining Club. The occasion was very convivial and wine was both good and plentiful; so when we found ourselves alone he turned to me with a question much more direct than one he would have allowed himself on a more sober occasion. 'I see you are not a fool, but I am told you hold *émigré* views about Russia: how can you?' And thus started the first of the many, indeed hundreds, of dialogues between us on politics, social philosophy, socialism, Russia, economics, methodology.

Professor Sir Michael Postan in his memoir of Hugh Gaitskell
published in a volume edited by W. T. Rodgers (1964)

I said at the outset of these remarks that your presence here *in partibus* on the coasts of Cambria raised a problem: how could your presence be justified? And my answer to that question is unhesitating: it is essential that the succession of those who can appreciate that tradition which is our England should be unbroken, and a not unimportant part of that tradition is bound up with the freedom of our modern university life, that freedom in which University College was a pioneer. It is when our possessions are menaced that we realise most fully their value. May you enjoy to the full, appropriate, make in a very true sense your own this your life in College: a Cockney student who is about to be discharged from service salutes his Cockney fellow-students and would wish each and all *Bon Voyage*.

Professor Norman H. Baynes in his Foundation Address on
'The Custody of a Tradition' delivered to UCL students at Bangor on the eve of his
retirement, 13 March 1942

The events of World War II threatened the survival of the College. Departments were scattered to ten different centres away from London. The historic buildings of the College were largely destroyed by enemy action, the extent of war damage being more severe than at all other university institutions in the country apart from medical schools. This is not the place to describe in detail the difficulties which resulted. Though much has been delayed, and though some departments have suffered frustrations and hard conditions, nothing in the spirit of the College or in its capacity to continue its major contributions in advanced studies has been destroyed.

Sir Ifor Evans in University College London [1956-1962] *(1962)*

319

T he enormous popularity of Sir Gregory Foster as Provost was shown by the tumultuous reception he was given in February 1926 on his return from a year's leave of absence spent in South Africa. Charabancs full of students provided an exuberant escort from his home to 'the largest number of students and staff ever gathered' in the Front Quad. There was much shouting of what had become – and was for some years to remain – the College chant:

Foster, Foster, Gregory Foster,
Gower Street, Gower Street, UCL.

While he had been away, his duties had been carried out by a triumvirate of Pro-Provosts: Seton, the Secretary; H. E. Butler, the Professor of Latin; and Col. H. J. Harris, the Senior Tutor – known collectively as the world, the flesh and the devil. Less than a year later, on the eve of the Centenary celebrations which he had done much to plan, Seton died suddenly. He was succeeded by C. O. G. Douie, an extremely able administrator from the Ministry of Education and a civilised man of wide interests and tastes.

At the end of 1929, Foster retired as Provost to concentrate on being Vice-Chancellor of the University under its new Statutes.

The second Provost was Sir Allen Mawer, a former graduate student of the College who had gone on to become Professor English at Newcastle and then at Liverpool. His great passion was English place names, and he did more than anyone to put their study on a rigorous basis.

The major innovation in the Faculty of Engineering between the wars was the creation of the

320

319. Sir Allen Mawer, FBA, Foster's successor as Provost, 1930-42.

320. The scene in the Front Quad as Sir Gregory Foster was welcomed back in 1926 after his year's leave.

321. C. O. G. Douie, Secretary of the College, 1927-38, as painted by Elizabeth Polunin of the Slade.

321

323

322

Department of Chemical Engineering in 1923. The first Professor of the subject in the country was E. C. Williams, who after putting the Department on its feet became Research Director for Shell in California. Both the new Chair and the laboratories that followed were a memorial to Sir William Ramsay, who had died in 1916. Half the money raised by the Memorial Fund was put towards the new Department, which also received substantial support from industry. The first temporary accommodation was opened in 1924 in the old St Pancras Vestry Hall; next door, the site of 21 and 23 Gordon Street was being used for the building of completely new laboratories, designed by A.E. Richardson, the first of many College buildings for which he was to be responsible. Postgraduate courses started from the beginning of the new Department, if with a good deal of improvisation; the undergraduate degree dates from 1938. The new laboratories, opened in 1931, suffered severe bomb damage in the war (see p. 215).

322. The pre-war Ramsay Memorial Laboratory of Chemical Engineering.

323. The formal opening of the Ramsay Memorial Laboratory by the Duke of Kent in 1931; on his left W. E. Gibbs, the second Professor, 1928-34, and on his right Lord Chelmsford.

324. The retirement gathering for E. J. Garwood, FRS, Professor of Geology, 1901-31, the architect of the modern Geology Department; many of his pupils over the thirty years are to be seen, including Marie Stopes.

324

Further expansion of the College buildings was made possible by the bankruptcy in the depression of the early 1930s of Shoolbreds, a once-famous department store in Tottenham Court Road. Their workshops and stables lay immediately to the south of the College site, and D. M. S. Watson decided that, suitably converted, they could contain adequate premises for the Department of Zoology and Comparative Anatomy which was outgrowing the quarters created for Lankester in the North Wing (see p. 113). Since succeeding to the Jodrell Chair in 1921, Watson had nurtured plans for a Zoology expansion parallel to Elliot Smith's development of human biology in the enlarged Department of Anatomy. The Rockefeller Foundation provided another endowment for this purpose. The acquisition of Shoolbred's Mews in 1931 was a good deal more than half funded by the sale in advance of rather less than a third of the buildings to the National Central Library, then being established with Carnegie money; in this skilful manoeuvre, the College's well-placed Highland connections were deftly deployed, as was, apparently, the necessary Talisker whisky over lunch. The rest of the utilitarian buildings, erected by Shoolbreds in the 1890s, were straightforwardly reconstructed as laboratories and teaching rooms by A. E. Richardson. Watson continued his important contributions to zoology and palaeontology until his retirement from the Jodrell Chair in 1951, and afterwards as an Honorary Research Associate until

325

326

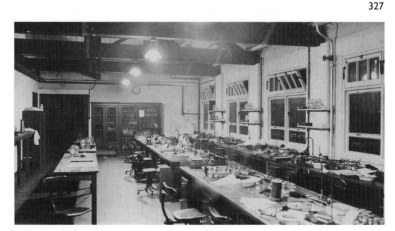

327

325. The new quarters for the Department of Zoology created out of the former Shoolbreds' warehouse and mattress factory – part of the addition to the College named Foster Court in honour of Sir Gregory Foster who died just before they were acquired in 1931.

326. The Earl of Athlone, as Chancellor of the University, on his way to open Foster Court in June 1933, seen through the Physiology Arch.

327. The Senior Laboratory in the new Department of Zoology.

328

328. The second oldest architectural feature of the College site, the Pewterers' Gate, dated 1668, and believed to have been designed by Sir Christopher Wren. It was removed from its original position at Pewterers' Hall in the City to its present site at the rear of what is now the Medawar Building in 1932 by Sir Albert Richardson as one of the several 'follies' among the College buildings for which he was responsible. Another curiosity of Richardson's, smaller but equally striking, is the 'Adam and Eve' door-handles of the Medawar building. The oldest architectural feature of the College is the fragment of brickwork and stone dated 1513, rescued by Richardson from the original Royal Navy shipyard at Deptford and re-erected in the entrance-hall of the Pearson Building in 1953, a time when the Bartlett School was still housed there.

1965, when his resignation ended fifty-three years of continuous service to the College. When the National Central Library building was re-acquired by the College in 1967, mainly for use as an annexe to the Library, it was renamed the 'D. M. S. Watson Library'. Both this and the western part of the Foster Court buildings at that time housing the Departments of Geography, English, Scandinavian Studies and Egyptology (the latter in the former stables) were long overdue for replacement. Plans were drawn up by Anthony Cox in 1972 for a major redevelopment involving a large new School of Medicine as proposed by a Royal Commission chaired by Lord Todd in 1968. Much thought was given to these proposals in the 1970s, but eventually the government withdrew its funding. The subsequent building developments took place elsewhere; the Foster Court buildings continued to be adapted and re-adapted for use by various academic departments.

329. J. P. Hill, FRS, Jodrell Professor of Zoology, 1906-21, and subsequently the pioneering Professor of Embryology, 1921-38.

330. D. M. S. Watson, FRS, Jodrell Professor of Zoology, 1921-51.

329

330

In the earliest years of the College, John Conolly and John Elliotson as professors of medicine had taken an interest in psychological problems (see pp. 53, 75) but the origins of a more systematic approach to the subject are to be found in the Department of Philosophy in the 1890s. James Sully, who succeeded Croom Robertson as Grote Professor, was more of a psychologist than a philosopher. He was a prime mover in the creation of the British Psychological Society, founded at UCL in 1902. A laboratory for experimental psychology was established in 1897. Housed originally in a small room that doubled as a library store, it was the first such laboratory in England, which in this respect lagged behind Germany and the United States. The new laboratory was equipped with apparatus brought from Freiburg, and put under the charge of W. H. Rivers, though he left after a year to take part in the famous Cambridge anthropological expedition to Torres Straits.

In 1903 William McDougall was made Reader in Experimental Psychology, but significant work in the new subject really began in 1907 with his successor, the German-trained Charles Spearman, and with the move to more spacious quarters in the South Wing. Spearman became Grote Professor in 1911, and later, in 1928, the Chair of Psychology was established for him. One of his earliest interests was in the concept of 'general intelligence' or 'G' and in ways of measuring it through the application to psychological problems of the techniques of correlation developed by Galton and Pearson (see p. 128). J. C. Flugel joined Spearman as his Assistant in 1909, and remained a member of the Department for virtually the rest of his life. He resigned as Assistant Professor of Psychology in 1943, finding life in war-time Aberystwyth intolerable, but became a Special Lecturer on the Department's return to London after the war until his death ten years later in 1955. For many years he gave pioneering lectures on Freudian psycho-analysis, and wrote an interesting book on *The Psychology of Clothes*.

331

332

333

334

The lines of research opened up by Spearman were developed by his successor, Sir Cyril Burt. In 1913 he had been appointed by the LCC to be the first official psychologist to an education authority, and in 1924 became Professor of Education at the Institute of Education. He conducted classic research on delinquent and maladjusted children, research that involved his becoming for a time a member of a criminal gang who accepted him as 'Charlie the parson'. His work on intelligence testing was one of the influences on the organisation of secondary education after the 1944 Act. Burt's thesis that differences in intelligence are to a considerable extent genetic has become the focus of much controversy since his death in 1971, and he came to be accused in the press of inventing not only some of his data, but also mythical female collaborators; these charges were rejected by his many admirers.

333. Charles Spearman, FRS, Grote Professor of Mind and Logic, 1911-28, and of Psychology, 1928-31.

334. Sir Cyril Burt, FBA, Professor of Psychology, 1932-50.

335. Experiments in progress in the Psychology Laboratory in the South Wing c. 1930.

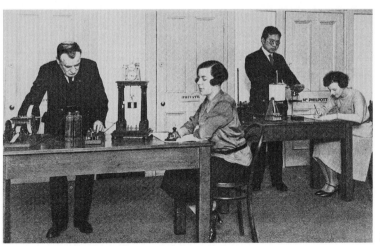

335

336

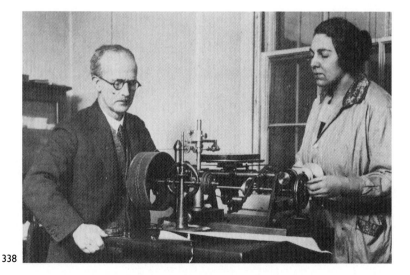

337

'antəni. 'frɛndz, 'roumənz, 'kʌntrimən, 'lɛnd mi: jɔːr 'iəz;
ɑi 'kʌm tu 'bɛri *'siːzə, 'nɔt tu 'preiz him.
ði 'iːvil ðət mɛn 'duː 'livz 'ɑːftə ðɛm;
ðə 'gud iz 'ɔft in'tɜːrid wið ðɛə 'bounz;

'antəni. 'frɛndz, 'roːmənz, 'kʏntrimən, 'lɛnd mi: juːr 'iːɹz;
ai 'kʏm tu 'bɛri 'seːzəɹ, 'nɔt tu 'prɛiz him.
ði 'iːvil ðat mɛn 'duː 'livz 'aftəɹ ðɛm;
ðə 'guːd iz 'ɔft in'taːrid wið ðɛːɹ 'boːnz;

336. Daniel Jones, creator of a new Department as Professor of Phonetics, 1921-49.

337. Three transcriptions of Antony's speech from Julius Caesar; the first two are by Jones and are in modern and Elizabethan pronunciation respectively; the third is in Alexander Melville Bell's 'visible speech'.

338. Work in progress in the Phonetics Laboratory, c. 1930, with the Lioretgraph, a device that obtained oscillograms of speech from a gramophone record.

The study of phonetics might be said to go back to the work of Alexander Melville Bell, who lectured on speech at the College between 1866 and 1870 and who devised a phonetic script which he called 'visible speech'; he was assisted by his son Alexander Graham Bell, then a student at the College and later the inventor of the telephone. It was not, however, until 1907 that systematic teaching began with the appointment of Daniel Jones. At first the courses were under the auspices of the departments of English and Modern Languages and were mainly offered to those who were intending to become language teachers. Jones worked alone for ten years, but by 1918 the subject had expanded to include more and more languages and also the historical aspects of phonetics; experimental phonetics too had obtained a toe-hold with the creation of a small laboratory in 1911. With encouragement from Gregory Foster, the subject expanded rapidly after the war and by 1921 Jones had become the first Professor of the subject and there were nine full-time assistants. In 1922 the Department moved to the Gordon Square premises which it has occupied ever since. By the time Daniel Jones retired in 1949, he had created a thriving Department with a world-wide reputation.

338

339

340

339-341. Three cartoons illustrating characteristic activities of A. H. Smith, Professor of English, 1949-67: meeting a place name with Sir Allen Mawer; at the Pierian spring; and travelling in style to his home at Alderton, near Tewkesbury.

The Department now includes Linguistics as well as Phonetics. The first step came in 1953 when the Communications Research Centre was set up as an experiment in interdisciplinary studies, to involve linguists, biologists and all interested in any form of communication both verbal and non-verbal. The enterprise was years ahead of its time, anticipating developments to be hailed as new and exciting a decade later in other universities. Its weakness was perhaps that it included too much and when M. A. K. Halliday was appointed Director in 1963, he recommended narrowing the range to human communication. In 1965 the Department of Linguistics was created, including the Centre. Six years later, it was merged with Phonetics.

Allen Mawer's main academic work, which he sustained after becoming Provost, was the methodical survey of English place-names. His initial interest came from his work on the Scandinavian influence on early England; from the inception of the English Place Names Society, which he inspired, he acted as its Director and was General Editor of its county by county survey. At UCL he found an energetic assistant in A. H. Smith, who came to the Department of English in 1930 and worked as one of its most devoted members for thirty-seven years, becoming Quain Professor of English in 1949. Smith was the man who kept the Place Names Survey moving, so that it remained a very vigorous element in UCL. He also acted as Director of Scandinavian Studies and was an active secretary of the Communications Research Centre in its early days, fostering two areas that grew into independent departments in the course

341

of the 1960s. It was also in his Department that the study of Medieval Archaeology was started by the appointment of D. M. Wilson, later Sir David and the Director of the British Museum from 1977 to 1992; the subject itself later moved into Scandinavian Studies, then into History and finally into the Institute of Archaeology, after its merger with UCL (see p. 16).

342

343

342. A cartoon of Mawer as Provost with R.W. Chambers and C. J. Sisson, Professors of English, triumphing over the problems of the 1930s, from the University College Magazine in 1934.

343. A student demonstration in 1933, revealing other political problems of the time.

344. Hugh Gaitskell, later Leader of the Labour Party, who taught economics at the College between 1928 and 1939, photographed in the Senior Common Room in conversation with C. O. G. Douie.

345. The Exhibition Room (see p. 193) in use as the staff dining room in the late 1930s.

National and international politics began to intrude significantly into student life from the late 1920s. In 1932, the first student political society, the Socialist Society, won recognition after a battle with the College authorities. One member of the staff with strong political interests was Hugh Gaitskell, who came as an Assistant in Political Economy in 1928 and rose to be Reader and acting Head of the Department, as well as Tutor to the Higher Civil Service students. He attended the *Tots and Quots*, a dining club, which met in Soho for scientific argument, founded by G. P. (Gip) Wells, later Professor of Zoology. In 1945, Gaitskell was offered the Chair of Political Economy, but declined it in order to stand for Parliament, becoming Chancellor of the Exchequer, 1950-51, and subsequently leader of the Labour Party until his premature death in 1963.

344

345

The College tradition of producing the cycle of 'Little Plays of St Francis' written by Laurence Housman, the brother of A. E. Housman, began in 1925 at the suggestion of Walter Seton. They became an annual event for the Dramatic Society until 1950. Housman himself was closely involved and granted the College the right to produce the plays free of royalty. In 1937 a performance was televised, and the Dramatic Society became the first amateur group to appear on television.

348

346

347

349

350

346. A. J. L. Cahill, Registrar of the College between 1954 and 1979, acting in one of the series of 'Little Plays of St Francis' together with their author, Laurence Housman.

347. A Slade Dance decoration of 1930 portraying Tonks, who retired in that year, and Randolph Schwabe, his successor as Slade Professor, 1930-48.

348. Three men who made their mark through their devotion to generations of students at the College: J. W. Jeaffreson, an inspiring teacher of French between 1919 and 1949.

349. H. J. Harris, second President of the Union in 1894, a teacher of mathematics until 1933, Senior Tutor, and Colonel of the University OTC.

350. N. Eumorfopoulos, a leading College figure while Demonstrator and Research Assistant in Physics from 1894 to 1942, for the last twenty-two years in an honorary capacity.

351. The Claude Rogers
portrait of J. B. S. Haldane,
FRS, which hangs in the
Haldane Room.

J. B. S. Haldane, who took his forenames from John Burdon Sanderson, his great uncle (see p. 110), came to UCL as Professor of Genetics in 1933 and became the first Weldon Professor of Biometrics in 1937. He had made his name by a series of papers showing mathematically how Darwin's theory would actually work in terms of Mendelian genetics. He was regarded by many as a

351

near-genius. He was also famous as one of the great popularisers of science, and moreover he had already shown his splendid patrician pugnacity against all forms of imposed authority. Throughout the thirties his politics moved leftwards; he began a remarkable series of scientific articles in the *Daily Worker*, though he did not actually join the Communist Party until 1942. His highest public fame came over the Lysenko controversy, when he stubbornly defended the Party's line, despite private misgivings both about Lysenko's theories and the Stalinist regime's exploitation of them.

His achievement as a scientific theoretician was formidable, but his achievement as professor at UCL was limited by his own perversity. Cantankerous to a degree, he became a legend for mismanaging business, terrorising secretaries and abusing administrators. In 1958, he made an improbable, though in the event successful, move to India. The departure was vintage Haldane, complete with bogus political motive (revulsion at the Suez adventure, though he had already decided to go), with allegations of bad faith by the College (promises made to him about the development of his Department had, he claimed, never been fulfilled) and a silly little scandal (his second wife, Helen Spurway, once a student, later a lecturer in the Department, insisted on going to prison after an incident outside the Marlborough Arms in which she trod on a police dog's tail). Haldane's stature as a scholar survives all the aberrations; the College honours his memory through the eponymous Common Room.

352. A plan showing the pre-war expansion of the College into most of the 'rectangle' bounded by Gower Street, Torrington Place, Gordon Street and Gower Place.

352

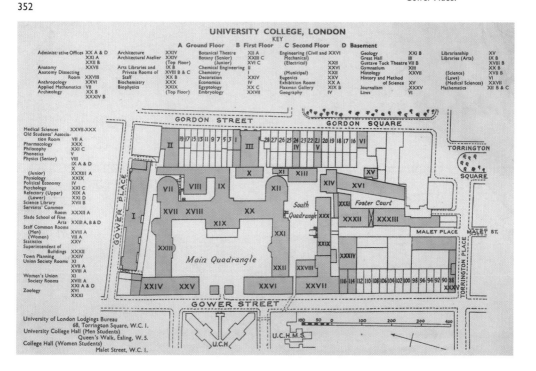

The Second World War did more damage to UCL than to any other British university or college. In September 1940 a bomb hit the buildings, entirely destroying the Great Hall and the Carey Foster Physics Laboratory. The Gustave Tuck and the Applied Mathematics Theatres were gutted, as was the Library north of the Dome. Serious damage was also done to other parts of the building. In April 1941 another air-raid led to considerable destruction by fire of the main building south of the Dome, and of the Dome itself.

The academic work of the College had already been dispersed. The crisis of 1938 had led to arrangements being made for evacuation, and in 1939 new entrants were refused and the departments immediately scattered to Aberystwyth, Bangor, Cardiff, Swansea, Sheffield, Southampton, Oxford, Cambridge and Rothamsted. The Faculty of Medical Sciences was subsequently reunited at Leatherhead, and an administrative headquarters was formed at Stansted

353

353. One of the series of elegant views of the College buildings drawn by J. D. M. Harvey in the years after the First World War.

Bury, near Ware, in Hertfordshire. The much reduced College continued in this extraordinarily far-flung way for the duration of the war. The decision to clear the College buildings was not taken without opposition: J. B. S. Haldane was in his element when he refused to budge, continuing his work for a time, 'subject' as he reported gleefully, 'to a certain amount of siege by the College authorities'.

The Library suffered most drastically from the air-raids. The manuscripts and rare books were evacuated to the solid rock cellars of the National Library of Wales at Aberystwyth, but some 100,000 books and pamphlets were destroyed as a result of the 1940 attack. The heaviest losses were to the Science Library, the English, German, Scandinavian and Phonetics collections, and the Mocatta Library. John Wilks, the Librarian from 1926 to 1954, had been a pupil of Robert Priebsch, the Professor of German (see p. 182), himself a noted bibliophile; they had built up the best working library of German scholarship outside the German-speaking countries. It is ironic that this was one of the collections largely destroyed.

354

354. A photograph taken during the Second World War, from virtually the same point as picture 353, showing the burnt Dome across the ruins of the Carey Foster Laboratory; it reveals the extent of the damage caused by the bombings of 1940 and 1941.

355. The war-time scene looking north from the Department of Pharmacology showing the extent of the destruction to the Mathematics Department, the Provost's office and the Council Room.

356. The site of the Great Hall and the Carey Foster Physics Laboratory after the bombing of September 1940.

355

356

357

358. The roof of the Library north of the Dome as it appeared in September 1940.

359. The interior of the Science library at the same date, revealing the massive extent of the damage sustained.

358

359

360 & 361. Books from the Library being dried out and inspected after the air-raid.

360

361

362. The ruins of the Ramsay Memorial Laboratory of Chemical Engineering in 1941, with (in military uniform) M. B. Donald, later to be Professor of Chemical Engineering, 1951-65.

362

363. Stansted Bury, the
war-time home of the
College administration and
of the Library.

364. The improvised
Physics Laboratory of 1942
in an old bicycle shop in
Bangor High Street.

The difficulties of life for the remaining students and staff in the dispersed elements of the College were considerable. In Physics, for example, sent to the University College of North Wales at Bangor, there were various demarcation disputes with the host department. It became necessary for Orson Wood, the Tutor to Science students, to improvise a laboratory in a converted bicycle shop in the High Street, blocking up the windows so that students could work unobserved by passers-by. Soon after the Faculty of Engineering moved to Swansea, the students claimed that their lodgings were disturbed by so many air-raids that they might as well move back to less makeshift accommodation in London.

In Oxford, the Slade was amalgamated with the Ruskin Drawing School under the joint direction of Randolph Schwabe as Slade Professor and Albert Rutherston, the Ruskin Master of Drawing, himself, like his brother Sir William Rothenstein, a former Slade student. The Slade students were considered to have contributed much to the gaiety of Oxford during the grim war years. Towards the end of the war, all the main College deeds were flooded in the place of safety to which they had been taken at Stansted Bury; now an unreadable solid mass, they are still preserved in the College safe until the papyrologists have time to apply the latest techniques of restoration. Many other records were destroyed at the time of the bombing of the College.

R. W. Chambers (see p. 164) visited the students in exile in Aberystwyth and Bangor and gave them brilliantly allusive lectures on the history of the College; but

363

364

365

on the way to deliver another such lecture in Swansea he collapsed and died, it was said of a broken heart following the destruction of so much of the Library he had created and of the College he had loved. Sir Allen Mawer died a few weeks later in 1942 on his way from Stansted Bury to a committee meeting in London. He had suffered from the strain of much travelling in his efforts to hold the scattered fragments of the College together.

365. The evacuated staff of UCL, mainly the Faculty of Arts, at Bangor.

366. Students and staff of the Department of Chemistry in evacuation at Aberystwyth.

366

367

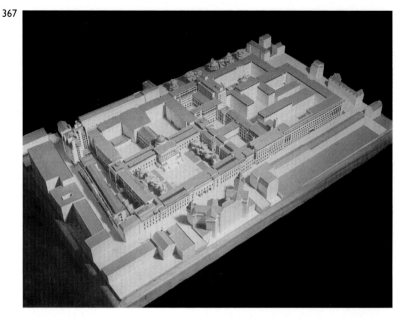

367. A model of the redevelopment of the College site hoped for in the early 1950s.

368. Sir David Pye, FRS, the third Provost, 1943-51.

369 (opposite). The first issue of the students' newspaper Pi, *named in Pye's honour, in 1946.*

D r D. R. (later Sir David) Pye became Provost of a deserted and ruinous College in 1943 in which 'there was hardly a square foot of glass'. He was an engineer with a considerable academic and administrative reputation. In Cambridge, he had done innovative work on the internal combustion engine and, as Director of Scientific Research for the Air Ministry, on the development of jet propulsion. He nursed the College through its extremely difficult move back to the blitzed buildings and the planning of the post-war rebuilding. 'Refectory accommodation in 1939 was totally inadequate', propounded the first plan for reconstruction

368

produced in June 1943. 'Common Rooms were equally so and were inconveniently scattered. It is regarded as an essential feature of the replanned College that the amenity accommodation shall be conveniently grouped round a central position...' The confident hopes of 1943 were never to be realised in the post-war world.

369

Next Month UCL Will Be
119 YEARS OLD

Societies Provide
Large-Scale Entertainment

PREPARATIONS for Foundation Week, which begins Monday, March 11th and continues until the 18th, are well advanced. A series of activities is planned which will extend over a fortnight. These activities will include a concert, two pre-Foundation Week plays, soccer and rugger matches, a debate, the Foundation Ball, and numerous dinners, parties and hops. The Foundation speaker this year will be the Very Reverend the Lord Bishop Barnes of Birmingham.

The festivities will begin as the Dramatic Society gives five performances of a double bill of two plays, between Wednesday, March 6th and March 8th. One of the plays is to be " Cain," produced by Christopher Beedell, and " The Lying Valet," produced by Alan Barlow. In spite of attacks of 'flu among the cast, rehearsals and stagework are progressing satisfactorily in the gymnasium. The Saturday matinee performance of the plays is to be given in aid of the Q-Camps for maladjusted children.

Dramatic Society's work ends as Foundation Week begins, and all connected with the plays hope to relax.

On Tuesday, March 12th, the Foundation Concert will be held in Friend's House. The 90-minute programme, starting at 6.30 p.m., will include Schubert's Sixth Symphony and performances by the Music Society Choir of Handel's " Acis and Galatea " and the " Danse Polotusienne," from Borodin's " Prince Igor."

University College teams take the field on Wednesday, March 13th, to play against King's. Phineas will be present. The matches to be played will include Soccer, Rugger, Men's and Women's hockey matches, Lacrosse and Netball. University College teams are determined to gain victories and avenge the defeats suffered during King's Commemoration Week. As a friendly gesture, however, King's teams may be invited to a Hop in the Gym. on the night of the game.

The Debating Society takes over on Friday, the 15th, during their Foundation Debate, which is to be held in the U.C.L. Gymnasium. Dr. Mathieux, Dean of St. Paul's, is among the speakers invited to hold forth on the motion " That the world is peopled by wicked sharps and good flats." There will be a Debates' Dinner afterwards.

Continued on page 4, column 1

Thursday February 21st, 1946.
Number 1.   Price 2d.

Success To New College Newspaper
—the Provost

In a College the size of ours communications are a difficult problem. University College is unique in the number and variety of Faculties and Departments within its walls. In no other College can Chemists and Physicists rub shoulders with the Fine Arts, or Engineers learn something of the ways of Lawyers, Phoneticians and Medicos. But to make the most of our opportunities we need to have a sense of corporate membership, which means, in effect, that the doings of each Department should be a matter of interest to all. There are passengers in every community who contribute little and look to others to provide for them ; but often they are passengers because nothing has yet awakened an interest in their surroundings which is latent nevertheless ; and so it must be in the College.

A Newspaper specially adapted to the needs and interests of Students, postgraduate as well as undergraduate, can be an ideal medium through which to promote a sense of corporate interest which embraces all the varied activities in the College. For this reason I welcome most warmly the appearance of my namesake.

I am told by the Editorial Committee that no one of their number is willing to accept responsibility for having suggested the name of their baby ; but that having been collectively evolved, the more it was queried, frowned upon, laughed out of Court, the more impossible it was either to neglect or to forget it. If the contents of Pi have the qualities of its name, success will be assured and Pi will extend as the mathematicians would have us believe, to an infinite series of numbers.

EXAMINATIONS PREVENT MEDICS JOINING FUN

MR. M. GREENBERG, a student of the Faculty of Medical Sciences, announced at a recent unofficial meeting that seventy medical students would be unable to participate in the Foundation Ball, owing to 2nd M.B. examinations commencing on March 18th. In a letter from the Medical Society to the Secretary of the I.U.S.C., it was suggested that the Ball should be held one week earlier, as this arrangement would be acceptable to most medical students, who would not mind spending a few of their pre-examination hours relaxing at the dance.

It appears that no compromise was possible, as it is extremely difficult to book a hall suitable for a U.C.L. function of this type and it was impossible to alter the date of the arranged booking.

When the date for Foundation Week was announced at a Union Society meeting held on December 8th, no serious protest was raised by the Medical member present, and therefore arrangements proceeded. An official recording has been made in the Inter Union Standing Committee's minutes to prevent recurrence of this unfortunate situation. Meanwhile, seventy medical students will not be present at the Foundation Ball. A further 60 Junior 2nd M.B. Students will be unable to attend since they go down on the 16th to make room for the senior examinations.

ELECTION RESULTS
HERE are the official results of the University College London Union elections, that have been announced up to the time of going to Press.
President .. J. Swainson.
Vice-Presidents F. A. Dutton and Hannah Steinberg.
Other results will be printed as soon as possible.
From the Union Office comes the following appeal to all students—
"Elections must finish this term. 40% of the electorate voting in every single election yet to come is needed to complete elections. Please do your bit. Watch the Union Notice Board every week for details of elections, and make use of your rights to vote. This is urgent."

RECONSTRUCTION DELAYED BY HOUSING PROGRAMME

PLANS for the rebuilding of University College, prepared by Professor Richardson, of Architecture, are now well advanced. This opportunity for replanning the College in a style worthy of its needs and traditions has been provided by the otherwise disastrous destruction of many buildings by high-explosive and incendiary bombs. Unfortunately, this important work has been temporarily suspended, as the critical housing situation has precluded the issue of the necessary permits for buildings other than dwellings.

In the office of Mr. Taylor, the Superintendent of Works, there is a large file of carefully drawn plans. But until the Ministry of Works issues a permit, and contracts are drawn up, no start can be made on the rehabilitation of the Main Building and the excavation of ground to the East of it for new quadrangles. This work involves the use of bulldozers. Mr. Taylor at present has at his disposal only a handful of men and they are engaged on maintenance work, site clearing, and what Mr. Taylor describes as " Odds and Ends."

There is, however, one chance that some of the work can be begun in 1946. The main building of the College is scheduled as a national monument, and it is hoped that an application for a permit on these grounds will be successful.

PHOTOELASTICITY : NEW SLANT ON CAMERA TECHNIQUE

Mr. Costa Mylonas, a post-graduate engineering student, is interested in the formation of a Photography Club. A native of Greece, Mr. Mylonas left Athens a few months ago to come to University College, where he is investigating Photoelasticity. Photo-elasticity is the study of the distribution of stresses in a structure by photographing transparent models in polarised light.

This research illustrates one of Mr. Mylonas' beliefs : that the art of photography can be combined with the science of Engineering to provide an invaluable research tool. In a recent statement, Mr. Mylonas said, " Now that peacetime conditions are gradually returning, there may be subjects you wish to photograph—an interestingly constructed bridge, a sunset, or even pages of a valuable manuscript you may wish to preserve photographically." Under present conditions of shortages, Mr. Mylonas feels, group work would be beneficial to all members of the group.

Any students who are interested in Mr. Mylonas' scheme to start a Photography Club in University College, can contact him through the Engineering Beadle.

This picture of the ruined Dome symbolises the extensive damage which is curtailing College activities

UCL's Problem

Professor Richardson's plans for the rebuilding of the College are extensive. It is proposed to erect entirely new buildings along Gordon Street to replace the row of blitzed houses backing upon the College. Together with the existing main building and Dome, these buildings will bound two quadrangles. Within the last two years the College has purchased from the Duke of Bedford's Estate the whole site running from the Ramsay Memorial Laboratory to the corner of Gordon Square.

SIX UCL STUDENTS OFF TO SWITZERLAND

HALF-A-DOZEN students from University College are soon to set off for Switzerland under an exchange scheme with Swiss Universities. They are part of a contingent of about forty students of German from colleges all over the country. They go this April, and remain abroad six months. In their place, Swiss students are coming here to study English.

370. The main building in 1954 after its post-war restoration by Richardson, seen across the huts at the rear.

371. The architect who was responsible for most additions to the College buildings between the 1920s and the post-war reconstruction: Sir Albert Richardson, Professor of Architecture, 1919-46, photographed soon after his appointment.

372. H. O. Corfiato, Professor of Architectural Design, 1937-46, and of Architecture, 1946-60, photographed in the Common Room after the war.

The first step in providing accommodation for the College after the return to its ruined buildings in 1945 was the construction of concrete huts in every available gap. Four were built in the Front Quad. Two were for the Union, which proposed naming them 'Cripps Cottage' and 'Bentham Bungalow'; they were used for debates, chamber music concerts and a full range of revived student activities. Other huts in Foster Court and on the bomb-sites to the rear of the college housed the Refectory, the Library and several academic departments. Once economic conditions permitted, the main building was finely restored and improved by Sir Albert Richardson, though it was not until 1951 that the General Library was re-opened and the building as a whole was only fully re-occupied in 1954.

370

371

372

373

373. Richardson's design for a proposed new Gower Street entrance gate, part of the completely unrealised 1943 reconstruction plans.

374. The old Seamen's Hospital in Gordon Street, converted for the Union and the Department of Mathematics in 1959.

375. The houses on the west side of Gordon Square, the early Victorian culmination of Georgian Bloomsbury, all of which were gradually acquired by the College.

374

375

376

376. The last committee of the Women's Union Society prior to its amalgamation with the all-male Union Society to form 'The Union' in 1946; the members include Hannah Steinberg, later Professor of Psychopharmacology, 1970-89.

Despite all the material difficulties, the academic work of the College was rapidly resumed after the war. The great Tudor historian, Sir John Neale, Pollard's effective successor since 1927, powerfully continued to dominate the Department of History. His *Queen Elizabeth* (1934) remains one of the greatest and most popular of all historical biographies, painstakingly researched yet fresh. Neale was also a popular College figure – the first edition of the *UCL Student's Song Book* (1926) was dedicated to him. In other departments, new heads were appointed to build up their subjects: the philosopher A. J. Ayer, for example, and H. C. Darby, whose great work was the reconstruction of the geography of eleventh-century England from the Domesday Book. A new Chair of Anthropology was established for Daryll Forde (see p. 233) while the Elliot Smith tradition of research was continued by N. A. Barnicot, who later became the country's first Professor of Physical Anthropology. In Town Planning, Lord Holford (as he was to become) succeeded Sir Patrick Abercrombie who had produced notable reports on the planning of Greater London; Holford himself was the planning consultant for the City of London's post-war rebuilding.

378

379

377

380

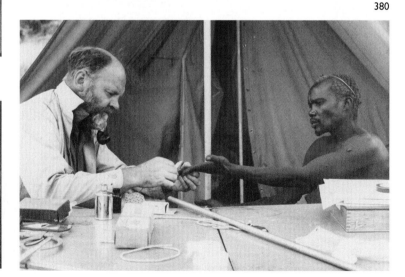

381

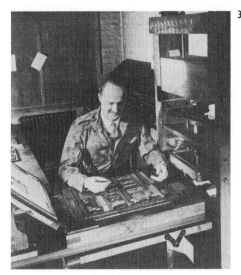

383

382

384

381. Lord Holford, Professor of Town Planning, 1948-70, examining a model of St Paul's in connection with his scheme for rebuilding the war-damaged precincts.

382. The facsimile of an Elizabethan printing press originally built in the Department of English in 1932 by A. H. Smith and reconstructed after its war-time destruction, here being operated by Arthur Brown, Professor of English, 1962-69, and of Library Studies, 1969-73.

383. A colophon from the printing press in the Department of English.

384. L. A. Willoughby (second from left), Priebsch's successor in the Chair of German in 1931, at a party marking his retirement in 1950, with Elizabeth M. Wilkinson, FBA (left), herself Professor of German, 1960-76, and W. Schwarz (second from right) later also Professor of German, 1964-72. A student at the College first in 1902, Willoughby was elected a Fellow of the College in 1910, and was the Senior Fellow at the time of his death aged 92 in 1977.

Chapter 8
The Evans and Annan Years, 1951-78

The leafless trees in Gordon Square stood black and gaunt against the façade of Georgian houses. The sky was cold and grey. It looked like snow. I hunched my shoulders inside my coat and set off briskly in the direction of the English department … Access to the English Department was through a small courtyard at the rear of the College. There seemed to be a lot of young people about, and I had to linger some moments before I caught the eye of Jones, the Beadle. I always make a point of catching the eye of beadles, porters and similar servants. Jones did not disappoint me: his face lit up.

'Hallo, sir. Haven't seen you for some time.'
'Come to see Mr. Briggs, Jones. There seem to be a lot of people about?'
'Undergraduates, sir,' he explained.

David Lodge, The British Museum is Falling Down *(1965)*

What bigotry 150 years ago denied the title of University has now become a university within a university. Why should University College pursue the fribble of independence from the University of London? The harness of attachment which used some years ago to chafe has become by skilful negotiations bands of silk; and anyway we all know that the greatest of all British universities, which has had such an extraordinary influence over the creation of new universities in the Third World as well as in our own country, all began here.

Lord Annan in his introduction to the first edition of this work in 1978

[Maurice Bowra] liked people to be quick, intelligent, and to delight in general ideas. It goes without saying that he expected them to come from the upper or middle classes, to grow up in a public school and to go to Oxford or Cambridge. He should have added the London School of Economics. These were the three places where ideas fermented. Of course other universities possessed influential scholars and scientists and lively students. In London the institutions that amalgamated to form Imperial College rivalled Cambridge as a scientific powerhouse after the war. University College London, a university within a university, excelled in science and engineering as well as being the foremost stronghold of what can be called British Museum scholarship. At Manchester there was Namier…

Noel Annan, Our Age: Portrait of a Generation *(1990)*

385

In 1951, Pye, ill, retired as Provost. He was succeeded by Sir Ifor Evans, who was destined to preside over the College in a period that saw rapid growth and change on an even greater scale than that witnessed in the Gregory Foster era. Sir Ifor Evans had himself been a student of English at the College in 1917, and he had led an active subsequent career as Professor of English at Southampton and Sheffield, as Education Director of the British Council during the war, and as Principal of Queen Mary College after it. For fifteen years he was to devote himself to UCL and its many problems of overcrowding and rebuilding at a time when national policy was demanding still further expansion. He faced all the difficulties fairly and firmly, and with a patience, tact and charm that minimised disappointment following difficult decisions. He did this while remaining a well-known literary critic, writer and broadcaster and also serving the *Observer*, the Arts Council and a good many other advisory bodies. Swift of despatch and easy of access, he was not only much admired in the College, but also much loved.

385 (opposite). Sir Ifor Evans, later Lord Evans of Hungershall, the fourth Provost, 1951-66, as painted by Sir William Coldstream. The portrait took seventy-three meticulous sittings spread over two years and Evans later confessed that he had wondered if he would live to see it completed. At the presentation following the eventual completion in 1960, Evans reminisced about meeting his wife at the College over forty years previously 'when I looked a little younger, and if I may venture to say so, a little more cheerful than when Professor Coldstream got to work on me'.

386. A characteristic view of the College buildings during the Evans era – the Physics Building (opened in 1953, and completed in 1959) and the New Refectory (opened in 1961) seen across an outbreak of the post-war huts. Some of these huts were later demolished to make way for the Central Collegiate Building, opened in 1968; the rest were not demolished until 1990.

386

387. Building underway to create the New Refectory, fashioned by Richardson out of what had originally been called the Brundrett Wing when built by Donaldson in 1849 (see p. 85), seen beyond the back of the old Birkbeck Laboratory (see p. 82).

388. The interior of the New Refectory under construction. The room, still sometimes in use as a refectory, provides space for three purposes: the Terrace Restaurant; a Common Room for the Graduate School; and the Jeremy Bentham Room ('JBR'), a common room for staff and students.

389. The New Refectory in use soon after its opening in 1961.

390. The Lower Refectory extended later in the brutal concrete of the post-Richardson phase of the College's rebuilding.

In the fine 'testimonial' presented to Sir Ifor Evans on his retirement in 1966, signed by nearly a thousand of his colleagues, he was addressed as 'an outstanding benefactor to the College, not only by your power to shape and order its affairs, but, to a singular degree, by being the cause of benefactions in others'. The government, through war damage compensation and through the University Grants Committee, provided substantial sums for the acquisition of property and for new buildings. But a good deal of the money for the expansion of the 1950s and 1960s had to come in the traditional way through appeals and gifts. In Evans' day this flow was faster than ever. The first appeal, coinciding with the centenary of Sir William Ramsay's birth, provided for a new storey on the Chemistry building. The second brought in £400,000 from industry for the Engineering Building on Torrington Place. Lord Marks gave £160,000 towards a new refectory and the start of the

387

390

388

389

Central Collegiate Building. Lord Samuel gave another £100,000; the Wolfson Foundation gave generously too, and through these and other benefactions the College's facilities and its accommodation for students began to be revolutionised.

391

391. The Biological Sciences Building under construction in 1959. It was opened in 1964, and involved the demolition of a number of Gower Street houses. One had belonged to Lady Diana Cooper; the murals by Rex Whistler (a Slade student in the 1920s) portraying the goddess Diana were moved from the house to the College in 1960, and have since graced the Refectory's Whistler Room.

392. Another of the demolished houses in Gower Street had been occupied by Darwin, as the blue plaque continues to testify on the Darwin Building, as the building was renamed in 1982 on the occasion of the centenary of Darwin's death.

392

393. The steel framework under construction for the large new Engineering Building designed by Corfiato.

394. The Engineering Building soon after its opening in 1961.

393

394

395. The Department of Mathematics in 1949, when Massey was still its head: the photograph includes, among many who were to achieve considerable scientific distinction, eight who were to become professors at UCL: M. J. Seaton, FRS (first right, front row), T. Estermann (third from left, second row), L. Castillejo (first left, third row), E. H. S. Burhop, FRS (fourth from left, third row), C. A. Rogers, FRS (third from right, third row), Sir Robert Boyd, FRS (third from left, top row), K. Roth, FRS (sixth from left, top row) and E. A. Power (fifth from right, top row).

395

396. Sir Harrie Massey, FRS, was one of the most outstanding of many scientists at UCL who during the post-war years achieved fame not only through research but through shaping leading departments in their fields. He came to UCL as Goldsmid Professor of Mathematics, 1938-50, and was then translated to the Department of Physics as Quain Professor, 1950-75, serving also as the second Vice-Provost of the College in 1969-73. (The first, when the office was instituted in 1965, was the lawyer Professor G. W. Keeton.)

397. Dame Kathleen Lonsdale, FRS, the crystallographer, Professor of Chemistry, 1949-68 – one of the first two women to be elected to the Fellowship of the Royal Society (in 1945) and the first woman to became a professor at UCL.

398. E. S. Pearson, FRS, Professor of Statistics, 1935-60, the son of Karl Pearson and one of the three men it took to succeed 'K. P.' in his various fields.

396

397

398

399

400

401

402

403

404

399 (opposite). J. Z. Young, FRS, Professor of Anatomy, 1945-74 (receiving a stuffed octopus presented by students on his retirement); his remarkably productive work on the mechanisms of memory using the creatures continued long after his retirement.

400. The first of four more leading scientists who headed distinguished departments: Sir Christopher Ingold, FRS, Professor of Chemistry, 1930-61.

401. D. Hughes, FRS, Professor of Chemistry, 1948-63.

402. E. N. da C. Andrade, FRS, Quain Professor of Physics, 1928-50.

403. Sir Peter Medawar CH, FRS, Jodrell Professor of Zoology and Comparative Anatomy, 1951-62, who was awarded the Nobel Prize for Physiology or Medicine in 1960.

404. The gathering of distinguished physiologists outside the Department of Physiology on the occasion of the retirement of Sir Charles Lovatt Evans, FRS, in 1949.

The Faculty of Arts followed a very different course from that of Science during the decades after the Second World War. It was larger than other Faculties, consisting by the late eighties of twenty-one Departments, varying considerably in size; of these, some had already gone over to the Course Unit system or to some other form of College-based degree, while others still strove to maintain the traditional University-based Final Examination, together with intercollegiate teaching. It also retained, to a far greater degree than elsewhere in College, the tradition of individual rather than group research projects. The achievements of some of its more prominent members, therefore, give a flavour of its character.

T. B. L Webster, a brilliant and prolific writer on the relations of art and literature in ancient Greece, was the founder of the University's Institute of Classical Studies; he takes credit also for offering Michael Ventris his only academic post as Honorary Research Associate in Greek after his revolutionary discovery that Linear B tablets were written in an early form of Greek.

Daryll Forde, originally a geographer who migrated to prehistoric archaeology and thence to social anthropology, created a Department of Anthropology which reflects in its structure his own range of interests; it is unique in offering to undergraduates courses in material culture as well as both physical and social anthropology. In French, Brian Woledge was the man responsible for widening the Department's range to include Renaissance and twentieth-century studies; his own work on early medieval literature was a pioneering application of computer analysis to the study of medieval texts. The Department of History developed an impressive range of interests. Following Pollard's footsteps, two more specialist Institutes were generated in the 1960s – for Latin

405. One of Michael Ventris's work-charts in his own hand, used in his pioneering study of Linear B texts, now preserved in the Institute of Classical Studies.

405

406. T. B. L. Webster, FBA, Professor of Greek, 1948-67.

406

407

408

America Studies, inspired by R. A. Humphreys, the first Professor
of Latin American History, and for United States Studies, under H.
C. Allen, Hale Bellot's successor as Commonwealth Fund Professor
of American History. Alfred Cobban, a member of the Department
from 1937 until his death in 1968; dealt lucidly and memorably with
modern French history and political ideas. The widest interests of all
were those of A. D. Momigliano, whose prodigious writings weave
a powerful counterpoint between the ancient world and the modern,
between ideas and social reality, between historical problems and
their historiography.

407. C. Daryll Forde, FBA, Professor of Anthropology, 1945-69.

408. A. D. Momigliano KBE, FBA, Professor of Ancient History, 1951-75.

409. A. B. C. Cobban, Professor of French History, 1953-68.

410. A cartoon of Brian Woledge, Fielden Professor of French Language and Literature, 1939-71, the first Englishman to hold a chair of French in London.

409

410

411

412

411. Reg Butler teaching sculpture in the Slade.

412. Sir William Coldstream, Slade Professor of Fine Art, 1949-75.

413. The Slade Antique Room, which was abolished in the 1960s.

S ir William Coldstream, Slade Professor from 1949 to 1975, had been a Slade student himself in the late twenties and then, after a period in film production, joined with Claude Rogers and Victor Pasmore to found the influential Euston Road School in 1937. As a painter, he is best known for portraits showing the scrupulous concern for empirical observation that is the hallmark of the Slade tradition. As Professor, however, tolerance and open-mindedness were the key words and the School's work broadened to include new studies and a wider range of styles and experiments. Sculpture already had an established tradition, to which Reg Butler

413

as Director of Studies between 1966 and 1981 added: but amongst the developments in Coldstream's time were postgraduate work in many areas, film studies, and the facilities for wood, metal and photographic work and the extension of a full range of print-making facilities. Meanwhile, as a committee man of wholly individual and quite devastating style, he became widely known and loved inside the College, and extremely influential in art education outside it. It was in fact the Coldstream Report on art education which led inside College as elsewhere to the expansion of art history teaching in the 1960s. The first Professor of the History of Art to become full-time – his part-time predecessors had included Sir Ernst Gombrich – was L. D. Ettlinger in 1964: he it was who created six joint-degrees with Art History and set up the Department, independent from the Slade, which expanded dramatically under Professor John White between 1971 and 1990.

In 1965 the College, with help from the Max Rayne Foundation, acquired the former offices in Endsleigh Gardens of the National Union of General and Municipal Workers. The building was given to the Faculty of Laws, which had been expanding rapidly and was previously inadequately housed in the Torrington Place building. It had become one of the strongest areas of College in terms of student demand for places. While maintaining its traditional interests in jurisprudence and Roman Law, it was also at the forefront of new developments in the undergraduate teaching of law. After 1967, it possessed what was for many years the only Professor of Air and Space Law; it was the first in the country to develop courses for undergraduates on International Air Law and Economic Law; and the first to offer options in Russian and Soviet Law, using these as a vehicle for the comparative study of law.

414. The present Laws building in Endsleigh Gardens, purchased in 1965 and previously the offices of the General and Municipal Workers, now re-named Bentham House.

415. The moot room of the Faculty of Laws, which contributes an important element to the experience of undergraduate lawyers, seen with Professor Jeffrey L. Jowell, Professor of Public Law since 1975, in the judicial seat.

415

414

*416. Bentham Hall,
converted out of houses
in Cartwright Gardens,
provided a hall of residence
for men students between
1952 and 1973.*

*417. Ifor Evans – Lord
Evans of Hungershall
– photographed outside
Ifor Evans Hall on the
occasion of its opening
in 1968. It now provides
accommodation for over
300 students, while Max
Rayne House, on the same
site in Camden Town,
provides for a further 300.*

416

417

The growth of student accommodation at UCL after the war was one of its greatest successes. In 1947, there were 47 student places available; by 1961 there were 350, and 1,500 by 1978, as well as nearly 500 students living in the 'intercollegiate' halls of the University of London.

From 1952, Bentham Hall for men and, from 1954, Campbell Hall for women, provided 250 places between them through the conversion of existing properties not far from the College site. A breakthrough came in 1961, when the College became the first university institution to attempt the provision of self-catering houses for students, first in Gordon Street and later in Bedford Way. But the long-term solution was to be found in purpose-built halls, and a series of extraordinary benefactions made the programme possible. The 'Anonymous Donor' provided for Ramsay Hall, the first phase of which was opened in 1964, and for Ifor Evans Hall, opened in 1968. Lord Samuel gave the airspace above a block of shops in Oxford Street for the building of Goldsmid House, also opened in 1968. Meanwhile the Max Rayne Foundation gave £50,000 a year for ten years to support the building programme and in particular Max Rayne House, opened in 1970.

418

419

420

418. Ramsay Hall photographed in 1987 just before the opening of the third phase of its building, showing the second phase (right) opened in 1971 and the original buildings (left) opened in 1964. It now provides accommodation for nearly 500 students, a few minutes' walk from the College rectangle.

419. Goldsmid House in Oxford Street, opened in 1968 as UCL's first purpose-built self-catering 'student house' (as distinct from a hall of residence, which provides communal meals). There were 134 single study bedrooms and 12 kitchens, as well as lounges, computer terminals, a music room and a launderette.

420. The pavilion of the Union's sports-ground at Shenley, opened in 1958 on land purchased in 1939 to replace Perivale (see p. 168). In 1971, new changing rooms were built and in 1977 a new bar was added. The excellence of the facilties at Shenley came to contrast with the limited accommodation of the Union building itself.

Noël Annan came to UCL in 1966 from Cambridge where he had been a lecturer in politics since 1948 and Provost of King's College since 1956. He became a Life Peer in 1965. A formidable reputation as scholar, administrator and orator preceded him, though it took the College time to adjust to a profound change of style from that of his predecessor. Events were to sharpen the contrast between the two periods, as the years of expansion gave way to economies, frozen posts and competition for diminishing funds. The years which followed required above all skilled diplomacy, not only to deal with severe cuts in establishment, but with the threat of student unrest and with far-reaching changes in the organisation and role of the College's non-academic staff. In 1966, as in 1951, the College was fortunate in finding the right man to deal with the problems of the time.

The momentum of expansion continued for a while: the Central Collegiate Building and its Theatre were opened in 1968; the first stage of the new Chemistry Building was completed in 1969, and formally opened as the Christopher Ingold Laboratories in 1970 for teaching purposes, though the old Chemistry Laboratories of 1915 continued to be used for research until the top floor was added to the new building in 1984. The Student Health Service, founded in 1945 and inadequately housed in Gower Street until 1973, received a new

421. Lord Annan, the fifth Provost, 1966-78, as painted at the end of his period of office by his friend Rodrigo Moynihan.

building thanks to a benefaction from the Wolfson Trust. The last major building of the Annan years was Wates House, built through a substantial donation from the Wates Foundation and opened in 1975 as a new home for the Bartlett School of Architecture and Planning.

422

423

424

425

422. The New Chemistry Building under construction in Gordon Street shortly before its completion in 1969, with (left) the Endsleigh Hotel, later demolished to make way for Wates House.

423. The Chemistry Building houses the Christopher Ingold Laboratories; the commemorative plaque recording that they were opened by Sir Christopher Ingold in 1970 was in fact unveiled by Lady Ingold, owing to the indisposition of Sir Christopher himself. Watching her is the Head of Department at the time, Sir Ronald Nyholm, FRS, later tragically killed in a car accident in 1971, at the height of a career of most productive research and outstanding administration.

424. The Health Centre, opened in 1973.

425. Wates House, opened in 1975 by Sir Ronald Wates, to house the Bartlett School of Architecture and Planning, the only Department in the Faculty of Environmental Studies, which had been created in 1969. Its name was changed in 1992 to the Faculty of the Built Environment, but in normal speech it continued as always to be called 'The Bartlett'.

426. The Observatory at Mill Hill, taken over by UCL when the Department of Astronomy was set up in 1951, having been originally built to house a 24-inch reflector presented to the University in 1928, with a second dome added in 1938. The modern successors of these are still in use for undergraduate teaching and also research.

427. Holmbury St Mary, near Dorking, where the Mullard Space Science Laboratory has been housed since 1966, when a donation from Mullard Ltd made possible the adaptation of a country mansion, Holmbury House.

428. The 'back-up' version of Ariel 1, the satellite launched in 1962 as a result of Anglo-American co-operation. Here seen on display at Holmbury St Mary, and now in the Science Museum: the founding artefact of a rich programme of international research projects, in which UCL has played a major role.

UCL continued to be the home of many distinguished scientists and engineers. For a long time, the College had the unusual distinction of having two Nobel prize-winners in Physiology or Medicine on the academic staff. In Engineering, the chair of Photogrammetry and Surveying established in 1946 was the only one if its kind in the country; the separate department was created in 1961 under E. H. Thompson who held the chair from 1951 until his death in 1976. Mechanical Engineering had been a separate department since the restructuring of the Faculty after the war; with Professor R. E. D. Bishop at the helm from 1957 to 1981, it developed particular interests concerned with the sea and the Navy, as the pre-war emphasis on photo-elasticity and the study of bodies at rest swung towards dynamics and the management of vibration. In 1967 the Department took over from the Royal Naval College at Greenwich the teaching for the Royal Corps of Naval Constructors, resulting in the creation of a very successful postgraduate course, based on a radical reappraisal of naval architecture. The first British postgraduate course in Ocean Engineering followed in 1972, established with an eye to the need for specialist engineers caused by the exploitation of the North Sea for gas and oil.

The Department of Physics and Astronomy was formed by amalgamation in 1972 establishing the largest and most far-flung of all College departments. The Observatory at Mill Hill had been

426

427

428

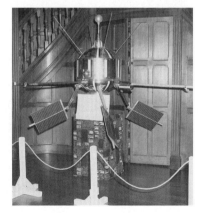

part of the College since 1951; space research had begun in the Department of Physics in 1956 when a group led by R. L. F (later Sir Robert) Boyd was set up. As a result of the successful launch of the Ariel I satellite in 1962, it became one of the most powerful research groups in Britain, taking full advantage of the American space research programme.

Sir Harrie Massey (see p. 230) was the instigator of this, as well as of other research groups including a particularly fertile one concerned with particle physics. Later, working as part of the European Organisation for Nuclear Research (CERN) at Geneva, fundamental discoveries were made about a range of elementary particles and the 'weak neutral current force'.

429. A tutorial in progress in the 1970s in the sub-basement of the Engineering Building involving the advanced 1000-litre fermenter, research which pioneered new processes in the manufacture of antibiotics.

430

429

431

430. A cartoon of Sir Andrew Huxley, FRS, Jodrell Professor Physiology, 1960-69, Royal Society Research Professor in Physiology, 1969-83, Nobel prize-winner in 1963 for his work on the transmission of nerve impulses, later President of the Royal Society and Master of Trinity College, Cambridge.

431. A second Nobel prize-winner working in the College was Sir Bernard Katz, FRS, who won his prize in 1970. One of several refugees from the Hitlerzeit to enrich the College's life since the 1930s, he was the first Professor of Biophysics, 1952-78.

432

433

432. Sir Eric Turner, FBA, Professor of Papyrology 1950-78, the only professor of the subject in the country at the time; it was he who inspired and organized the methodical publication of the papyri from Oxyrrhynchus in Egypt and so transformed our knowledge, for example, of the comic playwright Menander of Athens, whose works had been lost since antiquity.

433. A fragment from Menander's play, the Samia.

443. A speech therapist and a child using speech pattern displays developed in the Department of Phonetics and Linguistics for training in voice production and control. Much progress was made from the 1970s towards the transmission of voice information to totally deaf patients.

434

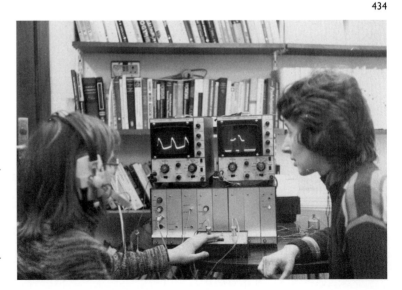

435

435. The Survey of Spoken English (later renamed the Survey of English Usage), one of the College's major research projects, arrived together with its originator Professor Randolph (now Lord) Quirk, FBA, from Durham in 1960. Its purpose is to provide a corpus of 'the grammatical repertoire of adult educated speakers of British English, using the evidence both of written and spoken language'. The project continues today, having survived the departure of its first Director to be Vice-Chancellor of the University.

436

436. Mary Douglas, Professor of Social Anthropology 1970-78, seen in the setting of some of the symbols of ambivalence through which she explored the significance of classificatory systems, ancient and modern, thus challenging orthodoxies in many fields of learning.

437

437. The Flaxman casts (see p. 92) in use for the teaching of Art History; the Department expanded rapidly in the course of the 1960s and 1970s, making the most of the many opportunities London offers for bringing classes face to face with the art of all periods.

ADMINISTR
UNIVEF

438

438. The administrative and library staff of the College assembled in 1955; the photograph includes 136 of the then total of about 200. Sir Ifor Evans as Provost sits in the centre; on his right is the Secretary of the College, 1947-64, E. A. L. Gueterbock, next to whom is the Assistant Secretary, 1948-68, Winifred Radley. Five places further along is L. J. Gue, at this time Publications Officer, who had already worked in the College for twenty-seven years; twenty-two years later, he retired as Deputy Secretary, having an unrivalled knowledge of the College's inner history in his time. On the Provost's left is J. W. Scott, who had been Librarian since 1954 and was to remain an unmistakeable figure in the College's life until his retirement in 1982; a fierce defender of the importance of scholarship and scholarly standards in the work of the Librarian, he is as well remembered for his skill in fighting his corner in the New Inn in the Tottenham Court Road as in the Librarian's office and on the Library Committee.

439

Panora Ltd.   56 Eagle Street,
London, W.C 1.

439. The 1977 photograph of the vigorous Department of Geography. Student life in UCL was and is based on the strong institution of the Department. The photograph illustrates how far dress and life-style had changed by the late 1970s compared to the immediate post-war years; those in ties can be assumed to be members of staff, those not in ties cannot necessarily be assumed to be students. Sitting at the end on the right is Professor W. R. Mead, the long-serving and much-liked Professor of Geography, 1961-81, who can still be seen around College as he approaches his 90th birthday.

440. The College Committee in session in July 1977. Under the terms of the new Charter later that year, it was to resume its nineteenth-century name of College Council as well as its formal responsibility as the College's governing body. In the Chair is Sir Bernard Waley-Cohen, who had served as the Committee's Chairman since 1971 and before that as Treasurer, 1962-70, following a family tradition of service to UCL that had begun in the College's earliest days. On Sir Bernard's left is Arthur Tattersall, the Secretary of the College, 1964-78, a firm but humane administrator, strikingly successful in maintaining close relations between the administration and the College community; three places along is the man who succeeded him in 1978, J. R. Tovell, who had been Finance Secretary since 1965.

440

441

442

443

444

441 (opposite). The strawberry tea in the Front Quad on the occasion of the Assembly of Faculties in 1962; this annual gathering occurred every year – apart from those of the second world war – between 1908 and 1966, when it was merged with the Union's Foundation week. It was revived between 1982 and 1988.

442. The Professorial Board assembling in June 1977. It too was re-named under the new Charter, becoming the Academic Board, but remained the controlling body on academic matters. All professors, a group of elected non-professors, and representatives of the student body comprised its membership. The students are here seen prominently in the foreground.

443. Allan Maccoll, Professor of Chemistry, 1963-81, and long-term supporter of the AUT, campaigning to 'rectify the anomaly' in a protest about the inadequacy of university teachers' salaries in November 1977.

444. A poster protesting at cuts in government spending on education in March 1977; it shows the meeting in progress that resulted in a short sharp confrontation, in which the students occupied some administrative rooms for two days and the Slade School for rather longer. Such incidents have been very rare and peacefully resolved; the campaign against cuts by successive governments has continued intermittently ever since, but with little or no success.

The College received a new Royal Charter in November 1977, in succession to the Deed of Settlement of 1826, the first Charter of 1836, the Acts of Parliament of 1869 and 1905, and the University of London's Act of 1926, which had previously governed the College. The changes introduced by the 1977 Charter were largely formal and titular, but they restored the College's status as an independent corporation, abandoning the 'incorporation' into the University of London (see p. 163). The new Charter was twelve years in the making; if the old constitutional machinery had been put to any serious test during this time, 'the creaking would have been heard from here to Timbuctoo', said Arthur Tattersall, the Secretary of the College. As soon as it was granted, the 1977 Charter began to be revised to provide for re-amalgamation with the Medical School.

The Queen Mother's visit in November 1977 marked the start of a series of celebrations for the sesquicentenary of the College, leading up to a great exhibition on 'UCL Past and Present' in May 1978, opened by Mrs Shirley Williams as Secretary of State for Education. The sesquicentenary was celebrated confidently, but it was a time of increasing financial uncertainty for universities in general and for London colleges in particular.

445. The Queen Mother, as Chancellor of the University, receiving one of the early prints of the College from Sir Bernard Waley-Cohen and Lord Annan during her visit in November 1977 to accept an Honorary Fellowship of the College.

445

ELIZABETH THE SECOND

by the Grace of God of the United Kingdom of Great Britain and Northern Ireland and of Our other Realms and Territories Queen, Head of the Commonwealth, Defender of the Faith:

TO ALL TO WHOM THESE PRESENTS SHALL COME, GREETING!

WHEREAS an humble Petition has been presented unto Us by Our most dearly beloved Mother Queen Elizabeth The Queen Mother, Chancellor of Our University of London, Sir Cyril Philips, then Vice-Chancellor of Our University of London and by the College Committee of University of London, University College: praying that We should grant a Charter of Incorporation for the purpose of re-constituting University of London, University College as a College of the University of London:

AND WHEREAS We have taken the said Petition into Our Royal Consideration and are minded to accede thereto:

NOW THEREFORE KNOW Ye that We by virtue of Our Prerogative Royal and of Our especial grace, certain knowledge and mere motion have willed and ordained and by these Presents do for Us, Our Heirs and Successors will and ordain as follows:—

1. University of London, University College is hereby re-constituted as a college of the University of London by the name and style of "University College London", hereinafter referred to as "the College".

2. The Council, the Academic Board, the Fellows and Honorary Fellows, the Academic Staff and Students of the College and all such other persons as may pursuant to this Our Charter and the Statutes and Regulations of the College become Members of the Body Corporate are hereby constituted and shall for ever hereafter be one Body Corporate and Politic by the name of "University College London" with perpetual succession and a Common Seal.

3. The objects of the College shall be to provide education and courses of study in the fields of Arts, Laws, Pure Sciences, Medicine and Medical Sciences, Social Sciences and Applied Sciences and in such other fields of learning as may from time to time be decided upon by the College and to encourage research in the said branches of knowledge and learning and to organise, encourage and stimulate postgraduate study in such branches.

4. The College, subject to this Our Charter and to the Statutes and Regulations of Our University of London (hereinafter referred to as "the University") shall in furtherance of the foregoing objects but not otherwise have the following powers:—

(1) To take over from the University the properties and liabilities hitherto entrusted to vested in or incurred by the University on behalf of the College by virtue of its incorporation in the University.

(2) To provide courses of instruction and facilities for research in the branches of knowledge and learning mentioned in Article 3 of this Our Charter, and for postgraduate study in such branches.

(3) To provide, maintain, alter and improve for the use of the Students

446

446. The Royal Charter issued to the College in November 1977.

UNDERSTANDING THE PAST · CHALLENGING THE PRESENT · SHAPING THE FUTURE

UCL

Chapter 9
The Years of Expansion, 1978-2004

The Council and the Academic Board have given unanimous support to an active policy aimed at preserving UCL's integrity in the face of current university enquiries. They both see the College as an administratively integral and topographically compact academic institution, strong in the humanities and law, fine arts and architecture, physical sciences and engineering, life sciences and medicine. They are determined to maintain this integrity, which allows an intimate spirit of collaboration within and among all those fields on UCL's 'Half Kilometre Square'. Furthermore, they see no case for attempting to widen that organisation in ways that would change the academic balance or the topographical compactness.

Sir James Lighthill writing in the UCL Annual Report, 1979-1980

My subject has always confused people and everybody who has had to introduce me has stumbled over the title of Molecular Pathology. Indeed, in contrast to those of you who profess subjects of great antiquity, molecular pathology was invented, I think, in the office of the Provost, Sir Derek Roberts, five years ago when he said, and I quote, 'If we are merging Molecular Biology and Chemical Pathology, that would make Molecular Pathology' – and so I became Professor of Molecular Pathology. I would still like to find out what it is, actually.

Professor David Latchman, now Master of Birkbeck,
in his Crabtree Oration delivered at UCL in February 1997

The level of excellence in research and teaching which is maintained at UCL is a direct result of the excellence and dedication of the staff. I find it remarkable that members of staff do perform at such a high level given the miserable way they have been treated by successive governments for two decades. The erosion of academic salaries, with respect to other professions, is a national disgrace. It was so when I came to UCL, and my biggest regret about my time here is that no improvement has been achieved – instead the converse is true.

Sir Derek Roberts writing in UCL Newsletter
in 1999 after his first retirement as Provost

447. Professor Harold Billett, Acting Provost, 1978-79, in a portrait by H.A. Freeth once displayed in the Housman Room.

In 1978 Lord Annan resigned as Provost in order to become the first full-time Vice-Chancellor of the University of London in preparation for the constitutional changes brought about by the University's new 1978 Act of Parliament. For the following academic year, 1978-79, Professor Harold Billett was Acting Provost. He had been a member of the staff since 1946, Professor of Mechanical Engineering from 1965, and a Vice-Provost since 1973. Professor Billett presided calmly and wisely over the College in an interregnum between two contrasting, commanding Provosts.

Sir James Lighthill was chosen as Provost in 1979. Like Lord Annan, he came to UCL from Cambridge with a formidable reputation, though an utterly different one. He was a brilliant mathematician, Lucasian Professor of Applied Mathematics at Cambridge at the time of his appointment, a product of Winchester and Trinity College, Cambridge, and had been a professor at Manchester at 26, an FRS at 29, and Director of the Royal Aircraft Establishment at Farnborough from 1959 to 1964. As Provost, he found, as he put it, 'something of an advantage' in being an applied mathematician who worked for many years on various applications of mathematics in the sciences, in engineering, and in medicine. There were few academic subjects in which he did not have some expertise, and there were no areas of the College on which he did not have considerable impact in the nine years that he devoted to the College. In 1988, Sir James Lighthill expressed the hope that the history of the College in the 1980s would be judged by the quality of the professorial appointments made during his Provostship –

over a hundred of them altogether. He put academic excellence first, but he also had many problems to deal with.

Already in 1979-80, a savings target of 3% of the recurrent grant from the UGC had to be imposed; there were problems, too, that were caused by the UGC's insistence that 'non-EEC students' should be charged fees on a new, higher scale. What the *Annual Report* called a 'traumatic sequence of body-blows' followed: in the 1981 budget, Mrs Thatcher's government announced a substantial cut in the resources to be provided for the university system as a whole; as a result, the College found that its grant for 1981-82 was to fall 15% short of the amount needed to maintain its 1980-81 levels of activity. Retrench-

447

448

ment was not easy, given that staff costs accounted for nearly 80% of all College expenditure. Lighthill introduced a 'seven-point plan' for economies, and was vigorous in hammering out painful plans for coping with the cuts. UCL adhered firmly to its policy of 'no redundancy', but an extensive early retirement scheme was launched, with a target of 160 retirements among members of the academic staff by 1984.

The target was achieved (though for many academics, it was only a technical retirement) and substantial one-off as well as on-going economies were made in various different ways, while at the same time the College embarked on a vigorous drive to increase its income from non-governmental sources. Industry as well as the research councils and charitable foundations were increasingly important sources of support. In the event, during a period of enormous financial difficulties, the College was so successful in obtaining alternative new funding that the number of staff in academic departments actually increased from 1,976 in 1978-79 to 2,014 in 1982-83. Despite the 'massive cuts' that marked the beginning of the decade, the 1980s turned out to be a remarkable period of growth, though most notably in the area of staff employed on research contracts.

Some of UCL's expansion derived from the intense period of 'restructuring' which the University of London embarked upon under the Vice-Chancellorships of Lord Annan, 1978-81, and of his successor, Professor Sir Randolph Quirk, 1981-85. The report by Lord Flowers in 1980 on medical education in the University was followed by an investigation into the organisation of all other subjects, conducted by Sir Peter Swinnerton-Dyer, later to be the Chairman of the UGC. A period of anguish and mergers ensued, coinciding with the 'cuts'. For many parts of the University it was dismaying and hurtful, but UCL was on the whole a beneficiary.

In 1982-83, a number of geologists were translated from Queen Mary College to enhance the Department of Geology (from 1985 renamed Geological Sciences and from 2002, Earth Sciences) under Professor Michael Audley-Charles; Bedford College's Department of Dutch moved to the College *en bloc*; the Department of Italian was strengthened by transfers from Bedford, as was the Department of Mathematics, which came to include Professor P. M. Cohn, FRS, as well as Dr Bill Stephenson (on whom see p. 294). Complex discussions with Westfield College did not lead to a merger, but in 1986 the Institute of Archaeology – a close neighbour, though an independent institute of the University – amalgamated with the College, retaining its separate identity as a Department within the Faculty of Arts.

The Bioengineering Centre in the Department of Mechanical Engineering was established in 1980, after the transfer from Roehampton of a DHSS group integrating engineering and medical

449

450

research. The D. M. S. Watson Library, after 're-structuring' of University library provision, became the Bloomsbury Science Library for a while after 1985. But the biggest changes of all were in medicine. In April 1980 the University College Hospital Medical School – a separate school of the University since 1907 (see p. 162) – was re-united with the College, forming the Faculty of Clinical Sciences within a new UCL School of Medicine. Soon afterwards negotiations began towards a further amalgamation with the Middlesex Hospital School of Medicine, a development achieved by November 1987 when the 'University College and Middlesex School of Medicine' was inaugurated. It included three formerly separate institutes, the Institute of Urology, the Institute of Orthopaedics, and the Institute of Laryngology and Otology. The enlarged UCL came to contain over 7,000 students.

During this period of expansion, the College acquired a new look. In 1979-80, the stone-cleaning of the Front Quad improved the outward appearance of the College dramatically, and in 1983-85 the Front Quad was closed to enable the building of a new main front entrance. The unsightly post-war huts were finally removed, and the College came to present a handsome front to the world. The Kathleen Lonsdale Building, containing the old chemistry laboratories, was elegantly reconstructed in 1985 to house the Sandoz (now Novartis) Institute for Medical Research, a signal example of co-operation with a major pharmaceutical company. All these changes, combined with some modest gardening expenditure as part of a 'greening of UCL' programme, significantly improved the rectangle site, which Sir James Lighthill liked to call the 'half-kilometre square'.

450. In December 1981, Sir James Lighthill, holding a copy of the agreement with the Sandoz Pharmaceutical Co to establish the Sandoz Institute for Medical Research at the College, receives a cheque from the officials of the company, gleefully watched (right) by John Tovell, Finance Secretary and Accountant, 1965-78, and Secretary of the College, 1978-82.

451. The centrepiece of the Appeal launched in 1981 was the long proposed 'filling of the gap' to complete the Gower Street entrance to the Front Quad. Sir Hugh Casson's own elegant sketch of the handsome pavilions he conceived on either side of the lodges was hung in the Royal Academy's summer exhibition in 1981.

452. The view from the Portico in 1985 after the construction of the two pavilions which completed the Front Quad, the Pearson Building to the north and the Chadwick Building to the south, on either side of the reconstructed lodges, with Waterhouse's University College Hospital towering beyond.

451

452

453

454

455

453. HM The Queen arriving at the College on 13th November 1985 and being introduced to Ian Baker, the retired general – formerly Assistant Chief of the General Staff for Operational Requirements and General Officer Commanding North-East District – who was Secretary of the College, 1982-91. Behind the Queen stands Dr Mary Fulbrook, then Lecturer in German History and Mayoress of Camden, later to be Professor of German History. Behind Ian Baker stands Lord Donaldson, Master of the Rolls and, as such, the College's Visitor under the 1977 Charter.

454. The Queen entering through the Portico accompanied by Sir James Lighthill as Provost and Sir Peter Matthews, Chairman of the College Council, 1980-89.

455. The inscription above the entrance in the Portico, as unveiled by the Queen, records that the Quadrangle started in 1827 was deemed complete in 1985. In her speech in the Donaldson Library she said, 'I confess that, sometimes, when I lay a foundation stone I am prey to faint worries about when, or even whether, the building will be finished. I wonder if, on that April afternoon in 1827 when he laid the first stone here, the Duke of Sussex had those same worries. Even if he did, I doubt if he would have guessed that it would be his great-great-grand niece, 158 years later, who would see the end of the process he began'.

456. The Middlesex Hospital, founded in 1745 and rebuilt in 1935, had had its own Medical School since 1835, when it was inaugurated – as was the Faculty of Medicine at UCL – by Sir Charles Bell (see p. 53). It was agreed that the Middlesex Hospital Medical School should amalgamate with the UCL Faculty of Clinical Sciences, as the former University College Hospital Medical School had become in 1980 when it re-united with the College, to create a new 'University College and Middlesex School of Medicine' within UCL. The first students were admitted to the Joint School in 1983 before the completion of the complex period of planning for full integration; projected for August 1987, the necessary Act of Parliament to give effect to this was delayed owing to the General Election of that year.

457. The formal inauguration of the University College and Middlesex School of Medicine was marked by the visit of HRH The Princess Royal – as Princess Anne had become – in November 1987. She spoke in the Edward Lewis Theatre in the presence of Professor D.V. I. Fairweather, Vice-Provost (Medical) and Head of the School (right of front row), Sir William Slack, the former Dean of the Middlesex Hospital Medical School who became Dean of the enlarged Faculty of Clinical Sciences (second from left, back row) and Professor A. P. Matthias, Dean of the Faculty of Medical Sciences (third from left, back row).

456

457

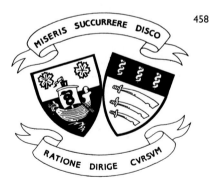

458

459

458. The first Grand Colours Dinner after the creation of the University College and Middlesex School of Medicine had on its cover the coats of arms and the mottos of the former University College Hospital Medical School and of the former Middlesex Hospital Medical School.

459. Soon afterwards a new logo was created for UCMSM, combining features from both the previous coats of arms.

UCMSM

460

461. The Royal National Throat, Nose and Ear Hospital

460. St Peter's Hospital in Covent Garden, established in 1860 to specialise in urological diseases, spawned the Institute of Urology as a research centre which in 1951 became one of the constituent parts of the British Postgraduate Medical Federation, itself a federal school of the University of London. The Institute of Urology along with two sister institutes – the Institute of Orthopaedics and the Institute of Laryngology and Otology – also joined the new UCMSM in 1987 as part of the enlarged UCL, bringing close connections with the Royal National Orthopaedic Hospital at Stanmore and the Royal National Throat, Nose and Ear Hospital in Gray's Inn Road.

461. The Royal National Throat, Nose and Ear Hospital, home since 1946 to the Institute of Laryngology and Otology, which joined UCL in 1987 while retaining its close links with the Hospital, seen here flying its 'Queen's Award for Technological Achievement'.

461

462. The Institute of Archaeology, which merged with UCL in August 1986, had been founded in 1937 as an institute of the University of London. The leading centre for archaeological research as well as undergraduate teaching in the field, it has been housed in this building in Gordon Square since 1948.

463. Sir Mortimer Wheeler, FBA, FRS, the founder of the Institute of Archaeology, in the portrait now hanging in the Institute's Common Room. Later well known as a pioneering tele-don, he had been a student at UCL in 1907 (see p. 147).

(see p. 147).

464. Professor Gordon Childe, FBA, Professor of Prehistoric Archaeology and Director of the Institute of Archaeology, 1946-56, the great populariser of Marxist theories of archaeology, in a somewhat eccentric photograph.

462

463

464

465. A group of powerful men: the Dean of the seven Faculties of UCL photographed on the Portico steps in 1986, together with the Provost, two Vice-Provosts and the Secretary of the College. Clockwise from Sir James Lighthill (second from right in back row) they are: Professor I. A. Harley, Dean of the Faculty of Engineering, Professor J. L. Jowell, Dean of the Faculty of Law, Professor D. Bishop, Dean of the Faculty of Environmental Studies, Professor A. P. Mathias, Dean of the Faculty of Medical Sciences, Professor John White, Vice-Provost, Professor J. W. Mullin, Vice-Provost, General I H Baker, the Secretary, Dr. P. J. Verrill, Dean of the Faculty of Clinical Sciences, Professor R. J. Audley, Dean of the Faculty of Science, and Professor M. M. Willcock, Dean of the Faculty of Arts. The financial problems of the 1980s had led to a significant increase in the power of the deans, who for some years came to exercise considerable control over the budgets of the Departments in their

465

466

466. The College Council photographed in March 1986, a month after a grand dinner was held to celebrate the 160th anniversary of the foundation of the College and the 150th anniversary of the establishment of the University of London. In the centre sits Sir Peter Matthews as Chairman of the Council with Sir James Lighthill as Provost on his right and Ian Baker as Secretary on his left. Besides members of the academic staff, the Council contains lay members and student representatives.

467. A group of women: a photograph of the Academic Women's Advancement Group (AWAG) which met in the College regularly from 1979 and was probably the earliest established women's academic group in the country. The time since its foundation has seen a substantial increase in the number of women professors at UCL, from the four of 1979 to the ninety-five of today (15% of all professors). In this photograph, the following can be seen: Professor Hannah Steinberg (Psychopharmacology), the Convenor of the Group, Professor Laura Lepschy (Italian), Professor Annette Lavers (French), Professor Mary Douglas (Anthropology), Professor Gertrude Falk (Biophysics), with Lady Lighthill and Jacqueline Dyson (Laws), who was Dean of Students 1990-96.

467

468

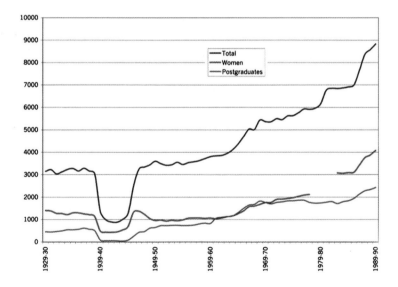

468. A photograph (courtesy of Pi) that provides an image for the 1980s.

469. A graph of student numbers in the sixty years from 1929 to 1989, showing the interruption of the second world war and the steady substantial post-war growth, leading on to the ever more rapid growth of the 1980s. The gap in the red line results from the short-lived belief in the late 1970s that it was no longer necessary to count women separately.

470. Sir Derek Roberts, FRS, the seventh Provost from April 1989, seen here shaking hands with his predecessor, Sir James Lighthill, in front of a portrait of Jeremy Bentham.

470

In April 1989 Dr Derek Roberts, FRS, was chosen to succeed Sir James Lighthill as Provost, an appointment that attracted much attention in the press, especially since the AUT was threatening a boycott of examination marking following the government's refusal to make an adequate salary settlement on top of its insistence upon the abolition of 'tenure' by legislation. Sir Derek Roberts, as he soon became, had held several visiting professorships (including one in the College's Department of Electronic and Electrical Engineering), but he was not an academic. His life had been spent in industrial scientific research and at the time of his appointment as Provost he was Joint Deputy Managing Director and Technical Director of GEC. The appointment, welcomed throughout the College, was seen as a sign of the times.

The times were indeed changing. An exhaustive report in 1985 in connection with Sir Alex Jarratt's investigation of the efficiency of universities had pronounced that 'the overall governance of UCL, in terms of its organisational structure and decision processes, is generally effective'. A new managerial and public relations style was becoming evident. David Bowles, the College's Finance Secretary and Accountant since 1978, became Director of Finance and Planning in 1989; an Alumnus Day was held on an entirely new basis; *UCL Universe* replaced the old *Annual Report*, and a glossy news-magazine, *UCL NEWS*, was launched in October 1989. Some of these developments had been foreshadowed before 1989. Dr Stephen Montgomery had been appointed Director of External Relations in 1985, and in 1988 the former ASU (Academic Services Unit, established in 1978) had been re-launched as UCLi, UCL Initiatives, a concerted effort to link UCL expertise to industrial and commercial opportunities. UCLv, UCL Ventures, a company with access to venture capital, was to follow. By the end of 1990, major new buildings were underway. UCL was choosing not to sit on its laurels.

471

472

473

471. For many years, the totally inadequate stage in the gymnasium, originally built for the Boys' School in 1878, had to serve for the many student dramatic productions, including the annual opera, a major feature of UCL life since 1951. The Music Society's policy has been to produce little-known operas and it has a number of premières to its credit. Since 1968 the operas have been staged in the first-class facilities of the Bloomsbury Theatre, employing aspiring professional singers in the main solo parts. The gym itself was finally pulled down in 1990-91 to make way for new buildings for medical research (see pp. 12-13).

472 & 473. Two recent photographs of the College's splendid theatre, opened in 1968 as the Collegiate Theatre, re-named in 1982 and now called the UCL Bloomsbury. It provides first-rate facilities for student activities and performances, as well as for visiting professional groups.

A sign of the times was the promotion of David Bowles, the much-respected Director of Finance and Planning, to Vice-Provost in 1991. As Director of Finance and Planning he was succeeded by Marilyn Gallyer, who also succeeded him as Vice-Provost in 1996. Both finance and planning came to play an ever more prominent role in UCL's decision-making. Many old-style committees of elected and appointed academics (plus since the 1970s, elected student representatives) gave way to new-style managerial structures. Under a Provost who believed in and practised quick decision-making, directors and managers appeared to proliferate, while members of the academic staff, who generally still preferred to talk of 'administrators', progressively lost the sense of contributing to College decisions. The growing number of unfilled elective places on the Academic Board provided an unhappy index of diminishing affection for UCL as a whole.

The drive to polish UCL's external image, however, continued to grow apace. After expert advice from Dr Henry Drucker, who had raised millions for Oxford, a new and more professional Development Office was developed under Rachel Hall as Director, 1994-98, Simon Pennington, 1998-2002, and Dr Alisdaire Lockhart since 2002. Fund-raising moved into a higher gear and better relations with UCL alumni were carefully cultivated through-out the world.

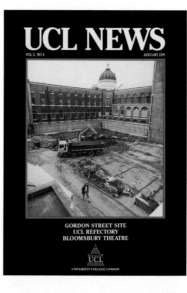

474

475

476

476. On the newly created terrace outside the Bernard Katz Building, a monument, inscribed in Japanese and English, to the pioneering Japanese students of 1863 and 1865 was unveiled in September 1993, symbolising enduring links with Japan and the international co-operation to which UCL is committed. Beside the monument is Professor John White, Durning-Laurence Professor of the History of Art, 1970-90, Vice-Provost 1986-88 and as Pro-Provost between 1990 and 1995 responsible for overseeing the drive into a new era of corporate public relations.

477. The very successful Language Centre at UCL was opened in 1991 in the refurbished former premises of the once famous book-shop H. K. Lewis & Co Ltd on the corner of Gower Street and Gower Place, since 2003 partly adorned with the paraphernalia of the 'congestion charge'.

477

L ord Annan may have thought in 1978 that the 'harness of attachment' which long chafed between UCL and the University of London had been turned into 'bands of silk'. Nevertheless, between 1929 and 1993, the grant from the UGC and its short-lived successor the UFC had been paid, not directly to UCL, but to the University of London, whose Court Department had the responsibility of dividing the annual grant between the constituent colleges, schools and institutes. It had long been believed in UCL, *pace* Lord Annan, that this system worked to the disadvantage of the larger colleges, and also that the system caused delay in the planning process. Both Lighthill and Roberts, in their different styles, maintained heavy pressure on a University that was in any case engaged in reform. The outcome of the sound and fury was that the HEFCE grant after 1993 was paid directly to UCL and to the other colleges, so treating them on the same footing as

478

478. The first 'graduation ceremony' at UCL was held in September 1992. The degrees awarded were still of the University of London, but the former centralised 'presentation ceremonies' in the Albert Hall gave way to devolved occasions organised by the colleges. They turned out to be very popular rituals; the first of them was reported in UCL Alumnus in Michael Freeman's first year as Director of Alumni Relations.

all other English universities. The University of London re-wrote its statutes in 1994, abolishing the Court Department and central control of finance and planning; there was to be no more top-slicing for federal activities.

479. Sir Derek Roberts as Provost welcomed Rachel Hall as Director of Development in 1994, guided by Dr Henry Drucker.

480. Michael Freeman was Director of Alumni Relations from 1991 to 1998, having been Administrator of the UCL Union 1970-91; he is photographed here, orating in July 2003 in the South Cloisters, on the occasion of his retirement as General Manager of the Bloomsbury Theatre.

479

480

In 1992, the UCL Graduate School was formed. It was a response to the increasingly clear separation of government funding for teaching and for research; at the same time there was a widespread feeling that the growing number of research students needed more support from the College in social life, in skills training and in interdisciplinary stimulus than the individual departments had been offering. The first Head of the Graduate School was Professor Tim Biscoe, Jodrell Professor of Physiology, and Vice-Provost 1990-92. As the number of research students grew towards the present total of 2,736, the Graduate School's most tangible impact on the lives of research students was as a source of funding for travel, conference-going and research expenses. An important intellectual development has been the creation of annual interdisciplinary awards, providing research students with an extra year's funding to make a serious study of a discipline additional to their own. Within a decade, the Graduate School had become a well-established presence within UCL.

481. Professor Tim Biscoe, the first head of the Graduate School, photographed with Professor Fred Bullock, Professor of Physics and Vice-Provost, 1993-98, on the Great Wall of China in 1998, while on a tour of Chinese academic institutions. In 1996, Professor Biscoe had become a Pro-Provost, a new office created in 1990 for senior members of the College given special responsibilities for a specific area, in his case relations with the Far East.

481

482

483

482. Professor Leslie Aiello has been Head of the Graduate School since 2002. She has taught in the Department of Anthropology since 1976; the photograph reveals her scholarly interest in evolution.

483. The Graduate School organises annual poster competitions for graduate students in all disciplines. Here, in the South Cloisters, graduate students inspect the 2002 display in biomedicine.

484

485

484. Sir Randolph (later Lord) Quirk, FBA, Professor of English, 1960-81, who became Vice-Chancellor of the University of London between 1981 and 1985, photographed in his office in the College, watched over by a bust of his illustrious predecessor W. P. Ker (see p. 146).

485. Professor R. E. D. Bishop, FRS, Kennedy Professor of Mechanical Engineering, 1957-81, before becoming Vice-Chancellor of Brunel University.

486. Sir Eric Ash, FRS, Pender Professor of Electrical Engineering, 1966-85, before becoming Rector of Imperial College.

487. Professor D. E. N. Davies, FRS, Professor of Electrical Engineering, 1971-88, before becoming Vice-Chancellor of the Loughborough University of Technology.

486

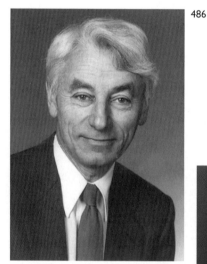

487

488

*488. Professor Ron Cooke
– later Sir Ron – taking
off on a balloon-trip in
1991 to celebrate the end
of his Headship of the
Department of Geography;
he was Vice-Provost
1991-93, before taking off
to become Vice-Chancellor
of the University of York.*

*489. Professor Roland
Levinsky, who had been
Director of the Institute of
Child Health from 1990
and who was UCL's Vice-
Provost for Bio-medicine
and Head of the Graduate
School, 1999-2002, before
sailing off to become Vice-
Chancellor of the University
of Plymouth.*

*490. Professor David
Latchman was Professor
of Molecular Pathology
and Director of the
Windeyer Institute of
Medical Sciences, before
becoming Professor of
Human Genetics and
Director of the Institute
of Child Health in
succession to Professor
Levinsky. In 2003, Professor
Latchman attained a
further evolutionary stage
by becoming Master of
Birkbeck College.*

489

490

491. Professor David Harris, Professor of Human Environment and Director of the Institute of Archaeology, 1989-96, photographed in the Institute's 'bone room', holding a skull of a dugong (sea cow) from the Torres Strait between Papua New Guinea and Australia.

491

492

492. Sir Lawrence Gowing, the Slade Professor of Fine Art, 1975-85, with one of his commanding canvasses.

493

494

495

493. Professor Geoffrey Burnstock, FRS, Professor of Anatomy, 1975-97, who for twenty-two years presided over the Department of Anatomy and Developmental Biology, which came to include six FRSs and twenty-one full Professors.

494. Professor Steve Jones, Professor of Genetics, achieved popular fame through his 1991 Reith Lectures on 'The Language of the Genes' and has ever since been a well-known broadcaster and writer.

495. Another member of academic staff well known as broadcaster and writer is Professor Lewis Wolpert, FRS, Professor of Biology as Applied to Medicine since 1987.

496. Dr Charles West, the founder in 1852 of the Hospital for Sick Children at 49 Great Ormond Street, whose programme from the beginning included child healthcare, medical research and the training of nurses. Wordsworth said that he was 'a man of hope and a forward-looking mind'.

497. Sir Alan Moncrieff, the first Director of the newly founded Institute of Child Health, 1946-64.

498. The new Wellcome Trust Building at the Institute of Child Health.

The Institute of Child Health was formally established in 1945 on the initiative of senior staff at the Great Ormond Street Hospital for Sick Children, with which the ICH has always had the closest links. Collaboration between curing patients and teaching students in fact goes back to the earliest days of the Hospital, when the founder Charles West and Sir William Jenner, himself also a UCL Professor, accepted students from its foundation in 1852. Regular courses were established by the end of the nineteenth century. From 1947 the ICH formed part of the British Postgraduate Medical Federation, the umbrella created by the University of London for various postgraduate medical institutes, several of which came to be such a major element in the expanded UCL. The first Director between 1945 and 1963 was Professor (later Sir) Alan Moncrieff, who presided over its early

496

497

498

499

development and encouraged specialisations in tropical medicine and in child-growth. In 1990, Roland Levinsky became Dean and it was he who presided over a period of re-organisation, expansion and eventually, in 1996, merger with UCL. The Institute now has over 500 members of staff and an annual turnover of over £27m.

The Institute of Neurology merged with UCL in 1997. It had been established in 1950 and retains its close links with the National Hospital for Neurology and Neurosurgery in Queen Square. It is the major national centre for postgraduate training and research in neurology and allied disciplines. It has over 350 staff and an annual turnover of £23m.

499. Queen Square: the National Hospital for Neurology and Neurosurgery, built in 1884, with the 1978 building of the Institute of Neurology towering above it.

*500 & 501.
Two distinctive plaques designed by A. J. J. Ayres on the 1937 extension to the Hospital symbolise the two functions of the Hospital and the Institute.*

500

501

502. Pioneer women students of medicine being taught anatomy in the Hunter Street building of what became the Royal Free Hospital Medical School for Women.

503. A portrait of Sophia Jex-Blake, who battled to found the London School of Medicine for Women.

504. Dr Elizabeth Garrett Anderson, the formidable Dean of the London School of Medicine for Women and of the renamed Royal Free Hospital Medical School for Women, 1883-1902.

The merger of the Royal Free Hospital Medical School with UCHMS has brought together three of the great nineteenth-century London medical institutions. The creation of the Royal Free Medical School derived directly from the struggle by women in Britain to be accepted for medical degrees and to qualify as doctors. In the summer of 1874, on the initiative of Sophia Jex-Blake, and with the somewhat reluctant support of Elizabeth Garrett Anderson, the London School of Medicine for Women opened with fourteen students – Sophia Jex-Blake among them – in a house in Henrietta Street, later extended to have a Hunter Street frontage. At first, no hospital would agree to accept them, until the Royal Free, nearby in Gray's Inn Road, came to the rescue in 1877, and the position was secured the following year by the University of

502

503

504

London's decision to open its degrees to women. Garrett Anderson emerged in 1883 as the Dean, as she was to be for the rest of the century. The name Royal Free Medical School for Women was adopted in 1897 and the last two words dropped when men were admitted as students for the first time after the second world war in 1948. The current hospital and medical school in Hampstead (see p. 17) was established between 1974, when the hospital moved, and 1982, when the pre-clinical departments completed their move. Less than ten years later, the Tomlinson Report recommended the merger that took place in 1998, so creating the Royal Free and University College Medical School. The Medical School is now perhaps the most prestigious in Europe, producing some 400 doctors a year, as well as conducting much fundamental research.

The following year, 1999, saw an important non–medical merger. The School of Slavonic and East European Studies had been founded originally at King's College in 1915, when it was inaugurated by Tomáš Masaryk; it became an independent institute of the University of London in 1932, relocating to the newly-built Senate House in 1939. Masaryk's interests in questions of national identity and self-determination, rooted in language, history, culture and society, continue to inform the School's activities with as much relevance today. SSEES, as part of UCL, is about to relocate again to its new building (see p. 16).

505. The bust of Tomáš Masaryk, still prominently displayed at SSEES. He inaugurated the original 'School of Slavonic Studies' at King's College in 1915, by giving a much-publicised lecture on 'The Problem of Small Nations in the European Crisis'. After the first world war he became the first President of Czechoslovakia.

506. A group of teachers from the School at King's in 1925. They include Sir Bernard Pares, Director, 1922-39, (front row, second from left) and R.W. Seton-Watson, FBA, the first Masaryk Professor of Central European History, 1922-45 (front row, extreme right). In the back row, fourth from left, is D. S. Mirsky, the émigré Prince who taught Russian literature at the School from 1922 to 1932, commuting from his residence in France. Later in the thirties, reconciling himself to the new order, he went back to Soviet Russia, only to die in a labour camp in Siberia in 1939.

505

507. Professor George Kolankiewicz, Director of SSEES since 2001.

506

507

508. Professor Salvador
Moncada, FRS, photo-
graphed in Gower Street
outside the former
University College Hospital,
now converted into the
Cruciform Building to house
the Wolfson Institute for
Biomedical Research, of
which he has been Director
since 1996. The Hospital
building, originally opened
in 1906 (see pp. 148-
49), was vacated by the
National Health Service in
1996 and restored for UCL
at a cost of £50m, raised
with contributions from the
Wellcome Trust, the Wolfson
Foundation and HEFCE,
with additional initial
funding raised through a
Private Finance Initiative.
Waterhouse's imposing
edifice now houses
more than 200 research
scientists and their state-of-
the-art research equipment,
besides teaching facilities
for the combined
Medical School.

508

509. Professor Sir John
Pattison, Professor of
Medical Microbiology at
UCL from 1984, Dean of
the UCL Medical School,
1990-98 and Vice-Provost,
1994-99, photographed
outside the renovated
Cruciform Building before,
in 1999, becoming
Director of Research
and Development of the
National Health Service at
the Department of Health.

509

510

511

510. The Eastman Dental Clinic, next to the Royal Free Hospital in Gray's Inn Road, was opened in 1931 by the American Ambassador in the presence of Neville Chamberlain. George Eastman, the American pioneer of popular photography, provided most of the funding. The Clinic was dedicated to providing dental care for children from the poor districts of central London, some of them seen here on the steps of the new building. In 1948, the Eastman Dental Institute, now independent of the Royal Free Hospital, became the postgraduate dental institute of the British Postgraduate Medical Federation; in 1999, it joined the enlarged UCL.

511. A student in her room in Astor College, opened in 1967 as the Middlesex Hospital Medical School residence, which, following the amalgamation with UCL in 1987, has formed part of the College's extensive stock of student accommodation. Several halls of residence have recently been added: Langton Close was converted from the former nurses home of the old Royal Free Hospital in 1994; Schafer House, named after the famous physiologist (see p. 111), was purpose-built in 1995; John Dodgson House, named after the much-loved Dean of Students, was built in 1996; James Lighthill House, named after the former Provost, was built in 1998; and Frances Gardner House, alongside Langton Close, named after a memorable Dean of the Royal Free Hospital Medical School, was opened in 2004. Now some 3500 places are available in UCL student accommodation, plus over 500 further places in University of London inter-collegiate halls; three-quarters of this accommodation is within a quarter of an hour's walk of the Gower Street

512. Professor Wendy Davies, FBA, Professor of History since 1985 and Head of the Department of History, 1987-92, was the last Dean of the old Faculty of Arts between 1991 and 1994 and the first Dean of the new Faculty of Social and Historical Sciences, when the old Faculty was divided in 1994-95. Since 1995, she has been Pro-Provost with responsibility for relations with Europe. She is seen here engaged on her 'Celtic Inscribed Stones' project, part of her innovative research into medieval societies in Brittany, as well as Wales and Ireland.

513. A completely new development has been the School of Public Policy, founded in 1997. Its academic discipline is political science, including political philosophy and political theory. It has rapidly built up an impressive research portfolio and an active graduate teaching programme. One of its three research groups focuses on the complexities, especially the current complexities, of the British constitution. Here Professor Robert Hazell, Director of the Constitution Unit, which he founded in 1995, is seen outside the Palace of Westminster.

512

513

514

514. Another research group within the School of Public Policy is the Jill Dando Institute of Crime Science, created in 2001 in memory of the well-known television journalist, as the first institute in the world devoted specifically to reducing crime. Its mission is to change crime policy and practice. Its Director is Professor Gloria Laycock, seen here in front of a picture of the late Jill Dando.

515. Among the many changes of the last twenty years has been the pervasive diffusion of computers in offices, libraries, laboratories and halls of residence. Many cluster-rooms have sprung up in various corners of the College, providing a new type of working environment for all academics and all students. This photograph provides a characteristic image of the twenty-first century university.

515

D erek Roberts' term as Provost had been extended to 1999, since his leadership was regarded as indispensable to the unprecedented process of expansion in the late 1990s. His successor was Chris (soon to be Sir Chris) Llewellyn Smith, a physicist who had been Professor of Theoretical Physics at Oxford, but who had been on secondment since 1994 as Director of the European-wide CERN research organisation at Geneva concerned with the basic particles of matter. Llewellyn Smith, on the advice of his predecessor, was the first to add the title President to that of Provost, so clarifying the status of the post particularly when visiting universities in the USA. He was shrewd enough to have recognised from the beginning the problem of running an institution whose size and complexity was in danger of outrunning its existing system of administration. He appointed three Vice-Provosts, each to have an area of responsibility (Humanities and Social Sciences; Medical Sciences; Science and Engineering) within which each exercised some of the Provost's powers, leaving himself freer to concentrate on planning, fund-raising and on the relations of UCL with the outside world. The sceptical felt that he was in fact taking on the role, not only the title, of an American University President.

516. Professor Sir Chris Llewellyn Smith, FRS, photographed standing dramatically on the dome above the portico, soon after becoming the eighth Provost in 1999.

Under Llewellyn Smith, UCL was successful in research bids in the Joint Infrastructure Fund ('JIF') competition and also received further funding for scientific research especially in biomedicine from the Science Research Investment Fund ('SRIF'); the total funding obtained from these sources was of the order of £100m. The plans had to be submitted within a short time-frame. The problems were

516

overcome triumphantly and a major building programme was soon underway. It was to be Llewellyn Smith's legacy to UCL, alongside his concern to see that these enhancements for the scientific side of UCL did not leave the non-laboratory subjects behind.

What should by rights have been a period of triumph soured rapidly. Early in the new millennium it was discovered that the financial situation was far worse than had previously been calculated. Previous efforts at savings, it was now realised, had failed to take enough factors into account and a new more stringent savings programme was adopted; despite this, the deficit went up and morale in the College went rapidly down. At the same time the Provost's proposals for academic re-structuring also attracted opposition. By the summer of 2002, the Chairman of Council, Lord Young, had been approached by some senior members of the College who conveyed extreme anxiety about the situation; they felt that there was no effective strategy in place and that the necessary decisive action was not being taken. Lord Young's discreet consultation among senior academics led him to advise the Provost that the College and the Council had lost confidence in his leadership. A statement was issued saying that Sir Chris was resigning to return to his research work. The news of this prompt action was received with some misgiving in parts of UCL, but by August the previous Provost, Sir Derek Roberts, had been pressed to return for one more year as Provost while the search for a new successor was carried on.

517. The Provost hosting a party at the European Student Conference on 'The Future of Europe' held at UCL in April 2002; the many international students attending, Sir Chris said, 'learned not only how difficult it is to reach agreement in the diverse Europe that we all enjoy, but also how much can be learned from trying'.

517

At first, the second coming of Roberts restored confidence. But early in the new academic year a proposal was made, initially on television by Sir Richard Sykes, the industrialist who had recently become Rector of Imperial College, that UCL and Imperial College should merge. The announcement implied that the new institution would continue to be divided between the Bloomsbury and South Kensington sites, but that Sir Richard would become the head of the whole enterprise and consequently that the search for a new Provost would be deferred. The main arguments put forward were that the size of the joint institution would place it among the most powerful universities in the world, second only to Stanford in research spending, and that this initiative would be strongly supported by the government, which was looking for means of making UK universities more globally competitive. Immediately, a rapidly devised structure of sub-boards and internal committees began examining the implications for both UCL and Imperial, reporting to a specially established joint board. UCL's Council insisted that there should be a tight deadline for this intense period of consultation and that a decision one way or the other should be made by Christmas.

518. Talks on the desirability of a merger between UCL and Imperial College are here seen beginning on 17th October 2002 in the Provost's office. Sir Derek Roberts and Sir Richard Sykes, the Rector of Imperial, are jointly chairing the board, attended by three Vice-Provosts of UCL as well as senior representatives from Imperial.

Resistance within UCL quickly emerged. The method of opposition to the proposal was innovative and illuminating: a web-site was set up to encourage comment and discussion, which before long attracted vigorously critical statements from staff and students across UCL and from distinguished alumni. It became clear that the proposed merger was not seen in UCL as the pooling of two equivalent institutions, but as the covert destruction of the tradition of independence and radicalism that had been an inheritance from the 1820s. The strength of feeling generated somewhat surprised the organisers, but surprised still more the advocates of the merger. The consultative process revealed many problems and within

518

weeks it was decided in UCL to withdraw from the merger. The talks were called off and the search committee for the new Provost resumed its interrupted work. Sir Derek was not after all destined to be the last Provost and President of UCL.

The consequences of the failure of this dramatic initiative were in some ways fortuitously very positive. For one thing, some areas of future co-operation between UCL and Imperial were identified. For another, the crisis had revealed a sense of community and purpose within UCL that many had thought lost in the years of expansion. The twenty-first century members of UCL – not least those from the several recently merged institutions – had proved to be far more in touch with the traditions and the ethos of the College than had come to be supposed.

519

Committee for UCL: Takeover	Page 1 of 9

The Committee for UCL   Revised 18-Nov-02 (new shortcut to mirror site www.cucl.org)

UCL lives on!

Applicants to UCL can now be sure that the university they wanted will be here

Announcement 18 November 2002, on UCL's web site
UCL and Imperial College have now completed an intense period of deliberation since it was first announced that the two Colleges were exploring the desirability and feasibility of merger between the two institutions. A number of areas for future collaboration have been identified, but the overall conclusion is that the best interests of the two institutions are not served by a formal merger. UCL is now recommencing its search for a new Provost from October 2003. Once in post the new Provost and the Rector of Imperial College may well continue discussions on developing the opportunities for collaboration identified in the last five weeks.
The news was first broken by Donald MacLeod in the Guardian: click here, and here

We thank the 24 distinguished signatories, the 119 senior staff and 362 other staff and students whose support brought about the survival of UCL, as well as the 7480 visitors (and 16243 hits) that this site has had in 22 days. The list was closed on 18th November 2002, apart from the late addition to the list of distinguished signatories of Jonathan Dimbleby, Bel Mooney and Sir Denis Rooke OM CBE FRS FREng.

Postscript: some press comments after the event

Lessons of a failed merger, (Matthew Lynn, Bloomberg News, 20-Nov-02) "Unfortunately for Sykes, the professors of Imperial and University College London were smarter than the last recipients of his strategic wisdom, the shareholders in the formerly independent drug companies Glaxo Wellcome and SmithKline Beecham. ": [get the pdf]

The biggest universities in the world are clearly not the best. So why do some British universities think that mergers will make them world class? (John Kay, 21-Nov-02) Financial Times) " The same empty phrases that were used in the 1990s to justify corporate mergers are today used to justify university mergers - the aspiration to be a "global player", the need to achieve "critical mass". But greater size is always the aspiration of those with no better strategic vision."

The proposed 'merger' of UCL and Imperial College

The end of 175 years of a Benthamite multi-faculty university?

No! -the start of the next 175 years of progress.

"The Stanford/UCSF merger experience, which ended in ignominious failure and an enormous debt, stands as a stark warning of blithely merging two distinct academic cultures, particularly when they are not geographically co-localized."
Phyllis Gardner MD (Stanford University)(signatory)

New information -merger committee reports: ● read here | 'Downsizing' -see SAVEUCL and comments

519. The 'Committee for UCL' web-site as it appeared on 18th November 2002 following the news that the merger project was being abandoned, after several weeks of intense agonising about the future of the College.

To attempt to portray the vast range and quality of research undertaken at UCL in the first decade of the twenty-first century would be an impossible task. The four examples given here provide mere glimpses into current research conducted in the world of UCL.

520. The painting analysis workroom in the Department of the History of Art where Libby Sheldon (left) and Catherine Hassall (right) carry out scientific investigations into the materials, techniques and conditions of paintings and painted objects. The painting in the foreground for example was established as being by J. M. W. Turner.

521. Libby Sheldon's research over many years showed that the 'Young Woman Seated at the Virginals' was painted by Vermeer. New techniques, including polarising light microscopy, and co-operation with Professor Robin Clark of the Department of Chemistry proved that the painting, previously considered a forgery, was painted by Vermeer in about 1670. This information enabled the picture to be sold at Sotheby's in 2004 for over £16m.

520

521

522

522. Professor Jonathan Edwards, Professor of Connective Tissue Medicine in the Medical School, and his team have developed an explanation for the causes of rheumatoid arthritis and a treatment for it. A drug was developed that dealt with the cells affected by autoimmune disease and has enabled severely affected patients to return to normal life.

523. Dr Linda Smith and Mark Westmoquette of the Department of Physics and Astronomy have captured a unique image of the 'starburst galaxy' known as M82, more than 10 million light years away from the Milky Way. The 'starburst galaxy' is created when a sudden burst of star formation is brought on by an encounter with another galaxy, sending plumes of hot gas tens of thousands of light-years into space.

523

524. A virtual reality map of London is being developed by Dr Andrew Hudson-Smith and Steve Evans at the Centre for Advanced Spatial Analysis (CASA) in the Bartlett School. The 3D map will provide London with information via the internet about planning and tourism; it is intended to encourage accessible debate about the way in which the environment of Londoners is shaped. The project is funded by the Greater London Authority.

524

525 & 526. A tradition of student protest continues to thrive, with the invasion of Iraq in 2003 providing an occasion for demonstration in the Front Quad and in Gower Street.

525

526

527. The front cover of pi
magazine in March 2004,
showing that the Student
Union is alive and well.

527

pi magazine
march 04 • issue 644   FREE

The Student Magazine of University College London Union

New Lonely hearts
dating column

Provost wants
pedestrianised
UCL campus

Spain
1 days
after 9/11

UC Opera
Vanda

Challenge

Varsity Rugby win
over Kings

Elections
controversy

UCL UNION

NEWS • MUSIC • INTERVIEWS • REVIEWS • COMPETITIONS • FILM • FASHION

528. The Front Quad in different mood, with the Union's summer arts festival.

529. The title of Fellow of the College has been bestowed since 1842 on former students achieving distinction in their careers, whether academic or non-academic. The new Fellows chosen in 2004 are photographed with the new Provost and Lord Young, the Chairman of the Council; among the distinguished group is Dame Antonia Byatt, the novelist and formerly Senior Lecturer in English, and Lynne Truss, the grammarian and former student of English.

528

529

530

531

530. Ricky Gervais was a student in the Department of Philosophy and worked at ULU before achieving celebrity status.

531. Jeremy Bowen graduated in History, before joining the BBC in 1984, since when he has become well known as a foreign correspondent and television presenter.

532

533

532. The band Coldplay, all UCL alumni who met up at Ramsay Hall. From left to right they are: Jonny Buckland, Chris Martin, Guy Berryman and Will Champion.

533. Lord Woolf, Lord Chief Justice of England, a Fellow of the College since 1981 and, like Lord Young, an alumnus of the Law Department, is to succeed as Chairman of the College Council later in 2005.

534

534. The Council of
UCL meeting in the Old
Refectory in Summer
Term 2004. It was the last
meeting of the Council
consisting of 35 members,
both academic and 'lay',
before the size of the
Council is reduced to 25.
Presiding over the meeting
is Lord Young (foreground,
wearing bow-tie). On
his right is Professor
Malcolm Grant, Provost
and President since 2003,
the New Zealander who
had taught Law at UCL
between 1986 and 1991,
before becoming Professor
of Land Economy and
Pro-Vice-Chancellor at
Cambridge. On his right is
Marilyn Gallyer, the Vice-
Provost (Administration).
In the centre of the
foreground is Dr Bill
Stephenson, a member
of the Mathematics
Department since 1982
and a combative leading
figure in the AUT both
in UCL and nationally,
attending his last meeting
of the Council.

535. The outlook from the Front Quad
in spring 2004: the new University
College Hospital building towers over
the northwest corner, while the glass
roof of the new Wellcome Building
rises over the Slade School.

535

536. Beadles traditionally maintained order at UCL; now, reinforced by new types of security guard, they maintain tradition, as here does the well-remembered Beadle Alfie Proberts.

536

Acknowledgements

This is the third edition of a book first published in 1978 at the time of the celebration of the sesquicentenary of the opening of University College London as the University of London. Essential backing was provided by Arthur Tattersall, the then Secretary of the College. The second edition was undertaken in 1991 at the prompting of Professor John White, the then Pro-Provost, and Dr Stephen Montgomery, then the Director of External Affairs. Many colleagues provided indispensable assistance in all manner of ways, which we acknowledged as fully as possible in the first two editions. We have not forgotten the many contributions of these colleagues, past and present, too many to be listed again here.

In approaching our task for the third time, we have accumulated many more debts of gratitude. Dr Alisdaire Lockhart, the Director of Development & Corporate Communications, started us off, and Purba Choudhury, the Deputy Director, spurred us on. Others in the Development & Corporate Communications Office provided invaluable help, especially Nicholas Tyndale, Leslie Bell and Gavin Blyth. UCL Press supplied us with an editor in Ruth Massey and a designer for the book in Richard Bryant of Past Historic, both of whom provided admirable expertise and enthusiasm.

Wise advice at various points was accepted with gratitude from Professor Malcolm Grant, the President and Provost, and from Lord Young of Graffham, the Chairman of the Council; Marilyn Gallyer, Vice-Provost (Administration) and her predecessor, David Bowles, each guided our steps and saved us from error. At various points, discussion with old members of the College, such as Bryan Bennett and Fred Gee, and with current colleagues, such as Professor Leon Fine, Professor David Bogle and Dr Nicholas Tyacke, helped us to achieve balanced judgements. Our aim has been to combine historical accuracy with lively selectivity so as to encapsulate as many different aspects as possible of the College over its hundred and seventy-five years.

Technological change has been especially rapid during the last thirteen years, and all the illustrations in the book have had to be reassembled in new digital format. Our successors in producing a fourth edition will have an easier technological time, while we have been heavily dependent on the staff of the Library, who were indefatigable in tracking down everything we needed, and we are particularly grateful to Gill Furlong, the Head of Special Collections, and Dan Mitchell of the Special Collections Room. In Media Resources, Mary Hinkley performed miracles with images. Mrs Rosamund Cummings and her colleagues in the Records Office did much searching, and Emma Chambers in the Strang Print Room was tirelessly helpful in connection with the College Art Collection.

Our debt to previous historians of the College remains very heavy, above all to Hale Bellot's *University College London, 1826-1926* (1929). To the debts mentioned in the second edition, we now have also made use of works such as Lynne Amidon's *Illustrated History of the Royal Free Hospital* (1996) and Ian Roberts's *History of SSEES* (1990). Help and advice about the recently merged parts of UCL was readily provided: we are indebted to Professor Neil McIntyre and to Victoria North, the Archivist, at the Royal Free Hospital; to Professor Mac Turner and Jeremy Nayler of the Institute of Child Health and to Nick Baldwin, the Archivist of the Great Ormond Street Hospital for Sick Children; to Louise Shepherd, the Librarian of the Institute of Neurology; to Karen Widdowson of the Eastman Dental Institute, and to Lesley Pitman, the Librarian of SSEES, and Maria Widdowson, the Secretary of SSEES.

Others who have provided help include Tim Perry and Paula Speller of the Registrar's Division, Tom Reilly of Human Resources, Anne Macdonald of the Graduate School, Professor John Foreman, the Dean of Students, and Karen Bowtell of the Finance Division. Andreas von Maltzahn in the Union keenly made many suggestions for images of student activity. Help in locating particular images was willingly provided by Dr Suse Keay in the Department of Geography, Professor Andrew Lewis in the Faculty of Laws, Professor Alwyn Davies in the Department of Chemistry, and Dr Kris Lockyear and Ian Laidlaw of the Institute of Archaeology. In the Department of History, Rachel Aucott helped at various points of crisis, especially involving computing, and also created the two graphs of student numbers, while Simon Renton beat off a virus attack that at one point threatened the whole enterprise.

Also in the Department of History, Kate Quinn proved an exceptionally able and resourceful assistant in checking innumerable details and helping with the compilation of the index.

Sources of Illustrations

Every effort has been made to identify the holders of copyright; we apologise for any omissions from the following list. Enquiries should be addressed to the Development Office, UCL.

Index